Colección Támesis

SERIE A: MONOGRAFÍAS, 245

THE PLACE OF ARGUMENT

ESSAYS IN HONOUR OF NICHOLAS G. ROUND

Nicholas Round is among international Hispanisms's most prodigiously gifted scholars. These essays in his honour embrace the three areas to which he has most memorably contributed. Within Medieval studies, Alan Deyermond illuminates the tradition of the true king and the usurper; David Pattison challenges conventional interpretations of women's place in the Spanish epic; David Hook uncovers the surprising 'afterlife' of medieval documents; John England examines Juan Manuel's views on money. Within Nineteenth-century studies, Geoffrey Ribbans analyses unexpected continuities between Galdós's *Marianela* and *El doctor Centeno*, Eamonn Rodgers discovers mythic dimensions in *El caballero encantado*, Rhian Davies explores *regeneración* in the *Torquemada* novels and the late Arthur Terry reflects on the non-realist bases of *El amigo Manso*, while Harriet Turner traces parallels between Alas's *La Regenta* and the trial of Martha Stewart. Within Translation studies and pedagogy, Jeremy Lawrance analyses sixteenth-century translation's contribution to the prestige of vernacular languages; Philip Deacon evaluates the Italian translation of Moratín's *El viejo y la niña*; Robin Warner explores the translation of cartoon humour; Patricia Odber contrasts ten translations of a poem by Gil Vicente; and Anthony Trippett and Paul Jordan reflect on the purpose and practices of higher education.

RHIAN DAVIES is Senior Lecturer, and ANNY BROOKSBANK JONES is Hughes Professor of Spanish, in the Department of Hispanic Studies at the University of Sheffield.

THE PLACE OF ARGUMENT

ESSAYS IN HONOUR OF NICHOLAS G. ROUND

Edited by

Rhian Davies
Anny Brooksbank Jones

TAMESIS

First published 2007 by Tamesis, Woodbridge

ISBN 978–1–85566–152–3

Tamesis is an imprint of Boydell & Brewer Ltd
PO Box 9, Woodbridge, Suffolk IP12 3DF, UK
and of Boydell & Brewer Inc.
668 Mt Hope Avenue, Rochester, NY 14620, USA
website: www.boydellandbrewer.com

A CIP catalogue record for this book is available
from the British Library

This publication is printed on acid-free paper

Printed in Great Britain by
Biddles Ltd, King's Lynn

CONTENTS

ACKNOWLEDGEMENTS

The editors' thanks are due to the following, without whose generous support publication of this volume might not have been possible: all the subscribers named in the Tabula Congratulatoria; the Modern Humanities Research Association Publications Fund; the Fundación Cañada Blanch; the Department of Hispanic Studies, University of Sheffield. We also gratefully acknowledge Hayley Rabanal's invaluable assistance with the editing process.

Modern Humanities Research Association

Cañada Blanch
FUNDACIÓN

Introduction
Celebrating Nick Round

ANNY BROOKSBANK JONES and RHIAN DAVIES

It is a truism of contemporary publishing that the mark of a strong collection of academic essays is its coherence. The Oxford English Dictionary
reflects this term's deployment in several quite different ways, according to
context: it foregrounds the action or fact of sticking together, logical connection, propriety and consistency, the harmonious connection of the several
parts of a discourse. For the generality – but thankfully not the totality – of
publishers, however, it is generally reserved for the precise congruence of a
set of essays with a designated target readership. It has been something of a
challenge, then, to assemble a coherent *Festschrift* in honour of a colleague
with the exceptional scholarly range and intellectual energies of Nicholas
Grenville Round.

Nick Round, as he is universally known, graduated from Pembroke College,
Oxford, with a double first in French and Spanish in 1959, completing his
DPhil – a monumental study of fifteenth-century *converso* translator Pero
Díaz de Toledo – eight years later. From 1962 to 1972 he taught Spanish,
first as Lecturer, then as Reader, at Queen's University Belfast, before taking
up the Stevenson Chair of Hispanic Studies at the University of Glasgow.
There he remained until 1994, when he left for the Hughes Chair at Sheffield,
becoming Emeritus Professor after his retirement in 2003.

This was a relatively settled career by today's standards. His scholarship,
by contrast, ranged prodigiously. A true polymath, his standing as one of the
most erudite academics of his generation is evidenced in books, pamphlets,
articles and translations that range with seamless authority from the medieval
to the contemporary periods, through narrative, drama and poetry, history
and philosophy, translation, linguistics and pedagogy. There are, in this sense,
many Nick Rounds. For some, he is a medieval and early-modern histo-
riographer of consummate intelligence, or the author of scholarly studies
of Fernando de Rojas and Juan Ruiz characterized by penetrating textual
and contextual insight. In the assessment of a distinguished medievalist and
friend, Alan Deyermond:

Nick's genius as a scholar flowers where literature, history and ideology meet, where the medieval shades into the early modern: in his first article on the Castilian aristocracy's attitude to humanism, his brilliant book on the fall of Álvaro de Luna, his magnificent edition of the earliest translation of Plato.

Others know him as a first-rate nineteenth-century scholar. His research into the nineteenth- and early twentieth-century novel and thought – including Alas, Unamuno and, pre-eminently, Pérez Galdós – is lit by a profound understanding of contemporary socio-cultural and intellectual contexts. It informs the critical guide to Unamuno's *Abel Sánchez* (Grant & Cutler, 1974), for example, and his fine translation of Galdós's *Torquemada en la hoguera* (Glasgow, 1985). In 1996, these interests led to the establishment of the University of Sheffield's online Pérez Galdós Editions Project and today, as Consultant Director, he remains an invaluable support for its current head, Rhian Davies.

But there are many, in and outside of Hispanism, who know Nick chiefly through his work on translation. A literary translator of the first order, his interventions in debates on the cultural and cognitive dimensions of translation have been enriched by his practice, generating highly original work on the knowledges of the translator, on translation and cultural influence, and on translation and poetic language. As former Sheffield colleague and fellow translation specialist Robin Warner notes, Nick's prodigious knowledge of comparative literature gives him privileged insight into the aesthetic dimension of writing, into what constitutes the literary qualities of a text and the challenges these present for translators. Important studies of the poetry of Manrique, Machado and Lorca testify to his expressive as well as his analytical powers. His rich and supple use of language and his sensitivity to the rhythms of speech are displayed to striking effect in his translations for the stage: most memorably, perhaps, of Tirso de Molina's *El condenado por desconfiado*, Buero Vallejo's *Las cartas boca abajo*, Galdós's *Realidad* (these last, broadcast on BBC Radio in 1973 and 1975 respectively), and the Duque de Rivas's *Don Álvaro o la fuerza del sino* for Scottish Opera in 1990. Colleagues at Sheffield remember his splendidly incisive surtitles for the 2003 production of Torrejón y Velasco's opera *La púrpura de la rosa*. In his plenary lecture to the anniversary conference of the Association of Hispanists of Great Britain and Ireland (Valencia, 2005), he observed that to translate poetry one needs to be a poet, and this lies at the core of his formidable powers. For all these gifts were brought to bear in his own poetry: often more personal in tone, it was produced chiefly during his time at Queen's University, Belfast, where his humanistic understanding of the conflict raging there was articulated in pieces of quite piercing verbal intensity. He was

associated with the Belfast Group (a poetry workshop established in 1955
by English Lecturer Philip Hobsbawm), which was then at its most active; as
well as the young Seamus Heaney, its organizers would include Arthur Terry,
who became a lifelong friend and whose essay for this volume is one of the
last completed before his sadly sudden death in 2004.

As a critic or historian, translator or poet, Nick's scholarship is driven
by a commanding intellect, and his encyclopaedic knowledge of his material and its contexts is sustained by exceptional powers of abstraction and
recall. The period in which the editors had the privilege of working with him
came towards the end of his academic career; yet he remained able to locate
at will the quotation he sought among the many hundreds of primary and
secondary texts lining his large office. Such are the hallmarks of the scholar
of international distinction, the Fellow of the British Academy, the recipient
(in 1989) of the Cruz de Oficial de la Orden de Isabel la Católica. The man,
the colleague and collaborator, is distinguished above all by great personal
generosity, wit, a principled humanism and, to borrow a term he has been
known to use himself, general *decency*. This was a man who would travel
miles by bus, tram and train on a filthy night to support a friend giving a late
lecture at another institution. These qualities combined with his combative
intellect to make him a fierce defender of his department, his colleagues and
students. A remorseless critic of institutional pragmatism and its distillation
in bureaucratic jargon, he deemed time spent exposing their flaws well spent.
On this and related matters the ample unfolding of his ideas tested a generation of Faculty Committee Chairs, while departmental meetings under his own
chairmanship could run on for several hours. Yet, as the editors witnessed at
the formal dinner following his Galdós Lecture in 2004, the wit, insight and
intellectual authority with which he speaks could, on occasion, enable him to
command the sustained attention even of colleagues whose elevated institutional position had weakened their capacity for extended listening.

At a time when the term 'unique' has lost much of its force through over-use,
how can this *truly* unique combination of qualities and concerns be reflected
in a single 'coherent' volume? The editors' response has been to invite contributions rooted in four areas: the first three – medieval, nineteenth-century,
and translation studies – are those to which Nick Round's scholarship has
contributed most resonantly; his commitment to the fourth, pedagogy, has
left its mark in eruditely polemical essays, in his daily professional practice,
on his colleagues, and, most enduringly, on the undergraduate and postgraduate students whose own academic aspirations have been enlarged by his
intellectual and personal example. Two of those former students, themselves
now eminent academics, are represented in this volume; so, too, are friends
of long-standing, former colleagues, and collaborators, many of them distinguished authorities in their fields.

The volume opens with four chapters on medieval topics. In the first, Alan Deyermond offers a masterly overview of the medieval tradition of the true king and the usurper, before exploring its development in three thirteenth-century examples: the *Cantar de Mio Cid*, the *Auto de los Reyes Magos*, and the *Libro de Apolonio*. His findings suggest that these works do not reflect contemporary crises in the monarchy but rather a more open interest in its nature, insofar as each 'shows either the survival and success of a king who recognizes that there may be more than one kind of kingship, or the defeat of a king who is incapable of recognizing it' (p. 13). A rather different type of tradition engages another distinguished medievalist, David Pattison, who challenges the widely held view that women play a subordinate and submissive role in the Spanish epic. Through an analysis of some particularly well-chosen examples – including Jimena and her daughters in *Poema de mio Cid*,[1] Doña Urraca, Queen Elvira, and the mother of Bernardo del Carpio – he presents them rather as an active, and often sexualized, force in the unfolding of the action and one that sometimes has clear political repercussions.

David Hook's contribution to the volume is an erudite illustration of 'the long afterlife' of medieval documents (p. 31). Taking his inspiration from Nick Round's study of Álvaro de Luna, he demonstrates that appropriations of medieval Spanish chronicles were not confined to later historiography and propaganda. His argument centres on an eighteenth-century memorandum found in a volume from the library of Sir Thomas Phillipps (1792–1872). The context of this memorandum was a debate concerning the monarchy's rights in the appointment and confirmation of bishops, and its author effectively exploits aspects of the 1482 Isabelline concordat (among other sources) as precedents to justify the maintenance of the *status quo*. The identification of specific manuscripts as the author's source, Hook argues, provides important clues concerning the contexts in which he was writing and researching, and underlines the potential value of political documents from Hapsburg and Bourbon Spain for research on the transmission of late medieval chronicles. In the final essay in this section, Sheffield colleague John England takes another essay by Nick, this time on Juan Ruiz, as his starting point for an examination of Juan Manuel's views on the use and abuse of money by individuals, communities and the state. The development of a monetary economy had been slow in medieval Castile, England notes, and while it was well under way by the first half of the fourteenth century, attitudes towards money were still evolving. Juan Ruiz, a cleric, uses traditional material to satirize its power: Juan Manuel, by contrast, offers an aristocratic layman's assess-

---

[1] Here, and throughout the volume, where alternative forms are available the spelling, capitalization, and accentuation are those preferred by the author of the chapter in question.

ment of the social necessity of money – its value both for a successful life on earth and for enhancing the possibility of salvation – and elaborates rules to limit its disruptive potential. While he notes that knowledge and wisdom are more important than wealth and possessions, argues England, this is partly because '*el saber* [...] empowers the individual in the proper acquisition, possession and sharing of wealth' (p. 53). In this sense, he concludes, Juan Manuel's observations can be said to form a coherent code of conduct from the perspective of the rich and powerful.

The volume's second section turns to the nineteenth-century novel, and begins with a chapter by the eminent *Galdosista* and Consultant Director of the Galdós Editions Project, Geoffrey Ribbans. He explores the surprising continuities between *Marianela* (1878) and *El doctor Centeno* (1883), two novels traditionally assigned to different periods of Galdós's development. Why, he asks, are these separated by three novels, despite the fact that the ending of the first explicitly anticipates the writing of what is, in effect, its sequel? Among the continuities highlighted by Ribbans are the tight intertwining of the stories of Marianela and Felipe (the eponymous Dr Centeno), close geographical and chronological links, and the many common themes: among them, social deprivation, charity, education, the conflict of reality and illusion. One partial explanation for the period separating the novels, he speculates, may be that Galdós produced an earlier draft of *El doctor Centeno* but abandoned it for more pressing business; or perhaps it is simply another example of the author's impressive ability 'to keep promising subjects on hold, archiving or hoarding them for later development' (p. 70).

Reflecting Nick Round's particular interest in the author, Galdós is also the focus of the next three chapters in this section. The first of these is an analysis of the novel *El caballero encantado* (1909) by another noted *Galdosista*, Eamonn Rodgers. To read the novel, as many have done, as 'merely an exercise in fantasy, an attack on *caciquismo*, an advocacy of socialist revolution' or a critique of *regeneracionismo*, he contends, 'is to overlook the larger mythic and historical dimensions of the novel' (p. 83). For Galdós sees immutable tradition and continuous revolution as inextricably intertwined, it is suggested, and the vision of the future projected in the novel is of a world that is more patriarchal and paternalist in character than is generally recognized. Rodgers draws out references to the *regeneracionista* debates of the time, while noting that Galdós's interest in them does not blind him to their idealistic and impractical aspects. Building on her own authoritative studies of *regeneración*, Rhian Davies develops this point in a chapter that tracks the concept's significance and implications in Galdós's *Torquemada* novels. Her focus is its philosophical dimension – which Nick Round has himself explored in several articles – and above all the question of Spain's representation as decadent in certain deterministic accounts of national character during the period. Davies teases out the novels' repeated allusions to decadence and determinism (in its biological, environmental and providential variants), but also registers a number of points where Galdós suggests that free-will and the regenerative potential of education might serve to moderate or correct those tendencies. That this possibility remains undeveloped in the novels should be read not as indicating Galdós's pessimism on the point, she argues, but as making his critical appropriation of aspects of *regeneración* more constructively open-ended.

The last two essays in this section both offer highly suggestive readings of nineteenth-century realism. In the first, the late Arthur Terry recalls that Galdós was writing realist novels dense with social detail at a time when the instability of 'reality' and the expressive and conceptual shortcomings of language were the subject of growing debate. With characteristic clarity and insight he goes on to trace the non-realist bases of Galdós's *El amigo Manso*: from its opening words '[y]o no existo' to the novel's end, in which the eponymous Manso dies only to find himself 'in a kind of limbo' from which he can continue to observe the behaviour of the other characters (p. 108). But what precludes readings of *El amigo Manso* as simply a realist novel in a fantastic frame, Terry argues, is a more general 'intensity of illusion' (p. 108). This rests partly on the expectations generated in readers by that non-realist frame; but it is most explicit in the fact that the novelistic illusion of Manso's life is structured around an enigma, and his gradual realization that the other characters are not as he had assumed them to be. The novel is best conceived, he concludes, in terms of George Eliot's metaphor of the 'web', in the sense that 'things are connected, not by a simple chain of cause and effect, but by an infinite number of differences and similarities which are only revealed by patient comparison' (p. 110). The metaphorical web that closes Terry's contribution opens Harriet Turner's own brilliantly provocative variation on the realist theme. In her case the web is that of 'el imaginario social', through which she insists on the intricate connections that bind the nineteenth-century realist techniques of Galdós and Clarín to those of the early twenty-first century (p. 112). Her analysis of Clarín's *La Regenta* has a double focus. On the one hand, it highlights startling parallels between the novelist's presentation of Ana Ozores and contemporary media representations of US celebrity Martha Stewart during her trial in 2004 for insider-trading. On the other, it explores how the novel's setting in Vetusta, being 'almost too imitative of life', has come to alter the cityscape of its model, Oviedo (p. 113). The analysis explores the processes by which the stories of the two women have been rendered 'melodramatic and *follestinesca* in their mixtures of high and low, truth and lies, fiction and reality' and through their continuing reworking as cultural products in bibliographies and tourist guides, the media and stock market listings (p. 122).

The volume's final section centres on translation studies and pedagogy, both of them areas in which Nick Round was active from the very earliest stages of his career. The opening essay, by distinguished medieval and Golden Age specialist Jeremy Lawrance, offers an elegantly erudite assessment of literary translation's role in augmenting the prestige of vernacular languages in sixteenth-century Spain and Italy. Within the scholastic linguistic hierarchy of the medieval period, he notes, vernacular languages could not aspire to the incorruptible nobility of Latin, its assumed distance from mere nominalism, or the aesthetic perfection of its grammatical patterns. But Dante's reversal of this hierarchy in *De vulgari eloquentia* (c. 1305) would have a profound impact on sixteenth-century debates on language. In Italy, these debates informed Speroni's affirmation that 'no language can be inferior to any other in its ability to express meanings' (p. 132); in France, they subtended du Bellay's view that if the vernacular is less able than Latin to express all knowledge then it is the responsibility of speakers of the vernacular to address this, 'cultivating and improving it by imitation of the wealth and excellence of more prestigious languages' (p. 132). This, Lawrance notes, was the theory behind the project to 'illustrate' vernacular languages, to make them illustrious through imitation. The specific manifestations of this project across early sixteenth-century Europe varied according to local conditions. Drawing on Nebrija, Garcilaso, Valdés, and Boscán, Lawrance elucidates significant variations in discourses on translation within Spain. This leads him to conclude that (contrary to convention) there were no significant developments there during the period in redefining the task of the faithful translator, as figures of the stature of Boscán and Garcilaso were ultimately more concerned with content than with style.

Sheffield colleague and eminent eighteenth-century scholar Philip Deacon maintains this transcultural focus in his discussion of the Italian translation of Leandro Fernández de Moratín's *El viejo y la niña* (1790). It was the practice in eighteenth-century European theatre, he notes, for the endings of dramatic works to be judged in relation to prevailing notions of moral justice. In the case of Moratín's play, the ending struck some members of its contemporary audiences as unduly sombre in a 'comedia', with its newly-wed protagonist only escaping the despotic behaviour of her 70-year-old husband by entering a convent. Whereas Moratín appeared to give an overall endorsement to the translation published in 1805 by Pietro Napoli Signorelli, other, more specific, comments attributed to the author are critical of changes made to this ending in response to Italian charges that it underestimated women and lacked verisimilitude. Deacon evaluates these comments by means of a detailed and nuanced comparison of the two versions. He argues that Moratín's criticism is not well-founded: that Signorelli's ending is, in fact, less jarring than the author claims, more closely aligned with contemporary notions of natural justice, and closer than the original to the author's own thinking when it was published – as evidenced when Moratín revisited related moral and social issues, in his play *El sí de las niñas*, in 1805.

From the cultural translation of drama the volume turns to that of poetry, with a contribution from Nick Round's former student and esteemed friend Patricia Odber de Baubeta. Her subject is ten English translations, by ten different translators, of Gil Vicente's 'En la huerta nasce la rosa'. From Sir John Bowring in 1824 to Steven Reckert in 1993, she traces cultural and other factors conforming their symbolic and wider allusive fields, their choice of genre, of prose or verse; their preference for complexity or simplicity, foreignization or domestication; their response to the poem's musicality. This analysis, and her shrewd assessment of the politics and pragmatics of the anthology, yield rich insights into 'the range of options and challenges that face translators of Gil Vicente, his Galician Portuguese predecessors and, indeed, translators of poetry in general' (p. 173).

The volume's last three chapters are all tributes from Nick's Sheffield colleagues. The first is by the recently retired linguistics specialist Robin Warner, a valued friend and the departmental colleague most attuned to Nick's work in cognitive linguistics. Here, Warner's focus is argumentation theory, an area of discourse pragmatics, and his shrewd and witty analysis draws on examples from Spanish, Latin American and English cartoons to illustrate its applicability to the translation of humour. For reasons that are not limited to specific lexical items, he notes, but embedded in a specific linguistic culture, verbal humour does not travel well. At issue here is something more than the questions of cultural translation explored by Lawrance, Deacon and Odber: 'the interlocking of formal linguistic features and socio-cultural elements in some types of jokes may be "so specific to a single language community that, beyond its frontiers, the joke is unlikely to succeed"' (p. 180, citing Chiaro). Cartoons, however, appear to travel better. Focusing on communicative function rather than linguistic form, Warner examines in detail the principal reasons for this, before concluding that 'many of the basic principles underlying the humorous use of [everyday argumentation] transcend differences between linguistic cultures' (p. 188–9).

The volume's last two contributions, by Tony Trippett and Paul Jordan, are inspired by Nick's abiding intellectual engagement with the purposes and practices of university education, with how, why and what we teach our students. Tony Trippett explores the first of two pedagogical questions that were central to Nick's activities as a teacher: how assessment can promote or inhibit students' development as active, confident and reflective individuals. And he begins with Nick's inimitable rejection of the functionalist hypostatizing of assessment grades: 'marks', he once reminded the School Examinations Board, 'are a metaphor' (p. 192) – a memorable example of his lifelong insistence on the larger purposes of what we do in the face of its routine recasting as strategy and convention. Paul Jordan considers the second of these questions: how literature in education can serve as a medium to draw students into engagement with a foreign culture. His argument surveys recent responses to the question from within and outside of British Hispanism and engages in some detail with Nick's published thoughts on the subject. It recalls, for example, his prescient call, back in 1980, for language departments to occupy the interdisciplinary centre of the Arts curriculum.

Jordan's essay can be read as a sequence of scenes in the battle for the heart of British Hispanism, and it seems an especially fitting point on which to close this Introduction to a volume celebrating the life and work of a man with a genuinely interdisciplinary cast of mind and an acute sense of intellectual purpose. We, his colleagues, are proud of the tributes paid to him here by distinguished scholars, respected collaborators and close friends. There are many others, in the UK and elsewhere, who wished to join in this celebration but whose areas of interest or, in some cases, major competing commitments made this impossible. Our warm thanks are due also to them; we have been much moved by their messages of support and good wishes. The encouragement at all stages of the project from colleagues in the Department of Hispanic Studies at Sheffield has been unstinting, and a fitting reflection of the collegiality that he was so active in shaping. Readers will make their own judgement as to the coherence of the volume now before them; but we hope they will feel that it reflects something of the comprehensive intelligence and broad humanity of the man to whom it is dedicated.

PUBLICATIONS OF NICHOLAS GRENVILLE ROUND

Books and Pamphlets

Unamuno: Abel Sánchez. A Critical Guide (London: Grant & Cutler, 1974)

Belfast Spanish and Portuguese Papers, edited with P. S. R. Russell-Gebbett and A. H. Terry (Belfast: Queen's University, 1979)

Fourth British Seminar of Judeo-Spanish Studies. Glasgow 1984. Abstracts of Papers, edited (Glasgow: Department of Hispanic Studies, 1984)

Readings in Spanish and Portuguese Poetry for Geoffrey Connell, edited with D. Gareth Walters (Glasgow: Department of Hispanic Studies, 1985)

Benito Pérez Galdós, *Torquemada in the Fire,* translated with introduction (Glasgow: Department of English Literature, 1985)

The Greatest Man Uncrowned: A Study of the Fall of Don Álvaro de Luna (London: Tamesis Books, 1986)

Tirso de Molina: *Damned for Despair,* edited and translated with introduction (Warminster: Aris and Phillips, 1986)

Re-reading Unamuno, edited, Glasgow Colloquium Papers, 1 (Glasgow: Department of Hispanic Studies, 1989)

On Reasoning and Realism. Three Easy Pieces (Manchester: University of Manchester, Department of Spanish and Portuguese, 1991)

Poetry and Otherness in Hardy and Machado, The Kate Elder Lecture, 3 (London: Queen Mary and Westfield College, Department of Hispanic Studies, 1993)

Libro llamado Fedrón: Plato's 'Phaedo' translated by Pero Díaz de Toledo (London: Tamesis Books, 1993)

Translation Studies in Hispanic Contexts, edited with introduction, *Bulletin of Hispanic Studies,* 75, no. 1 (January 1998)

New Galdós Studies. Essays in Memory of John Varey, edited with introduction (Woodbridge: Tamesis Books, 2003)

'What is the Stars?': Galdós and the Measures of Mankind, The Seventh Annual Pérez Galdós Lecture (Sheffield: University of Sheffield, 2004)

Articles

'Renaissance Culture and its Opponents in Fifteenth-Century Castile', *Modern Language Review,* 57 (1962), 204–15

'La rebelión toledana de 1449. Aspectos ideológicos', *Archivum* (Oviedo), 16 (1966), 385–446

'Five Magicians or the Uses of Literacy', *Modern Language Review,* 64 (1969), 793–805

'Politics, Style, and Group Attitudes in the *Instrucción del Relator*', *Bulletin of Hispanic Studies,* 46 (1969), 289–319

'Garci Sánchez de Badajoz and the Revaluation of *Cancionero* Poetry', *Forum for Modern Language Studies*, 6 (1970), 178–87

'The Fictional Integrity of Leopoldo Alas' *Superchería*', *Bulletin of Hispanic Studies*, 47 (1970), 97–116

'Rosalía Bringas' Children', *Anales Galdosianos*, 6 (1971), 43–50

'Time and Torquemada: Three Notes on Galdosian Chronology', *Anales Galdosianos*, 6 (1971), 79–97

'The Medieval Reputation of the *Proverbia Senecae*: A Partial Survey Based on Recorded MSS', *ProcRIA*, 72, C, 5 (1972), 103–51

'How Not to Read the *Lusiads*', *Vida Hispánica*, 21, 3 (1973), 33–8

'The Myth of National Character and the Character of National Myth', *EMU* (University of Glasgow), 4 (1974), 7–22

'Approaches to the 1898 Generation', *Vida Hispánica*, 24, 2 (1976), 5–14

'Versiones protestantes del *Nuevo Testamento* en el *Diario íntimo* de Unamuno', *Cuadernos de la Cátedra Miguel de Unamuno*, 25 (1978), 169–81

'Las traducciones medievales catalanas y castellanas de las *Tragedias* de Séneca', *Anuario de Estudios Medievales*, 9 (1974–79), 187–227

'The Shadow of a Philosopher: Medieval Castilian Images of Plato', *Journal of Hispanic Philology*, 3 (1978–79), 1–36

'Exemplary Ethics: Towards a Reassessment of Santillana's *Proverbios*', in *Belfast Spanish and Portuguese Papers* (Belfast: Queen's University Department of Spanish, 1979), pp. 217–36

'Thinking about Thody: Language and Culture in the University Discipline', *Modern Languages*, 61 (1980), 155–64

'Conduct and Values in *La Celestina*', in *Medieval and Renaissance Studies on Spain and Portugal in Honour of P. E. Russell*, ed. F. W. Hodcroft et al. (Oxford: Society for the Study of Medieval Languages and Literatures, 1981), pp. 38–52

'La correspondencia del Arcediano de Niebla en el Archivo del Real Monasterio de Santa María de Guadalupe', *HID*, 7 (1981), 215–68

'Naturalismo y feminismo en *La Tribuna*', *Estudios ofrecidos a Emilio Alarcos Llorach*, V (Oviedo: University of Oviedo Press, 1983), 325–43

'Galdós' *Realidad*: Novel into Drama', *Forum for Modern Language Studies*, 20 (1984), 30–48

'Formal Integration in Jorge Manrique's *Coplas por la muerte de su padre*', in *Readings in Spanish and Portuguese Poetry for Geoffrey Connell*, ed. Nicholas G. Round and D. Gareth Walters (Glasgow: Department of Hispanic Studies, 1985), pp. 205–21

'The Revolution of 1383–84 in the Portuguese Provinces: Causality and Style in Fernão Lopes', *Dispositio*, 10 (1985), 65–84

'Villaamil's Three Lives', *Bulletin of Hispanic Studies*, 62 (1986), 19–32

'Fifteenth-Century Guadalupe: The Paradoxes of Paradise', in *Medieval and Renaissance Studies in Honour of Robert Brian Tate*, ed. Ian Michael and Richard A. Cardwell (Oxford: Dolphin, 1986), pp. 135–50

'The Top Favorite: Michael Geddes Looks at Álvaro de Luna', *Dieciocho*, 9 (1986), 219–38

'On the Logic of Unamuno Criticism', in *Volumen-Homenaje a Miguel de Unamuno*, ed. D. Gómez Molleda (Salamanca: University of Salamanca Press, 1986), pp. 683–705

'Celestina Secundum Litem: Miguel Marciales' *Carta a Stephen Gilman*', *Celestinesca*, 11 (1987), 25–40

'From "Talk in Context" to "Texts and Culture"', *Journal of the Modern Language Association of Northern Ireland*, 20–1 (1988–89), 11–26

'Stephen Gilman 1917–1986', *Bulletin of Hispanic Studies*, 64 (1987), 245–7

'The Presence of Mosén Diego de Valera in *Cárcel de Amor*', in *The Age of the Catholic Monarchs, 1474–1516: Literary Studies in Memory of Keith Whinnom*, ed. Alan Deyermond and Ian Macpherson (Liverpool: Liverpool University Press, 1989), pp. 144–54

'"Without a City Wall". *Paz en la guerra* and the End of Realism', in *Re-reading Unamuno* (Glasgow: Department of Hispanic Studies, 1989), pp. 101–20

'Lectura intertextual de *Nada menos que todo un hombre*', in *Actas del Congreso Internacional Cincuentenario de Unamuno*, ed. D. Gómez Molleda (Salamanca: Salamanca University Press, 1989), pp. 595–8

'Literatura moderna peninsular', *25 años de Tamesis*, ed. A. D. Deyermond, J. E. Varey and C. Davis (London: Tamesis, 1989), pp. 38–45

'The Antiquary Reassessed; Floranes and the Liberal Tradition', in *The Eighteenth Century in Spain. Essays in Honour of Ivy L. McClelland, Bulletin of Hispanic Studies* Special Homage Volume, ed. Ann L. MacKenzie (Liverpool: Liverpool University Press, 1991), pp. 107–23

'Alonso de Cartagena and John Calvin as Interpreters of Seneca's *De Clementia*', in *Atoms, Pneuma, and Tranquility*, ed. Margaret J. Osler (New York: Cambridge University Press, 1991), pp. 67–88

'The Fictional Plenitude of *Angel Guerra*', in *Galdós' House of Fiction: Papers Given at the Birmingham Galdós Colloquium*, ed. A. H. Clarke and E. J. Rodgers (Llangrannog: Dolphin, 1991), pp. 143–67

'Sobre las "Coplas" de Jorge Manrique', in *Historia crítica de la literatura española, I/1 Edad Media: primer suplemento*, ed. A. D. Deyermond (Barcelona: Ed. Crítica, 1991), pp. 277–80

'The Speakable and the Unspeakable', in *Prologue to Performance*, ed. L. Fothergill-Payne (Lewisburg: Bucknell University Press, 1992), pp. 113–35

'The Tragic Sense of *Niebla*', in *Bulletin of Hispanic Studies* Special Homage Volume, *Hispanic Studies in Honour of Geoffrey Ribbans* (Liverpool: Liverpool University Press, 1992), pp. 171–83

'The Three *caballeros*: Don Guido and his Relations', in *'Estelas en la mar': Essays on the Poetry of Antonio Machado (1875–1939)*, ed. D. Gareth Walters, Glasgow Colloquium Papers, 2 (Glasgow: Department of Hispanic Studies, 1992), pp. 83–99

'Alonso de Espina and Pero Díaz de Toledo: *Odium Theologicum* and *Odium*

Academicum', in *Actas del X Congreso de la Asociación Internacional de Hispanistas*, 4 vols (Barcelona: PPU, 1992), vol. II, pp. 319–29

'*Celestina*, Aucto I: A Platonic Echo and its Resonances', in *'Celestina': Approaching the Fifth Centenary*, ed. Joseph T. Snow and Ivy A. Corfis (Madison: Hispanic Seminary of Medieval Studies, 1992), pp. 93–112

'Celestina', in *The International Dictionary of the Theatre, I (Plays)*, ed. M. Hawkins-Dady (London: St James Press, 1992)

'The Politics of Hispanism Reconstrued', *Journal of Hispanic Research*, 1 (1992–93), 134–48

'*Misericordia*: Galdosian Realism's "Last Word"', in *A Sesquicentennial Tribute to Galdós 1843–1993*, ed. Linda M. Willem (Newark: Juan de la Cuesta, 1993), pp. 155–72

'Platonism', in *Dictionary of Iberian Literature*, ed. G. Bleiberg, M. Ihrie and J. Pérez (Westport, CT: Greenwood Press, 1993), vol. II, pp. 1298–1300

'Towards a Typology of Quixotisms', in *Cervantes and the Modernists: The Question of Influence*, ed. E. Williamson (London: Tamesis, 1994), pp. 9–28

'Translation, Cultural Influence and Semantics: Notes towards a Theoretical Convergence', in *Translation and Meaning, Part 3 (Proceedings of the 2nd Maastricht/Lodz Duo Colloquium)*, ed. M. Thelen and B. Lewandowska-Tomaszcyk (Maastricht: Hogeschool Maastricht, School of Translation and Interpreting, 1995), pp. 175–84

'Frei Luís de Sousa: Romantic and Postromantic', in *Portuguese, Brazilian, and African Studies (Studies Presented to Clive Willis on His Retirement)*, ed. T. F. Earle and N. Griffin (Warminster: Aris & Phillips, 1995), pp. 187–98

'La "peculiaridad literaria" de los conversos ¿unicornio o snark?', in *Judíos, Sefarditas, Conversos: La expulsión de 1492 y sus consecuencias*, ed. Ángel Alcalá (Valladolid: Ámbito, 1995), pp. 557–76

'Interlocking the Voids: The Knowledges of the Translator', in *The Knowledges of the Translator*, ed. M. Coulthard and P. Odber de Baubeta (Lewiston/Lampeter: Mellen, 1996), pp. 1–30

'Some Preliminary Thoughts on the Unamunian Speech Act', *Revista Canadiense de Estudios Hispánicos*, 21 (1996), 219–36

Introduction to Federico García Lorca, *Four Major Plays*, trans. John Edmonds (Oxford: Oxford University Press, 1997), pp. ix–xxxvii

'Juan Ruiz and Some Versions of *Nummus*', in *The Medieval Mind: Hispanic Studies in Honour of Alan Deyermond*, ed. R. Penny and I. Macpherson (Woodbridge: Boydell & Brewer, 1997), pp. 381–400

'Rojas' Old Bawd and Shakespeare's Old Lady: Celestina and the Anglican Reformation', in *Estudios en homenaje de Louise Fothergill-Payne, Celestinesca*, 21, nos. 1–2 (1997), pp. 93–109

'"Perdóneme Séneca": The Translational Practices of Alonso de Cartagena', *Translation Studies in Hispanic Contexts, Bulletin of Hispanic Studies* 75, no. 1 (January 1998), 17–29

'Monuments, Makars and Modules: A British Experience', in *Rimbaud's*

Rainbow: Literary Translation in Higher Education, ed. P. Bush and K. Malm-kjaer (Amsterdam: John Benjamins, 1998), pp. 11–20

'Versión y subversión: volver a soñar *La vida es sueño*', in *Aproximaciones a la traducción*, ed. A. Gil de Carrasco and L. Hickey (Madrid: Instituto Cervantes, 1999), pp. 131–52

'Combined Tactics in Translating Lorca', in *Fire, Blood, and the Alphabet: One Hundred Years of Lorca*, ed. S. Doggart and M. Thompson (Durham: Durham University Press, 1999), pp. 225–35

'Horrible Children', in *Spain's 1898 Crisis*, ed. J. Harrison and A. Hoyle (Manchester: Manchester University Press, 2000), pp. 94–110

'Sex, Lies and Dinner with the Dead', in *Essays on the Representation of the Don Juan Archetype in Myth and Culture*, ed. A. Ginger, J. Hobbs and H. Lewis (Lewiston, Lampeter: Mellen Press, 2000), pp. 7–32

Preface to *Dissolving Frontiers: Second Postgraduate Colloquium on Hispanic Research*, ed. A. Cutting and A. Fernández Guerra (University of Manchester: Department of Spanish and Portuguese, 2000), pp. vii–x

'Boat Race Night: P. G. Wodehouse and his Spanish Translator', *Cadernos de Tradução*, 5 (2000), 133–60

'What Makes Mabbe So Good?', in *Context, Meaning and Reception of 'Celestina', A Fifth Centenary Symposium*, ed. I. Michael and D. Pattison, *Bulletin of Hispanic Studies*, 78, no. 1 (January 2001), pp. 145–66

'Lost Lady Found: The Countryside as Redemptive Space in Tirso de Molina's *La República al revés*', in *Spanish Theatre: Studies in Honour of Victor F. Dixon*, ed. C. Cosgrove, J. Whiston and K. Adams (London: Tamesis, 2001), pp. 157–76

'Cognitive Engines: Notes on the Presentation of History in Galdós's *Novelas españolas contemporáneas*', *Anales Galdosianos*, 36 (2001), 231–41

'Alonso de Cartagena's *Libros de Séneca*: Disentangling the Manuscript Tradition', in *Medieval Spain: Culture, Conflict, and Coexistence. Studies in Honour of Angus MacKay*, ed. R. Collins and A. Goodman (Basingstoke and New York: Palgrave Macmillan, 2002), pp. 123–47

'Una vida escondida: "La Regenta" y "Middlemarch"', in *Leopoldo Alas: un clásico contemporáneo (1901–2001)*, ed. A. Iravedra Valea, E. de Lorenzo Álvarez and A. Ruiz de la Peña, 2 vols (Oviedo: Oviedo University Press, 2002), vol. II, pp. 673–92

'Galdós Rewrites Galdós: The Deaths of Children and the Dying Century', in *New Galdós Studies* (Woodbridge: Tamesis, 2003), pp. 125–39

'Lovers in Hell: *Inferno* V and Íñigo López de Mendoza', in *Dante Metamorphoses. Episodes in a Literary Afterlife*, ed. Eric G. Haywood (Dublin: Four Courts Press, 2003), pp. 11–42

'*In memoriam* Arthur Terry (1927–2004)', *Boletín de la Asociación Internacional de Hispanistas*, 10, 3 (2004), 44–5

Preface to *Essays on Luso-Hispanic Humor*, ed. Paul W. Seaver (Lewiston, Queenston, Lampeter: Mellen Press, 2004), pp. i–iv

'Translation and its Metaphors: The (N+1) Wise Men and the Elephant', *SKASE Journal of Translation and Interpretation*, 1, 1 (2005), 47–69
'Arthur Terry (1927–2004)', *Bulletin of Hispanic Studies*, 82 (2005), 241–7
'Lenguaje poético y lenguaje traductivo', in *Antes y después del 'Quijote' en el cincuentenario de la Asociación de Hispanistas de Gran Bretaña e Irlanda*, ed. Robert Archer, Valdi Astvaldsson, Stephen Boyd and Michael Thompson (Valencia: Biblioteca Valenciana, 2005), pp. 425–45

Translations Published, Performed, etc. (in chronological order)

Segundo Serrano Poncela: *Redín the Philanthropist* (short story), *Arena*, 14 (1963), 68–77
Antonio Buero Vallejo: *The Cards Face Down* (play), broadcast, BBC Radio 4 (1973)
Luís de Sttau Monteiro: *The Moon Still Shines* (play), public reading, Lyric Theatre, Belfast (1973)
Benito Pérez Galdós: *In Real Life* (play), broadcast, BBC Radio 4 (1975)
Federico García Lorca: 'Died of Love' (poem), *Literary Review* (July 1984)
Duque de Rivas: *Don Álvaro or the Power of Fate*, translation commissioned by Scottish Opera and adapted as *Fate: Verdi's Tragic Tale Retold*, Tron Theatre, Glasgow (January 1990)
Almeida Garrett: *Frei Luís de Sousa*, translation commissioned by the Anglo-Portuguese Foundation and adapted as *The Pilgrim* for production by Young Vic Theatre in January 1991. Original translation produced at the Prince Theatre, Greenwich (September 1998)
Alfonso el Sabio: *Cantigas* (selections), Glasgow: Scottish Early Music Consort (1992)
'*Jabberwocky* in Translation: *La Jipijaraguera*', in *Alice in Translation: A Homage to Lewis Carroll*, ed. P. A. Odber de Baubeta, *Fragmentos* (Florianópolis), 16 (1999), pp. 135–6
English surtitles for Calderón/Torrejón de Velasco, *La púrpura de la rosa*. University of Sheffield, Department of Music/Department of Hispanic Studies (2003)

Reviews

Between 1964 and 1992, 57 reviews published, mainly in *Bulletin of Hispanic Studies, Modern Language Review*, but also in *Al-Masaq, Anales Galdosianos, Journal of Ecclesiastical History, Journal of Hispanic Philology, Medium Aevum, Romanistiches Jahrbuch, Vida Hispánica*.

MEDIEVAL STUDIES

'¿Rei otro sobre mí?': The Exile of the True King in Thirteenth-Century Castilian Literature

ALAN DEYERMOND

Introduction

The dramatic power of the contrast between the true and rightful king and the usurper who exiles him runs through many works of medieval Castilian literature. That power derives from the theme's part in Biblical narrative, in folklore, and in the political life of the Middle Ages. It fits into a wide tradition of the divided nature of monarchy, which manifests itself in diverse ways. The division may be conceptual, most notably in the idea of the king's two bodies – one physical and mortal, the other political and continuous – studied by Ernst Kantorowicz (1957). It may flow from the incompatibility between two kinds of authority; the obvious case in the Middle Ages is the recurring tension between sacred and secular authority, the pope's against the king's, a tension that is heightened because both claimed to derive their power from God (this is clearly seen in the title of Holy Roman Emperor), and that makes Thomas Becket its most notable victim. Another kind of division may be embodied in the machinery of state, when the nominal power is vested in the king, the real power in a palace official: the Mayors of the Palace and the Merovingian kings in eighth-century France (a duality that ended when the Mayors of the Palace took power), or the Shoguns and the emperors in Japan from the seventeenth to the mid-nineteenth century (here the duality reached the opposite conclusion when the Emperor retook power).[1] It was just such a duality that, the nobles alleged, threatened the social fabric of Juan II's Castile when much of the real power was exercised by Álvaro de Luna, 'the greatest man uncrowned'. Luna's fall, brilliantly analysed by Nicholas Round (1986), prevented the division of

The second section of this chapter draws on an unpublished seminar paper given (there was never a written text) in collaboration with David Hook (Hook and Deyermond 1982). Professor Hook has very kindly allowed me to make use of that paper.

[1]   Another aspect of the difference between real and apparent authority is discussed in C. S. Lewis's paper, written in 1944, on 'The Inner Ring' (1965).

power from being institutionalized, but although Santillana and his allies probably knew nothing of Mayors of the Palace, and could not have foreseen the Shoguns, it was such an institutionalization that they feared.[2] Finally, the crown could be claimed by two members of a dynasty, one relying on primogeniture or legitimate birth, the other on assertions of incapacity or monstrous conduct by the monarch, assertions accompanied by powerful support within the ruling elite. It was that kind of rivalry that darkened the closing years of Alfonso X's reign, when, after the purported deposition of Alfonso in 1282, both he and Sancho, his eldest surviving son, claimed royal authority; in the mid-fourteenth century it triggered Juan Manuel's resentment of Alfonso XI (a resentment that made great literature, openly in the *Libro de las tres razones*, covertly in *El Conde Lucanor*); it led, four generations after the deposition of Alfonso, to the murder at Montiel in 1369, and four generations after that to the Farsa de Ávila in 1465.

The theme of the true king rejected and exiled has equally deep roots in the medieval literature of other languages, and in Castilian literature of the Golden Age (*La vida es sueño*, for instance), but my concern in this chapter is with the treatment of the theme in three works of the thirteenth century: the *Cantar de Mio Cid*, the *Auto de los Reyes Magos*, and the *Libro de Apolonio*, each of them surviving in a single manuscript. I shall take these in what now seems to be their chronological order – that is, the order in which the texts as represented in the extant manuscripts were composed. This is not necessarily the same as the chronological order of the manuscripts, and it is very different from the order of the stories embodied in the Castilian texts: the Epiphany story dramatized in the *Auto de los Reyes Magos* is, of course, found in the Gospels, and its dramatic form is widely represented in Latin and the European vernaculars (see Sturdevant 1927); the story of Apollonius of Tyre goes back at least to the closing years of classical antiquity (see Archibald 1991); and even the fictionalization of the Cid's life goes back more than a century before the *Cantar*, to the *Carmen Campidoctoris* (see Montaner and Escobar 2001). The order of composition of the Castilian texts provides a convenient way of arranging the material, but this arrangement does not imply a chronological development in Castilian treatments of the theme.[3]

[2] Francisco Bautista (2005) shows how fear can pervade even a work that appears to have no connection with contemporary politics.

[3] If I were to argue the case for the dates that I give, there would be no room left for the subject of this chapter. I therefore state briefly what I believe, in the light of the latest research, to be the most likely dates.

The *Cantar de Mio Cid*

The *Cantar de Mio Cid* was probably composed around 1207, though the extant manuscript is clearly later (this dating, which would at one time have been highly controversial, is now widely accepted).[4] It was certainly preceded by Latin texts about the Cid, and it is quite possible that one or more Castilian heroic poems about him circulated orally in the twelfth century, but the *Cantar* that we have is so unlike the general run of epic poetry that it is likely to be the work of a literate and innovative poet; he may have drawn on earlier poems, but I do not believe that his text is a reworking of them (see Deyermond 1982).

The poem begins with Rodrigo Díaz de Bivar setting out on his journey into exile, stripped of his public honour by the decree of King Alfonso; it ends with him triumphant, his daughters married to the heirs to the thrones of Navarre and Aragon, and, after his death, conferring honour on kings descended from him. This remarkable transformation is, as the narrative progresses, hinted at and, eventually, stated openly. As he rides into Burgos on his way to the frontier, the citizens say, as if with a single voice, '¡Dios, qué buen vassallo, si oviesse buen señor!' (l. 20).[5] Many articles have been written on the exact meaning of this line, but on any reading it tells us that the Cid has the qualities of a good vassal and that Alfonso does not have the qualities of a good lord; moreover, it calls on God to witness these judgements. Since, in medieval social theory (and to a large extent in practice), everyone except a serf is both vassal and lord (the king is God's vassal), and since someone who is a bad vassal is likely to be a bad lord also – an idea given great dramatic force in one of the best of the plays set in medieval Spain, Lope de Vega's *Fuenteovejuna* – Alfonso is found wanting in one capacity and, implicitly, in the other. That is a bold statement for the citizens to make, but what follows is even more striking. Turned away from his lodging in Burgos by order of the King, the Cid rides to the monastery of San Pedro de Cardeña, where his wife and daughters have taken refuge:

> Llamavan a la puerta, í sopieron el mandado,
> ¡Dios, qué alegre fue el abbat don Sancho!
> Con lunbres e con candelas al corral dieron salto,
> con tan grant gozo rreciben al que en buena ora nasco.
>
> (ll. 242–5)

The full implications of this scene were not understood until Conrado

---

4   See Lacarra (1980: 222–54) and, among more recent studies, Hernández (1994) and Bayo (2002).

5   All my quotations from the *Cantar* are taken from Michael (1978). In all quotations from medieval Spanish I supply modern accents where necessary, and I regularize the use of i/j, u/v, and c/ç.

Guardiola (1982–83) pointed out that the monastery at Cardeña was Benedictine, and that the Benedictine rule at the time required that if the king
came to visit, the abbot himself must instantly go to the gate to welcome him.
In this scene, therefore, the abbot is treating the impoverished and disgraced
exile as if he were a king. This is not an assurance of ultimate triumph, such
as is given by the archangel Gabriel in lines 405–12. There is a series of
such assurances, which runs parallel to the series of intimations of the Cid's
royal status; the two series sometimes coincide, and they both point to the
triumphant last lines of the poem, but they are distinct. Assurances of a hero's
success are common enough in medieval narrative, but it is far less common
to find intimations, at first implicit but later explicitly pronounced (in this
case by King Alfonso), that the hero is, indeed, of the stature of kings.

The fact that the Cid, after the capture of several towns and villages,
is able to exact tribute from the great city of Saragossa is a sign of his
increasing military power, but it does not tell us of a progress towards royal
status. That progress is, however, amply demonstrated after the capture of
Valencia. First, the Cid appoints don Jerónimo as Bishop of Valencia:

> 'en tierras de Valencia quiero fer obispado
> e dárgelo a este buen christiano [...].'
> Plogo a Álbar Fáñez de lo que dixo don Rodrigo;
> a este don Jerónimo yal' otorgan por obispo,
> diéronle en Valencia ó bien puede estar rrico.
> ¡Dios, qué alegre era todo christianismo
> que en tierras de Valencia señor avié obispo! (ll. 1299–1306)

An exiled *infanzón*, however successful militarily, had of course no authority to
appoint bishops. This was a matter for the king, and by making the appointment
the Cid is acting as if he were king of Valencia (see Socarrás 1971). What is
more, no one queries his right to do so.

The next piece of evidence comes from the King himself, when he says:

> viniéssem' a vistas, si oviesse dent sabor. [...]
> Dezid a Ruy Díaz, el que en buen ora nasco,
> quel' iré a vistas dó fuere aguisado,
> dó él dixiere í sea el mojón. (ll. 1899b and 1910–12)

It was for the king to choose when and where to have a formal meeting (*vistas*)
even with a vassal of high rank, let alone an exiled vassal who had not yet been
pardoned, but Alfonso invites the Cid to choose the place, which he does: the
banks of the Tagus. In return, the Cid asks Alfonso to choose the time:

> Sobre Tajo, que es una agua cabdal,
> ayamos vistas quando lo quiere mio señor. (ll. 1954–5)

The only circumstances in which it would be normal for one party to the meeting to choose the place and for the other to choose the time would be in a diplomatic exchange between monarchs. There is, of course, no question of the Cid's claiming royal status; indeed, he prostrates himself before Alfonso at the *vistas* (ll. 2021–5). Yet he behaves as if he had the privileges of a king, and Alfonso, far from objecting, treats him as if he had them.

The implications of the arrival at Cardeña, the appointment of the bishop, and the fixing of the *vistas* show a poet with legal training at work.[6] The next piece of evidence requires no legal training; it stems from a widely diffused part of the medieval world-picture. One of the best-known episodes in the *Cantar* is that of the Cid's lion. Having escaped from his cage and caused 'grant miedo [...] por medio de la cort' (l. 2283), the lion submits as soon as he sees the Cid:

> El león, quando lo vio, assí envergonçó,
> ante Mio Cid la cabeça premió e el rrostro fincó. (ll. 2298–9)

This episode is far more complex than it at first seems to be, and a number of traditions and of narrative sequences intersect here, so it is natural that a number of interpretations should have been offered by critics, but some (e.g. Bandera-Gómez 1969) have been shown to be invalid.[7] The lion is not the one familiar to us in the bestiary; the 'viga del lagar' behind which one of the Infantes de Carrión hides does not, except perhaps parodically, represent the Cross (l. 2290). The central meaning of the episode – not its central narrative function, which lies elsewhere – is that of hierarchy (see Olson 1962). Specifically, the lion defines the Cid's hierarchical status: by his immediate submission the king of beasts recognizes a king among men.[8]

First, the spontaneous verdict of the people of Burgos, then a series of episodes with legal implications, and then confirmation from the natural world. All of this builds up to the dénouement of the poem. At the *cortes* convened by Alfonso to hear the Cid's complaint against the Infantes de Carrión, he is invited by the king to join him in the seats of power:

> El rrey dixo al Cid: 'Venid acá ser, Campeador,
> en aqueste escaño quem' diestes vós en don;
> maguer que a algunos pesa, mejor sodes que nós. (ll. 3114–16)

6   For this aspect of the poem, see Russell (1952), Socarrás (1971), Smith (1977), Hook (1980), and Lacarra (1980: 1–102).

7   The best account of the episode is in Hook (1976).

8   Such correspondences within what has been called the 'Great Chain of Being' are frequent in medieval thought, literature and art. See Lovejoy (1936) and Tillyard (1943: 77–93).

The hero modestly declines, but the point has been made. It is made again, clearly and triumphantly, in the famous last lines of the poem:

> ¡Ved quál ondra crece al que en buen ora nació
> quando señoras son sus fijas de Navarra e de Aragón!
> Oy los rreyes d'España sos parientes son,
> a todos alcança ondra por el que en buen ora nació. (ll. 3722–5)

The transformation is complete. The Cid, nominally never more than an *infanzón*, attains equality with kings in his lifetime and superiority to them in death.

The *Auto de los Reyes Magos*

A different kind of sovereignty is presented in the *Auto de los Reyes Magos*, the oldest Castilian vernacular play. It was long accepted that the *Auto* was composed in Toledo in the mid-twelfth century, but although the place has been confirmed the date has been shown to be considerably later. Lucy K. Pick, in a closely argued chapter, shows that in all probability the play comes from the circle of Rodrigo Ximénez de Rada, Archbishop of Toledo (she does not exclude the possibility of his authorship), and gives dramatic form to the ideas set out in his *Dialogus libri vite*.[9] The date is likely to be late in the second decade of the thirteenth century, that is to say some ten years after the *Cantar de Mio Cid*.[10]

The *Auto* tells the familiar story of the Epiphany in an often unfamiliar way: most strikingly, it omits the arrival of the Magi at the manger. This is not a case of an ending lost because of a leaf missing from a manuscript; the scene was deliberately omitted, and the ending that we have is the one that was intended.[11] We shall see in due course how important that ending is for the theme of divided sovereignty and the exile of the true king.

The title – a modern one, provided because the manuscript gives no title – is misleading. The three wise men from the East are nowhere referred to as kings, and they address each other as 'senior(es)'.[12] It is true that 'senior' is used in the sense of 'lord, ruler':

[9] 'If Rodrigo was not himself the author of the *Auto*, it was certainly he who sponsored the work and decided its form, message, and content' (2004: 185, also 199).

[10] This discovery invalidates the closing lines of Deyermond (1989a), though not, fortunately, the main argument of the article.

[11] See Hook and Deyermond (1985). This conclusion is endorsed by Pick (2004: 190–1).

[12] All my quotations are taken from Pérez Priego (1997). Some of what I say here about the *Auto* is based on Deyermond (1989a) and on the section of Hook and Deyermond (1985) for which I was primarily responsible.

> senior á a seer da oriente
> de todos hata in occidente (ll. 25–6)

but it is not used of the Magi in that sense. There is, however, increasing emphasis on the royal and/or divine nature of the new-born child, beginning with Caspar's words in lines 5–6, going on to Baltasar's (just quoted) and Melchior's (ll. 40–3), and culminating in the discussion on how to establish the child's nature:

> CASPAR ¿Cúmo podremos provar si es homne mortal
> o si es rei de terra o si celestrial?
> MELCHIOR ¿Queredes bine saber cúmo lo sabremos?
> oro, mira i acenso a él ofreçremos.
> Si fure rei de terra, el oro querá;
> si fure omne mortal, la mira tomará;
> si rei celestrial, estos dos dexará,
> tomará el encenso quel' pertenecerá. (ll. 65–72)

The baby will, of course, take all three gifts, since he is mortal man, king, and God, but this must, in the absence of the scene at the manger, be deduced by the sophisticated audience for which the play was written.

The Magi come to the court of Herod (the only king who appears in the action of the play) and, in response to his question about the purpose of their travel, Melchior says:

> Imos en romería aquel rei adorar,
> que es nacido in tirra, nol' podemos fallar. (ll. 77–8)

This causes extreme agitation: Herod asks five questions in two lines. Melchior responds with:

> Rei, un rei es nacido que es senior de tirra,
> que mandará el seclo en grant pace sines guerra. (ll. 84–5)

The Magi seem to know that two kinds of kingship are involved, and the juxtaposition of the two uses of 'rei' reinforces this. This does not occur to Herod, who can see only a threat to his position. He dissembles until the Magi have left, and then bursts out:

> ¿Quién vio numquas tal mal?
> ¡Sobre rei otro tal!
> ¡Aún non só io morto
> ni so la terra pusto!
> ¿Rei otro sobre mí?

Numquas atal non vi.
El seglo va a çaga,
ia non sé qué me faga. (ll. 107–14)

I have discussed elsewhere the typological significance of 'El seglo va a çaga'. What is important in the present context is that it shows that Herod cannot imagine any kind of kingship other than his own earthly one.[13] The play ends before he orders the slaughter of the first-born, and before the exile of the new-born king in Egypt, but this will inevitably have been in the minds of the audience as they witnessed his rage. Unlike Alfonso he cannot accept, or even envisage, a king who will complement his rule instead of destroying it, and this lack of understanding brings about the destruction that he fears. In the last scene, the dispute between the rabbis (unusual in literature of the period and unprecedented in Epiphany plays, as Winifred Sturdevant (1927), found), we see the foundations of Herod's court crumbling.

Libro de Apolonio

Both the *Cantar de Mio Cid* and the *Auto de los Reyes Magos* are rooted in history – secular and recent in one case, sacred and distant in the other – but the *Libro de Apolonio* is not only fictitious, it makes no serious attempt to present itself as historical. It is the earliest of the Castilian works deriving from the *Historia Apollonius regis Tyri*, and in form it, like other poems in *cuaderna vía*, is indebted to the *Libro de Alexandre*. It is harder to date than either the *Cantar de Mio Cid* or the *Auto de los Reyes Magos*, but it is likely to have been composed round about the middle of the thirteenth century.[14]

---

[13] James F. Burke, pointing out that the theme of the world upside-down is 'very characteristic of carnival', argues that 'interlaced with [the *Auto*'s] orderly program is almost certainly an intertext derived from this widespread opposing face of medieval culture' (1998: 88). Burke goes on to cite evidence, from medieval texts and from folklore, that links the Epiphany and the Feast of the Innocents with burlesque paradramatic activities such as the Boy Bishop and the Feast of Fools (1998: 89–92). It is obviously true that Herod's rage is, among other things, comic (the same may be said of the dispute of the rabbis), and I agree that there may well be 'a connection between the context of the play and one of the most important of the themes of the December celebrations – the role of the mock king' (93). However, I do not believe that there is evidence in the text of the play that 'both Christ and Herod can be seen as temporary carnival rulers' (93), or that the comparisons adduced by Burke impose such a reading of Christ's role in the *Auto*. Seeing Herod as a temporary carnival ruler is consistent with what I have said about him, but to see the new-born Jesus in the same light conflicts with what, in my reading of the play, the dramatist is showing us.

[14] Among recent editors, Manuel Alvar dates it at c. 1260 (1976: I, 79 and 96) and Carmen Monedero at c. 1240 (1987: 14–15). Both acknowledge the impossibility of greater precision, and in his *editio minor* Alvar is even more cautious: 'bien mediado el siglo XIII' (1984: xvi).

The plot is essentially that of the *Historia Apollonius regis Tyri*, though the structure is improved and some of the inconsistencies are resolved. In the prologue the poet describes Apolonio as courteous and loyal to his wife and daughter (st. 1d, 2d).[15] The action begins with incestuous rape committed by the widowed King of Antioch upon his only daughter (st. 6–7). From the outset, then, Tyre is fixed in the reader's or listener's mind as a centre of virtue, Antioch as a centre of vice, a polarity equivalent to that between Jerusalem and Babylon, or between the two cities in Augustine's *De civitate Dei*.[16] Antioco conceals his crime, and, because many princes seek to marry his daughter (st. 5a), he devises a riddle ('un argument cerrado', st. 15b), which all suitors must try to solve; those who fail will be killed, the one who succeeds will win the princess's hand (she is never named, and seems to lack an independent identity). Apolonio alone is able to solve the riddle, thereby revealing Antioco's guilt. Antioco, not surprisingly, denies that this is the correct solution, and he gives Apolonio another chance (a concession not offered to any of the previous suitors). Apolonio is a king, as is Antioco, so what gives one the power of life and death over the other? We are never told of a connection between the two kingdoms; Tyre is not a client state of Antioch, and there is no mention of suzerainty. Antioco's dominance is, it seems, one of greater political and military power.

Apolonio returns to Tyre and shuts himself in his library, but can find no other solution to the riddle (st. 31–2). Antioco sends an assassin after him, but Apolonio, who has foreseen this, flees the country, beginning a series of Mediterranean voyages, shipwrecks, and other adventures. It does not occur to him to defend himself in his own country, and like the Cid but in very different circumstances, he becomes an exile. In the fullness of time Antioco is punished, and the news is brought to Apolonio, who has married another princess:

> Dil' [a Apolonio] que es Antioco muerto e soterrado,
> con él murió la fija, que le dio el pecado,
> destruyólos a amos un rayo endiablado.
> A él esperan todos por darle el reinado. (st. 248)

Most modern readers, I should think, find it surprising and distasteful that Antioco's daughter should receive exactly the same punishment as her father, but we have no way of knowing how a thirteenth-century audience reacted. This is, however, not a question that affects the subject of the present chapter (I discuss it in Deyermond 1989b). What is important in the present context is that with Antioco's death Apolonio's exile ends, and that the throne of Antioch passes to him. Why should it? The only explanation that occurs to me is that by solving

---

15 My quotations from this poem are taken from Alvar (1984).
16 Here and at other points in this section I draw on Deyermond (1989b).

Antioco's riddle Apolonio has won the princess as his bride, that she is regarded as being *de jure* his wife, and that he inherits from her. There is, of course, a problem here: if Apolonio has been married to Antioco's daughter all along, what becomes of his marriage to Luciana, heir to the throne of Pentapolis? The question is not raised in the poem, so we must assume that it was not something that troubled the poet, and for the purposes of the present study it must be bypassed.

When Architrastres, King of Pentapolis and Apolonio's father-in-law, dies, Apolonio succeeds him:

> Cuando fue el buen rey d'este sieglo passado,
> com' él lo merescié, noblemient soterrado,
> el gobierno del rey e todo su dictado
> fincó en Apolonio, ca era aguisado. (st. 629)

This stanza makes explicit (though it does not explain) the line of succession to the throne of Pentapolis, confirming that this is what happened in the case of Antioch. We are reading about a world in which (presumably in the absence of a direct male heir) son-in-law succeeds father-in-law. More surprisingly, Apolonio now reigns also over Tarsus and Mitylene (the territory of his son-in-law Prince Antinágora), as the people of Tyre point out:

> El poder de Antioco, que te era contrario,
> a tú se es rendido, a tú es tributario,
> ordenest' en Pentapolín tu fijo por vicario,
> Tarso e Mitalena tuyas son sin famario. (st. 646)[17]

All these realms are his to dispose of as he wishes. The suzerainty that Antioco lacked, so that he had to rely on force, is now vested in Apolonio. In some cases we are not told the reason, but the impression given is that all this is a reward for his virtue. He is a different, and greater, kind of king.

Conclusion

Other works of the same period show other kinds of divided or disputed sovereignty. The *Libro de Alexandre* (first years of the thirteenth century) shows the taking over of an empire; in stanzas 127–85 of Gonzalo de Berceo's *Vida de Santo Domingo de Silos* (1230s) we are shown a clash between royal and abbatial authority; the *Poema de Fernán González* (third quarter of the century?)

[17] *famario* = 'duplicity'.

shows, in striking contrast to the *Cantar de Mio Cid*, the transformation of a vassal, albeit a powerful one, into an independent ruler, in the teeth of his king's opposition.[18] None of them, however, deals with two kinds of kingship as in the three works that are the subject of the present chapter, and none with the exile of a king (the future Santo Domingo is exiled, but there is no suggestion that he is a king).

It is natural to wonder whether the treatment of kingship in the *Cantar de Mio Cid*, the *Auto de los Reyes Magos*, and the *Libro de Apolonio* had a contemporary political purpose. María Eugenia Lacarra (1980: 105–212) and Colin Smith (1980–81) have argued for different, though not necessarily incompatible, motives for the composition of the *Cantar*, but neither of these involves a dispute over the nature of kingship at the court of Alfonso VIII. The *Auto* clearly aims at the conversion of the Jews, and this fits its revised date of composition as well as its traditional one, but there is nothing in it to suggest arguments about the nature of kingship early in the reign of Fernando III. And although the fact that the *Libro de Apolonio* is an adaptation of a much older Latin narrative does not in itself exclude a political motivation (I have suggested elsewhere (1985) that rivalry at the court of Alfonso X may have been responsible for the translation from Arabic of the *Libro de los engaños* or *Sendebar*), it is hard to relate its plot or themes to events in the last years of Fernando III or the first years of Alfonso X. It seems, therefore, that these works reflect not contemporary crises in the monarchy but rather a continuing medieval interest in the nature of monarchy, an interest that is most obviously manifested in the genre of the *speculum principis*. Each of them shows either the survival and success of a king who recognizes that there may be more than one kind of kingship, or the defeat of a king who is incapable of recognizing it. In the *Cantar de Mio Cid*, King Alfonso comes to accept the Cid's royal quality, and he thereby ensures not only his own survival on the throne but also that of his descendants. Herod, in the *Auto de los Reyes Magos*, is unable to adjust, is convinced that the world is turned upside-down, and witnesses in the last scene the dispute between the rabbis that gives dramatic intensity to the crumbling of his power. In the *Libro*

18 The *Libro de Alexandre* was previously thought to have been composed in the mid-1220s, but Amaia Arizaleta has argued convincingly for the first years of the century (1999: 19–26). Enzo Franchini (1997) and Gerold Hilty (1997) present evidence for a later date. The earliest extant manuscript of the *Vida de Santo Domingo de Silos* is c. 1240, but the archetype was probably c. 1236 (Dutton 1978: 18–20). On the basis of historical evidence, the *Poema de Fernán González*, previously believed to be c. 1250, is dated at about 1276 by María Eugenia Lacarra (1979), and at 1280–85 by Jean Paul Keller (1990: 92–9). More recent studies have, however, returned to the idea of composition soon after the middle of the century: in particular, Itzíar López Guil questions some of the historical evidence and, on the basis of linguistic evidence, concludes that the poem was composed in the 1250s (2001: 17–27). The question remains open.

de Apolonio the point is made not with the subtlety of the *Auto* but brutally, when Antioco is destroyed by a thunderbolt. 'Rei otro sobre mí?' The new king will return from exile in triumph, come what may, but whether that triumph permits the survival of the old order depends on whether the new kind of king is accepted and welcomed.

List of Works Cited

Alvar, Manuel (ed.), 1976. *'Libro de Apolonio': estudios, ediciones, concordancias*, 3 vols (Madrid: Fundación Juan March & Castalia)

—— (ed.), 1984. *Libro de Apolonio*, Clásicos Universales Planeta, 80 (Barcelona: Planeta)

Archibald, Elizabeth, 1991. *Apollonius of Tyre: Medieval and Renaissance Themes and Variations* (Cambridge: D. S. Brewer)

Arizaleta, Amaia, 1999. *La Translation d'Alexandre: recherches sur les structures et les significations du 'Libro de Alexandre'*, Annexes des *Cahiers de Linguistique Hispanique Médiévale*, 12 (Paris: Séminaire d'Études Médiévales Hispaniques de l'Université de Paris-XIII)

Bandera-Gómez, Cesáreo, 1969. *El 'Poema de Mio Cid': poesía, historia, mito*, Biblioteca Románica Hispánica, 2.124 (Madrid: Gredos)

Bautista, Francisco, 2005. 'Nobleza y bandos en la *Cadira de honor*', in *Juan Rodríguez del Padrón: Studies in Honour of Olga Tudorică Impey*, ed. Alan Deyermond and Carmen Parrilla, I: *Poetry and Doctrinal Prose*, Papers of the Medieval Hispanic Research Seminar, 47 (London: Department of Hispanic Studies, Queen Mary, University of London), pp. 103–35

Bayo, Juan Carlos, 2002. 'La datación del *Poema de Mio Cid* y el problema de la tradición manuscrita', in *'Mio Cid' Studies: 'Some Problems of Diplomatic' Fifty Years On*, ed. Alan Deyermond, David G. Pattison, and Eric Southworth, Papers of the Medieval Hispanic Research Seminar, 42 (London: Department of Hispanic Studies, Queen Mary, University of London), pp. 15–35

Burke, James F., 1998. 'The Other Side of the Diptych: The *Auto de los Reyes Magos*', in his *Desire against the Law: The Juxtaposition of Contraries in Early Medieval Spanish Literature* (Stanford: Stanford University Press), pp. 79–95 and 258–61

Deyermond, Alan, 1982. 'The Close of the *Cantar de Mio Cid*: Epic Tradition and Individual Variation', in *The Medieval Alexander Legend and Romance Epic: Essays in Honour of David J. A. Ross*, ed. Peter Noble, Lucie Polak, and Claire Isoz (Millwood, NY: Kraus International), pp. 11–18

——, 1985. 'The *Libro de los engaños*: Its Social and Literary Context', in *The Spirit of the Court: Selected Proceedings of the Fourth Congress of the International Courtly Literature Society*, ed. Glyn S. Burgess and Robert A. Taylor (Cambridge: D. S. Brewer), pp. 158–67

——, 1989a. 'El *Auto de los Reyes Magos* y el renacimiento del siglo XII', in *Actas*

del IX Congreso de la Asociación Internacional de Hispanistas, ed. Sebastian Neumeister (Frankfurt am Main: Vervuert for AIH), I, pp. 187–94
——, 1989b. 'Emoción y ética en el *Libro de Apolonio*', *Vox Romanica*, 48: 153–64
Dutton, Brian (ed.), 1978. Gonzalo de Berceo, *Obras completas*, IV: *La vida de Santo Domingo de Silos*, Colección Támesis, A74 (London: Tamesis Books)
Franchini, Enzo, 1997. 'El IV Concilio de Letrán, la apócope extrema y la fecha de composición del *Libro de Alexandre*', *La Corónica*, 25.2: 31–74
Guardiola, Conrado, 1982–83. 'La *hospitalitas* en la salida del Cid hacia el destierro', *La Corónica*, 11: 265–72
Hernández, Francisco J., 1994. 'Historia y epopeya: el *Cantar del Cid* entre 1147 y 1207', in *Actas del III Congreso de la Asociación Hispánica de Literatura Medieval (Salamanca, 3 al 6 de octubre de 1989)*, ed. María Isabel Toro Pascua (Salamanca: Biblioteca Española del Siglo XV and Departamento de Literatura Española e Hispanoamericana, Universidad de Salamanca), I, pp. 453–67
Hilty, Gerold, 1997. 'Fecha y autor del *Libro de Alexandre*', in *Actas del VI Congreso Internacional de la Asociación Hispánica de Literatura Medieval (Alcalá de Henares, 12–16 de septiembre de 1995)*, ed. José Manuel Lucía Megías (Alcalá de Henares: Universidad de Alcalá), pp. 813–20
Hook, David, 1976. 'Some Observations upon the Episode of the Cid's Lion', *MLR*, 71: 553–64
——, 1980. 'On Certain Correspondences between the *Poema de Mio Cid* and Contemporary Legal Instruments', *Iberoromania*, 11: 31–53
——, and Alan Deyermond, 1982. ' "Ipse Rodericus, rex quondam, rexque futurus"?: Intimations of the Cid's Royalty in the *Cantar de Mio Cid*', paper read at the Medieval Hispanic Research Seminar, Westfield College (12 February)
—— and ——, 1985. 'El problema de la terminación del *Auto de los Reyes Magos*', *Anuario de Estudios Medievales*, 13: 269–78
Kantorowicz, Ernst, 1957. *The King's Two Bodies: A Study in Medieval Political Theology* (Princeton: Princeton University Press)
Keller, Jean Paul, 1990. *The Poet's Myth of Fernán González* (Potomac, MD: Scripta Humanistica)
Lacarra, María Eugenia, 1979. 'El significado histórico del *Poema de Fernán González*', *Studi Ispanici* [no volume number]: 9–41
——, 1980. *El 'Poema de Mio Cid': realidad histórica e ideología* (Madrid: José Porrúa Turanzas)
Lewis, C. S., 1965. 'The Inner Ring', in *Screwtape Proposes a Toast and Other Pieces* (London: Collins, Fontana Books), pp. 28–40
López Guil, Itzíar (ed.), 2001. *Libro de Fernán González*, Clásicos de Biblioteca Nueva, 29 (Madrid: Biblioteca Nueva)
Lovejoy, Arthur O., 1936. *The Great Chain of Being: A Study of the History of an Idea* (Cambridge, MA: Harvard University Press)
Michael, Ian (ed.), 1978. *Poema de Mio Cid*, Clásicos Castalia, 75, 2nd edn (Madrid: Castalia)

16

Monedero, Carmen (ed.), 1987. *Libro de Apolonio*, Clásicos Castalia, 157 (Madrid: Castalia)

Montaner, Alberto, and Ángel Escobar (ed. and trans.), 2001. *'Carmen Campidoctoris', o poema latino del Campeador* (Madrid: España Nuevo Milenio)

Olson, Paul R., 1962, 'Symbolic Hierarchy in the Lion Episode of the *Cantar de Mio Cid*', *MLN*, 77: 499–511

Pérez Priego, Miguel Ángel (ed.), 1997. *Castilla*, Páginas de Biblioteca Clásica: Teatro Medieval, 2 (Barcelona: Editorial Crítica)

Pick, Lucy K., 2004. 'Polemic and Performance: The *Dialogus* and the *Auto de los Reyes Magos*', in her *Conflict and Coexistence: Archbishop Rodrigo and the Muslims and Jews of Medieval Spain* (Ann Arbor: University of Michigan Press), pp. 182–203

Round, Nicholas, 1986. *The Greatest Man Uncrowned: A Study of the Fall of Don Álvaro de Luna*, Colección Támesis, A111 (London: Tamesis Books)

Russell, P. E., 1952. 'Some Problems of Diplomatic in the *Cantar de Mio Cid* and their Implications', *MLR*, 47: 340–9

Smith, Colin, 1977. 'On the Distinctiveness of the *Poema de Mio Cid*', in *'Mio Cid' Studies*, ed. A. D. Deyermond, Colección Támesis, A59 (London: Tamesis Books), pp. 161–94

——, 1980–81. 'The Choice of the Infantes de Carrión as Villains in the *Poema de Mio Cid*', *Journal of Hispanic Philology*, 4: 105–18

Socarrás, Cayetano J., 1971. 'The Cid and the Bishop of Valencia: An Historical Introduction', *Iberoromania*, 3: 101–11

Sturdevant, Winifred, 1927. *The 'Misterio de los Reyes Magos': Its Position in the Development of the Mediaeval Legend of the Three Kings*, Johns Hopkins Studies in Romance Literatures and Languages, 10 (Baltimore: Johns Hopkins University Press; Paris: Presses Universitaires de France)

Tillyard, E. M. W., 1943. *The Elizabethan World Picture* (London: Chatto & Windus)

The Role of Women in Some Medieval Spanish Epic and Chronicle Texts

DAVID G. PATTISON

The received wisdom about the role of women in Spanish epic, specifically in the *Poema de mio Cid*, has been that they have subordinate, submissive roles. In 1995, María Eugenia Lacarra wrote, '[l]a importancia de las mujeres se relaciona directamente con la política matrimonial de los protagonistas, de ahí que su presencia se deba a las relaciones de parentesco que tienen con ellos y que su papel se ciña a su función de madres, hijas o esposas' (1995: 41). And in more general terms, Gloria Beatriz Chicote wrote in 1996 'la épica románica surge en la Edad Media europea como el vehículo de expresión de un mundo de hombres' (1996: 75); and María Luzdivina Cuesta in 1997, 'la familia sólo incidía en la narración en cuanto formaba parte de la identidad del protagonista y compartía su honra y honor' (1997: 94).

Some thirty years ago, Lucy Sponsler, in her book *Women in the Medieval Spanish Epic and Lyric Traditions*, provided us with perhaps the most typical – and, from modern perspectives, slightly naïve and possibly anachronistic – view of the role of women in the *Poema de mio Cid*. She wrote,

> Jimena and Rodrigo are deeply in love and happily married. Through the pages of the *Poema* Jimena emerges as an ideal wife, whose deep respect, love, and obedience to her husband stimulate the admiration of the poet and the reader. Epithets [...] continually indicate that the medieval poet respects Jimena's prudence and understanding, her virtue and moral qualities [...]. (1975: 7)

Versions of this paper were read at the annual conference of the Association of Hispanists of Great Britain and Ireland (as a Presidential Address), at Cork in April 2002, and at the Third Conference on The Medieval Chronicle, at Utrecht in July 2002. I am grateful to those who participated in discussions, both formal and informal, on those occasions.

Again, she wrote, 'there can be no doubt that the main aim of the poem is the glorification of a masculine hero, and in achieving this, woman, from a modern standpoint, is viewed in a subordinate and submissive role'; or, 'Jimena can bask in Rodrigo's reflected honor and glory, and she can inspire him to great heights by being present to buttress his masculine pride; yet these are secondary roles dependent on a man for their fulfilment. Rodrigo respects and loves Jimena because she is a devoted mother and because she appreciates his masculine strength and valor, but he and the poet clearly view the ideal wife as lacking any role outside the marital and family structure'; and, on the Cid's daughters, 'The limited role played by Doña Elvira and Doña Sol in finding mates for themselves illustrates how restricted were the rights the medieval Spanish woman possessed even before she found herself subdued in the marital relationship' (1975: 8, 9, 10). This is, then, the received wisdom, and although one might argue that the last critic quoted, at least, is rather too ready to read into the text aspects – love, devotion, prudence, virtue, respect – which are at best implied and, one might argue, matters of inference from a twentieth-century perspective, the fundamental premise of the subordinate, not to say submissive aspect of women's role cannot be gainsaid.

However, even in the case of the *Poema de mio Cid*, it is important not to play down the importance – the functional importance, one might say – of the feminine role. In Lacarra's words, 'las mujeres son imprescindibles, porque a través de ellas el héroe establece su linaje, transmite sus bienes y poder a sus legítimos herederos y preserva también su fama a las generaciones venideras' (1995: 39). Joseph Duggan also makes the point of the crucial nature of the marriage of the Cid's daughters in the *Poema*: 'The Cid's daughters' two sets of marriages are imbedded in this framework. They serve a predominantly economic purpose in that they allow the exchange of the hero's wealth first for an ephemeral prestige based solely on the values of inherited rank, then for a lasting one that joins his lineage with the royal families of Navarre and Aragon' (1989: 147).

In the *Mocedades de Rodrigo* – the other surviving extant poetic epic text of the period – Jimena plays a much more obviously active role than she or her daughters do in the *Poema de mio Cid*, by demanding marriage to the young Cid as reparation for his having killed her father. Gloria Chicote wrote of this that 'se presenta en las *Mocedades* en una posición activa [...] haciendo uso de su derecho de pedir reparación [...] y merced' (1996: 79); Lacarra's words are that she 'actúa como dueña de iniciativa' (1995: 45).

For other epic material we have to depend on later indirect evidence found in chronicle prosifications (the late thirteenth-century tradition begun by Alfonso X, *el sabio*, drew extensively on epic material) and on ballads. Questions of genre arise here and will be taken up in my conclusion.

Turning to the first category, chronicle prosifications of lost epic texts, the first legend to be considered, that of Bernardo del Carpio, conforms well to the stereotype: the female character who provides, in a way, the starting point of the story, is the sister, Jimena, of the ninth-century Leonese king Alfonso II; she has an illicit relationship and clandestine marriage to a nobleman, the conde San Díaz de Saldaña, and from this liaison is born Bernardo. The outraged king imprisons the count and sends his sister to a convent, but has the young Bernardo brought up at his court; the rest of the story follows Bernardo's military career and has as its climax a scene in which the rebel Bernardo so embarrasses the king (by this time it is Alfonso III) that he is able to insist on his father's release: too late, for the count has died; but he is 'resurrected', bathed, dressed and mounted on horseback in a scene reminiscent of a later and better known one describing the Cid's posthumous victory over the Moors after his death in Valencia. In this story the role of the woman, Jimena, is passive and minimal. In no chronicle version do we hear anything of her after she is sent to the convent, and Bernardo shows no interest in her fate: this is stereotypical treatment of a woman whose role is simply that of providing the initial situation from which the male-dominated action flows. As Andrew Beresford remarked, 'given the significance of female characters in other epics, Ximena's presence is somewhat perfunctory' (2000: 44).

In the story of Fernán González, first count of an independent Castile, the most important female character is called Sancha, and she is a princess, sister of King García of Navarre. That king captured and imprisoned the Castilian count; but the princess hatched a plot for his release, on condition that he agreed to marry her. The actual escape seems simple (she is, after all, the king's sister, and presumably she is used to obedience from the staff); she is, by the way, a strong woman in every respect: the count is still in chains as they make their way across country, and we read in the *Estoria de España* that, 'porque el conde non podie andar por los fierros que eran muy pesados, ouole la infant a leuar a cuestas una grant pieça' (Menéndez Pidal 1955: 413 b 28–31); she shows further evidence of strength, guile, self-confidence and even shamelessness in an episode which follows: the two fugitives are assailed by a lecherous cleric who wants to have his wicked way with the princess as his price for not turning them in to the authorities; she pretends to comply, and tells the archpriest to undress and leave his clothes with Fernán González and then come with her to a more private spot. The narrative continues: 'et el arçipreste cuedando luego complir la su uoluntad, trauo della et quisola abraçar. Mas la inffant, como era muy buena duenna et muy esforçada, trauo del a la boruca et dio una grand tirada contra si', whereupon the count arrives with a knife and, 'mataronle alli amos a dos' (Menéndez Pidal 1955: 414 a 35-40, 43-4). (The meaning of the word *boruca* is not entirely clear; it may mean 'testicles', and one chronicle version of the story substitutes the euphemistic but perfectly clear *verguenças* for it, while others bowdlerize the story to the extent of simply saying, 'trauo del muy esforçadamente/ reziamente'.)

Doña Sancha is also involved in another later episode of Fernán González's life, when he is once again imprisoned, this time by the Leonese King Sancho I, *el gordo*. On this occasion she comes to ask the king for permission to spend the night with her husband; then we have the rather old story of the release facilitated by the couple changing clothes: having learned, perhaps, from earlier experience, she also asks that his irons be removed; the king agrees, making a somewhat earthy reference to a possible reason with the words 'que el cauallo trauado nunqua bien podie fazer fijos' (Menéndez Pidal 1955: 421 a 1–2) – something else that various rather more prudish chroniclers omit, together with any reference to beds or to the couple sleeping together.

One notes the obviously sexual nature of much of this narrative and specifically of Sancha's part in it; more significant is that she is much more than her predecessor Jimena in the story of Bernardo del Carpio, or indeed than the other Jimena and her daughters in the *Poema de mio Cid* – that is, subsidiary and submissive participants in the action, bound up indeed in a web of family and matrimonial ties by no means lacking in thematic significance, but ultimately passive. This woman is a doer, one who influences the action by her own daring and takes control of the situation at crucial moments.

She does so, as it should be clear, in a wholly positive and admirable way; she is a heroine in the popular sense of the word, while not being the principal protagonist of the story. Yet the next two female characters to be discussed are far from being exemplary: they are Doña Lambra, who plays such a central role in the story of the *Siete Infantes de Lara*; and the eponymous Condesa Traidora. Doña Lambra is the woman at whose wedding there develops a feud between her and her husband on the one hand and, on the other, the seven noble brothers, the *infantes* of the title. Believing herself insulted (there is a lot of interesting and deeply symbolic business involving the throwing of a blood-filled cucumber) she incites her husband, Ruy Blásquez, to avenge the slur on her reputation and he duly arranges a treacherous ambush by the Moors in which the seven young men are killed and their severed heads taken to Córdoba. There, their father is languishing in prison (as a part of the same vendetta-like plot instigated by Doña Lambra); a Moorish noblewoman is sent to comfort him, they fall in love and she becomes pregnant. The son of this union, by name Mudarra, grows up and eventually travels to Castile, where he makes his business the avenging of the death of his half-brothers, the *infantes*. He challenges Ruy Blásquez, defeats him in single combat and takes him to the count for execution; but the narrative spends rather longer describing the sequence by which he takes revenge on Doña Lambra, who is clearly considered the real villain of the piece. In the *Estoria de España* we find simply the laconic remark that, 'priso a donna Llambla [...] et fizola quemar' (Menéndez Pidal 1955: 448 a 18–19), but in a later version, the *Crónica de 1344*, there is a more extended description of her death: after an unsuccessful appeal to Count Garçi Fernández, she hears the count's sentence:

> Mentides como grande alevosa, ca vos basteçiestes todas estas trayçiones e males que el [Ruy Blásquez] fizo [...], de aqui adelante non vos atreguo el cuerpo, e mandare a don Mudarra que vos faga quemar viva, e que espedaçen canes vuestras carnes e la vuestra alma sera perdida para siempre.
>
> (Menéndez Pidal 1951: 235–6)

We are then told that on her eventual capture by Mudarra, 'mandole dar tal muerte como dio a Ruy Vasquez', which in this chronicle version was in fact a gruesome one involving his being speared and dismembered on a *tablado*, and then stoned (1951: 235–6).

If Doña Lambra provides an example of a female character whose behaviour, far from being passive, is not only active but malignantly and disruptively so, the Condesa Traidora is yet more devious and potentially damaging. The story tells of the two wives of Count Garçi Fernández, the son of Fernán González and the second count of Castile. The first wife is a French woman called Doña Argentina, who becomes unhappy with her marriage to the Castilian count and runs away with a visiting French count (it might be said that by the very act of elopement she shows herself to be, in Andrew Beresford's words, 'another example of ardent females taking their fates into their own hands' [2000: 53]). Her husband eventually recovers from the illness (Patricia Grieve argues that there may be a hint of impotence: she says 'it would not be impossible to make a case for Garci Fernández's sexual inadequacy' [1987: 320]); he tracks her down to her new home in France, but does so in disguise, as a beggar. He is recognized as a man of quality by the French count's daughter Sancha, who then promises to help him avenge his dishonour at the price of marriage to her. The stratagem by which she does so is an interesting, if faintly comic one: Sancha hides Garçi Fernández under her parents' bed (actually, of course, her father's and stepmother's) with a string tied to his toe. When she is sure they are asleep, she pulls on the string as a signal, whereupon he emerges and decapitates them: the point there is that he is able to return to Castile with tangible proof (in the form of severed heads) that he has expunged the stain on his honour. He duly keeps his word and marries Doña Sancha, but she turns out to be even more treacherous than her predecessor: she wishes to marry a Moorish king (Beresford says, 'yet another example of female assertiveness with regard to sexual union' [2000: 53]), and brings about her husband's death by weakening his war-horse before a battle against the Moors, feeding it bran instead of barley. She then turns her attention on her son Sancho, the new count, and plots to kill him by poisoning his wine. However, her plot is discovered by a neat twist (also with sexual overtones): her plot is overheard by one of her maids who is having an illicit relationship (the phrase used in the chronicle is 'fazia mal de su fazienda') with one of the count's squires or bodyguards; the count, returning from a hard day's fighting against the Moors, is offered the poisoned wine but, forewarned by his faithful squire, forces his mother to drink from the cup first; she duly dies.

Beresford's remarks, which I have quoted in passing, are indeed significant: both *condesas* – assertive women, to be sure – are indeed driven by sexual passion to an extent which it would be hard to parallel in other texts of this kind; and I wholeheartedly agree with Alan Deyermond's conclusion that in this story, 'el argumento y el interés sexual se extienden' and 'la sexualidad se intensifica en el desenlace también' (1988: 774, 775). Patricia Grieve, again, has an interesting point to make in her summing up: 'Sancha began her individual quest with a personal vendetta, but she became a 'public woman' by moving increasingly into the sphere of political concerns, even though the motivating forces for her actions – lust and a desire for social status – remain personal aims' (1987: 324).

Often closely associated with the *Condesa traidora* story is that usually called *El infant García*. García was in fact not only a prince but – briefly – count of Castile, succeeding his father Sancho (the protagonist of the final part of the story just discussed). The young García, on succeeding his father, was betrothed to the sister of the king of León, also, perhaps confusingly, called Sancha. On travelling to León to meet his bride, García was confronted by rebellious nobles exiled by his father, the sons of *el conde* Don Vela. We are told how the *infante* was murdered in cold blood, and that his fiancée Doña Sancha was also maltreated, one of the murderers slapping her face, taking her by the hair and throwing her down the stairs. Although the young couple had known each other only a short time, we are told in the chronicles that it was a case of love at first sight, and that the princess was so affected by García's death that she tried to throw herself into his grave. It is in the epilogue to the story, however, that the unfortunate Doña Sancha comes into her own, as it were: she prevails on King Sancho of Navarre – who had accompanied the Castilian count to León (he was his uncle by marriage) – to put her vengeance in hand. This he does willingly, capturing the Vela brothers and burning them at the stake after the customary torture. However, their accomplice Fernán Laínez was the perpetrator of the personal violence on Doña Sancha, and she resolves to bring him to justice herself. Interestingly, she becomes betrothed to the son of King Sancho of Navarre and, in

Beresford's words, 'soon realises that her sexuality is an important weapon, for [...] she resolves that she will not consummate the marriage until Fernán Laínez has been captured and killed' (2000: 61). The king obliges, whereupon we find what is probably one of the most gruesome acts of judicial violence in medieval Spanish literature:

> Tomo un cuchiello en su mano ella misma, et taiole luego las manos con que el firiera all inffant et a ella misma, desi taiol los pies con que andidiera en aquel fecho, despues sacole la lengua con que fablara la traycion; et desque esto ouo fecho, sacole los oios con que lo uiera todo. Et desque ouo parado tal, mando adozir una azemila et ponerle en ella et leuarle por quantas uillas et mercados auie en Castiella et en tierra de Leon do el fiziera aquella traycion, diziendo et pregonando sobrel cada logar que por la muerte que aquel Fernant Laynez basteçiera al inffant Garcia et fuera ell en ella, padecie ell aquello. (Menéndez Pidal 1955: 472 b 19–32)

Suffice it to say that here we have another example of an assertive female, and moreover one whose role occupies both the private and the public space, as the exemplary punishment meted out to Fernán Laínez is a consequence both of his violence towards her personally and of his involvement in regicide; what is more, the means she uses to achieve her end – the refusal to consummate her marriage with the *infante* Fernando – has clear dynastic implications and so is 'public' in this respect also. Alan Deyermond draws eminently valid conclusions from the role played by women in the stories so far discussed (what is often referred to as the Cycle of the Counts of Castile): 'In every epic of the Counts cycle which has come down to us in verse or prose, part at least of the action is strongly influenced by a woman [...]. The women generally have dominant personalities, and several prove capable of great savagery' (1976: 287–8).

Of my final two examples, one concerns a well-known figure, the other may be rather less familiar. The first is Doña Urraca, daughter of Fernando I and sister of Sancho II and Alfonso VI, who plays a leading part in the fratricidal wars which followed on the death of her father, and particularly in the siege of Zamora. That series of episodes formed the subject matter of another lost epic poem, and has survived both in an interesting set of chronicle prosifications and in an almost equally flourishing ballad tradition. It is with a ballad that I want to begin: it is the well known one describing the deathbed of Fernando I, best known in the form beginning 'Morir vos queredes, padre'.

The context is that the king has distributed his lands among his three sons, Sancho, Alfonso and García, making no provision for his daughters. Urraca's complaint at this is as follows:

a mi porque soy muger dexays me deseredada
yrme yo por essas tierras como vna muger errada
y este mi cuerpo daria a quien se me antojara
a los Moros por dineros y a los Christianos de gracia [...].

(Díaz Roig 1976: 140)

This plan of so-to-speak selective prostitution has the effect of making the king change his plan to the extent of bequeathing to Doña Urraca the city of Zamora, 'la bien çercada' (one notes the use of a threat with sexual overtones to achieve her aims).

The story continues with Sancho's dispossession of his two brothers and culminates in his attempt to wrest Zamora from his sister; the city is besieged, and Doña Urraca receives an offer of help from one Vellido Adolfo or Dolfos. The Princess makes him a promise which, in the *Estoria de España*, is a veiled one: 'non a omne en el mundo que a mi hermano tolliesse de sobre Çamora et me la fiziesse descercar que yo non le diesse quequier que me demandasse' (Menéndez Pidal 1955: 510 a 5–8). Vellido duly murders King Sancho and returns to Zamora; in the *Estoria de España* version he is imprisoned, but nothing more is heard of him as the chronicler moves on to the challenge issued to the city by Diego Ordóñez and the return and accession of Alfonso as king. It is true that the *romancero* does hint at a sequel in the ballad 'Guarte, guarte, rey don Sancho', with Vellido Adolfo returning to the city with the words, '[t]iempo era, doña Urraca, de cumplir lo prometido' (Díaz Roig 1976: 145).

A later chronicle version, the fourteenth-century *Sumario escrito en el reinado de Enrique II por el despensero de la reina doña Leonor*, a version deriving from the earlier *Crónica de 1344*, throws some light on this aspect. In it we are told that Urraca's 'promise' to Vellido was a false one or at least one with serious mental reservations: 'como quiera que propuso a su voluntad de lo complir por manera que desonor non le viniese et cumpliese lo prometido segun gelo fizo como mas adelante oyriedes'; and the sequel is so curious that it deserves quoting: 'Doña Urraca tornose a Çamora et fizo atar de pies et de manos al dicho Vellido Dolfos et mandolo meter en un costal et liaronlo bien et por tener en la promesa mandolo echar en la cama donde ella dormio et doña Urraca se acosto vestida bien arredrada en aquella misma cama' (*Sumario*, quoted in Reig 1947: 76). In this version, she goes on, incidentally, the next morning, to have Vellido executed by having his hands and feet tied to four horses and consequently being dismembered as they depart in different directions: so she follows her mother Sancha in a taste for bloody punishment of a kind we should call cruel and unusual – but we should not, of course, take an anachronistic viewpoint.

However, there is no clear ancient tradition to suggest that in all this Urraca was doing more than uttering an ambiguous promise. The American critic Charles Fraker took the view that the older *cantar*, as reflected in the *Crónica Najerense*, did give credence to such a story, which was then expunged or sanitized by the later Alphonsine chroniclers – perhaps to be revived in the fourteenth-century version I have just quoted. Fraker writes, 'in the Sancho narrative of the Nájera chronicle, which is in all probability based ultimately on an older *Cantar*, Urraca simply offers her person and her wealth to the man who breaks the siege', and he goes on '[the *Crónica Najerense*] shows her as unchaste, proposing a love relationship with the savior of Zamora. To the narrator her lust is one of the most damning things about Zamora itself; the sinfulness of the princess accrues to the discredit of the city' (1996: 47, 51).

Whether or not any of this is true, Urraca does have an ambivalent reputation in the tradition; there are hints of a relationship with the Cid, most obviously in another ballad ('Afuera, afuera Rodrigo') where she says to Rodrigo, 'que pense casar contigo mas no lo quiso mi pecado' (Díaz Roig 1976: 141), and later chronicle accounts go to some pains to insist that there was no impropriety between Urraca and the Cid: after explaining how Rodrigo came under the protection of King Fernando and was brought up in his household, the author of the *Crónica de 1344* refers to the special relationship between Urraca and Rodrigo: 'ella amaualo mas que a nenguno de sus hermanos', but feels it necessary to add 'e non entendades que este amor que le ansi auia que era por nenguna otra manera que y ouiesse, nin de cuydo nin de fecho' (*Crónica de 1344*, quoted in Pattison 1983: 87, n. 16).

There even seems to have existed a legend of illicit, indeed incestuous love between Urraca and her brother Alfonso. That, at least, was the conclusion of Ramón Menéndez Pidal when he wrote, 'podemos sentar como históricamente cierto que hubo relaciones incestuosas entre Alfonso VI y su hermana Urraca', basing this contention on both the insistence of official historiographers on denying such a relationship and the acceptance in popular poetic sources of a secret wedding between the king and his sister, confirmed by a reference in the work of an Arab historian (1952: 86). Carolyn Bluestine also discussed these aspects, noting that 'there were persistent rumors of incest between Urraca and Alfonso', and that 'sexual intriguing between Vellido and Urraca is implied too' (1986: 57).

Without entering into the historical controversy about Urraca's sexual life, it must be accepted that the received picture of this eleventh-century princess was morally dubious to say the least. She may have slept with her brother Alfonso; she may have slept with the Cid; she may have offered herself to Vellido Dolfos as a reward for his killing her other brother Sancho. Whether or not this is historically true, that is the view of Urraca which emerges; and although we are here dealing with a much more firmly-based historical

character than in most of the other cases discussed above, the important part
of the message seems to be that – in legend and possibly in life also – we are
dealing with a sexually active woman who is prepared to use her sexuality
for political purposes: a worthy sister of the Sancha who was such a useful
asset to Fernán González, and the other Sancha (Urraca's mother, in fact)
who made such a good if bloody job of avenging the murder of the *infante*
García.

The last character to be examined is perhaps the least well known of the
heroines described here. Her name is Elvira – not the daughter of the Cid,
but the wife of King Sancho *el mayor* of Navarra. I devoted an article to
this legend some years ago, calling it 'The Legend of the Sons of Sancho
el Mayor' (Pattison 1980), but an alternative title of the story, and the one
favoured by Menéndez Pidal, was *La reina calumniada*, the 'slandered
queen'. According to the *Estoria de España*, Sancho inherited the County of
Castile, on the death of the *infante* García, through his wife Elvira, daughter
of the *infante*'s sister (another Sancha). King Sancho had two legitimate sons,
García and Fernando, and a third illegitimate one, Ramiro. The story goes
that the king had a favourite horse, of which he was so proud that it slept
in the palace; while the king was absent elsewhere in the kingdom, his wife
took special care of the horse; and when the eldest son, García, wanted to
ride it, she refused, on the advice of a 'cauallero que seruia en la casa de la
reyna' (Menendez Pidal 1955: 474 b 47–8). The prince, with the connivance
of his younger brother Fernando, thereupon made a false accusation against
his mother, claiming that she 'auie amiztat con aquel cauallero que estoruara
con ella quel non dio el cauallo' (Menéndez Pidal 1955: 475 a 5–7). The king
had the queen imprisoned and brought to trial, and the consensus was that
her honour should be defended by a champion, if one could be found. The
only man to come forward was the king's illegitimate son, Ramiro: 'ueno
estonces don Ramiro, fijo del rey, que era de barragana, omne muy fermoso
et muy esforçado en armas, et dixo por corte que el querie lidiar por la reyna'
(Menéndez Pidal 1955: 475 a 25–8). In fact the contest never took place, the
queen being vindicated from another source – García's confessor who was
quite happy to break the seal of the confessional in a good cause – but she
insisted, as her price for pardoning her malicious sons, that the eldest, García,
should not succeed his father as king of Castile (which was part of her own
inheritance) but that the second son, Fernando, should be king of Castile
– which he duly became as Fernando I – while García had to be content with
Navarre. She also used her good offices to ensure that her stepson Ramiro,
who had offered to fight for her honour, should receive his reward, and at
her instance he became king of Aragon: 'que era como logar apartado desto
al, por amor que non ouiesse contienda con sus hermanos' (Menéndez Pidal
1955: 475 b 11–13).

When writing about this story in 1980, I made the point that although the *Estoria de España* contains most of the important details, one – which is to be found in the much earlier *Crónica Najerense* and which subsequently resurfaces in later chronicle elaborations – is missing. This is the symbolic adoption by the queen of her stepson, the illegitimate Ramiro. The *Crónica Najerense* version reads as follows:

> Itaque regina [...] Ranimirum intra uestes coram regali curia recipiens, et quasi parturiet illum de sub uestibus eiciens in filium adoptauit, et in regno habere fecit portionem. (*Crónica Najerense*, quoted in Pattison 1980: 42)

With this, compare the version in the *Crónica de 1344*:

> E entuençe lo tomo & lo metio por una manga de la piel & sacolo por la otra, segunt que era costunbre en aquel tienpo de tomar los fijos adoctivos. (*Crónica de 1344*, quoted in Pattison 1980: 44)

The detail is a folkloric one; it appears also in the later and fuller version of the story of the Infantes de Lara, where Gonzalo Gustioz's wife Sancha adopts her stepson Mudarra – also illegitimate – in a very similar way:

> doña Sancha [...] reçibiolo por fijo como manda el fuero de Castiella: entonce tomolo, e metiolo por una manga de una falifa de çicatron que tenia vestida, e tirolo por la otra.
> (*Crónica de 1344*, in Menéndez Pidal 1951: 223)

Doña Elvira, the 'slandered queen', is interesting, I suggest, because she is shown as, first, a woman in a dangerous position; but then as one who profits from that position to influence dynastic and political events – the disposition of her husband's kingdom after his death – and in doing so, by her symbolic act of adoption, a kind of simulacrum of childbirth, reminds us of her female status, of the very status which put her in the vulnerable position setting in train the potentially disastrous sequence of events.

It is time to summarize: or rather, to say that few definite conclusions should be drawn from the above examples. Some of the women discussed – Jimena and her daughters in the *Poema de mio Cid*, arguably also the other Jimena, mother of Bernardo del Carpio – do seem to fit the stereotype of woman as a subsidiary and submissive figure; although even as such, by their very presence and the consequences of their passivity, they acquire a level of importance; to repeat Joseph Duggan's words about the Cid's daughters quoted above: '[their] two sets of marriages [...] serve a predominantly economic purpose in that they allow the exchange of the hero's wealth first for an ephemeral prestige based solely on the values of inherited rank, then for a lasting one that joins his lineage with the royal families of Navarre and Aragon' (1989: 147). Other women are unashamedly active, often in a sexual way; one thinks of the two Doña Sanchas, wives of Fernán González and of his son Garci Fernández (the second Condesa Traidora), arguably also of the third Sancha, who wreaked such bloody vengeance for the death of the *infante* García; or Doña Lambra in the story of the *Infantes de Lara*, whose reaction to a supposed slight sets in train such a disastrous sequence of events; and perhaps one might put the *infanta* Doña Urraca at least tentatively into this same category of voracious women to whom the words 'subsidiary' and 'submissive' could never rightly be applied.

The remaining women are the most interesting: it is not so much that they are active, or not specifically in any sexual or violent sense. They are the Doña Sancha of the *Infante García* story, whose insistence on bringing Fernán Laínez to justice before she will consummate her marriage with the *infante* Fernando has clear political repercussions; and, perhaps above all, the last case discussed, the slandered queen Elvira, whose reactions to the situation in which she finds herself are shown to have had such an important outcome in terms of the dynastic history of the Northern kingdoms.

At this point it is worth returning briefly to the generic question mentioned earlier. It is impossible to know the extent to which the compilers of chronicles or the authors of ballads added elements or nuances to the material they inherited from epic. It might be argued that in the epic, women tended to be passive, in chronicles active and even vengeful, and that ballads tended to stress the erotic; but such generalizations can only ever be speculative.

We may conclude, then, by saying that there exists a range of ways in which women are important in the epic, chronicle and ballad material of medieval Spain. Above all, we have to resist the notion that they are limited to subordinate roles or even that, though passive in themselves, they acquire a functional importance merely by virtue of their relationship to the hero and the part they play in perpetuating his lineage and honour. Some at least of the female characters examined take an active role in both their personal and their public lives, and by doing so give the lie to the kind of generalization quoted in the opening paragraphs above.

List of Works Cited

Beresford, Andrew M., 2000. ' "Cortol la cabeça e atola del petral ca la querie dar en dona a Galiana": On the Relationship between Death and Sexuality in Four Epic Legends' in *Textos épicos castellanos: problemas de edición y crítica*, ed. David G. Pattison, Papers of the Medieval Hispanic Research Seminar, 30 (London: Department of Hispanic Studies, Queen Mary and Westfield College), pp. 41–63

Bluestine, Carolyn, 1986. 'Traitors, Vows, and Temptresses in the Medieval Spanish Epic', *Romance Quarterly*, 33: 53–61

Chicote, Gloria Beatriz, 1996. 'Jimena, de la épica al romancero: definición del personaje y convenciones genéricas', in *Caballeros, monjas y maestros en la Edad Media (Actas de las V jornadas Medievales)*, ed. Lillian von der Walde, Concepción Company, and Aurelio González, Publicaciones de *Medievalia*, 13 (Mexico: Universidad Nacional Autónoma de México, Colegio de México), pp. 75–86

Cuesta, María Luzdivina, 1997. 'Notas sobre las relaciones paterno-filiares en la narrativa castellana medieval', *Scriptura*, 13: 93–106

Deyermond, Alan, 1976. 'Medieval Spanish Epic Cycles: Observations on their Formation and Development', *Kentucky Romance Quarterly*, 23: 282–303

——, 1988. 'La sexualidad en la épica medieval española', *Nueva Revista de Filología Hispánica*, 36: 767–86

Díaz Roig, Mercedes, 1976. *El romancero viejo* (Madrid: Cátedra)

Duggan, Joseph J., 1989. *The 'Cantar de mio Cid': Poetic Creation in its Economic and Social Contexts*, Cambridge Studies in Medieval Literature, 5 (Cambridge: Cambridge University Press)

Fraker, Charles F., 1996. 'Sancho II: Epic and Chronicle', in *The Scope of History: Studies in the Historiography of Alfonso el Sabio* (Ann Arbor: University of Michigan Press), pp. 44–84 [original publication, 1974]

Grieve, Patricia E., 1987. 'Private Man, Public Woman: Trading Places in *Condesa Traidora*', *Romance Quarterly*, 34: 317–26

Lacarra, María Eugenia, 1995. 'Representaciones de mujeres en la literatura española de la Edad Media', in *Breve historia feminista de la literatura española (en lengua castellana)*, II: *La mujer en la literatura española*, ed. Iris M. Zavala (Barcelona: Anthropos), pp. 21–68

Menéndez Pidal, Ramón, 1951. *Reliquias de la poesía épica española* (Madrid: Espasa Calpe)

——, 1952. 'Alfonso VI y su hermana la infanta Urraca', in *Miscelánea histórico-literaria* (Buenos Aires: Espasa Calpe), pp. 79–88 [original publication, 1948]

——, 1955. *Primera crónica general de España*, 2nd edn (Madrid: Gredos) [1st edn 1906]

Pattison, D. G., 1980. 'The Legend of the Sons of Sancho el Mayor', *Medium Ævum*, 51: 35–54

——, 1983. *From Legend to Chronicle: The Treatment of Epic Material in Alphon-*

sine Historiography, Medium Ævum Monographs, 13 (Oxford: Society for the Study of Mediæval Languages and Literature)

Reig, Carola, 1947. *El Cantar de Sancho II y Cerco de Zamora*, Anejos de la *Revista de Filología Española*, 37 (Madrid: CSIC)

Sponsler, Lucy A., 1975. *Women in the Medieval Spanish Epic and Lyric Traditions*, Studies in Romance Languages, 13 (Lexington: University Press of Kentucky)

Chronicle as Precedent: Some Aspects of Quotation from Late Medieval Chronicles in an Eighteenth-Century Crisis Memorandum

DAVID HOOK

Among the numerous acute insights offered by Nicholas Round's study of Álvaro de Luna is his awareness of the significance of the long afterlife of the medieval Spanish accounts of the Condestable, including the work of Michael Geddes (1715), which he describes as 'an astute, well-documented political biography', and which might, with good reason, be honoured as one of the earliest serious works of British scholarship concerning medieval Spain (1986: 218, n. 11). The use of medieval Spanish chronicles in later historiography and propaganda in Spain and elsewhere in Europe is, of course, common enough; less well known is the extent to which these texts were exploited in other contexts. An example of this use is a memorandum concerning the appointment and confirmation of bishops, datable to around 1718 (and whose author was therefore roughly contemporary with Geddes, although firmly on the other side of a significant religious divide from the latter), which cites as sources various medieval historical texts both documentary and narrative. The memorandum in question is found in MS 4140 from the library of Sir Thomas Phillipps (1792–1872); entitled on the spine 'Varios Politica y Gobierno', this was volume VI of fifteen volumes of 'Papeles Espagnoles' [sic], of which the provenance given by Sir Thomas's printed catalogue is somewhat imprecise ('Thorpe ex Bibl. de la Serna Santander,

A preliminary version of part of this study was presented at the Conference of the Historians of Medieval Iberia, held in Liverpool in September 2003, and some problems posed by so-called miscellany manuscript volumes in general were discussed in a paper given at the IVth Bristol Colloquium on Hispanic Texts and Manuscripts, in June 2003, part of which used this manuscript. I am grateful to those present on both occasions for their comments. The manuscript is now MS L-6 in my library.

Yriarte, et Astorga').[1] Although the catalogue recognizes only twelve, the MS contains thirteen separate items, of which this anonymous and untitled memorandum of thirty-four unfoliated, unpaginated leaves is the second.[2] The date of this text is established by its author's allusions to the interval that has elapsed between the significant events of 1482 (when a serious dispute between the Papacy and the Catholic Monarchs over issues arising from the appointment of a bishop to the vacant see of Cuenca gave rise to a concordat between the two parties that governed relations between Crown and Church in this matter for a considerable period thereafter) and the date of writing; he asserts, for example, that 'con que seria cosa dura, y de gravisima dificultad, que lo que el año 1482. estaba tan establecido, y asegurado, se disputase ahora con otros 236. años de aquiescencia' (f. 30v), and argues from an hypothesis '[p]ues demos el caso de no estar echa la Concordia, y asegurada con una practica de 236. años, y que oy durase la disputa' (f. 32r).[3] The date of 1718 for the composition of the memorandum seemingly given by these two statements will suffice *pro tem* pending possible future identification of the precise moment of controversy that provoked its appearance, which is not specified in the text beyond an oblique reference to 'la dificultad presente' (f. 2v). The further series of chronological indicators provided by the publication dates of various works cited as sources by the anonymous author is of no assistance whatsoever in refining this dating, since all these are works printed before 1700.

The 'dificultad' during which the memorandum was composed appears to be one in which an active debate on policy concerning the monarchy's rights in the appointment and confirmation of bishops provoked in its author consciousness of a certain urgency in advising, as his preferred course of action, the maintenance of the arrangements enshrined in the Isabelline concordat; the intensity of his appeal in arguing against any attempt to extend royal rights, or to limit the involvement of the Papacy in the confirmation of bishops, gives the impression at times of someone striving to avert a crisis. He traces the history of the appointment of bishops from the earliest days of

---

[1]   The history of Phillipps's printed catalogue of manuscripts is complex; there is a modern facsimile edition of its fullest state (Munby 2001). For these manuscripts, see Munby (2001: 60–3), with MS 4140 at p. 60. All quotations in this paper follow the orthography of the source quoted; resolved contractions are printed in italics, and missing letters are supplied within [brackets]. My foliation is supplied for citing the memorandum; all other folio and page references are those of the originals cited.

[2]   Item 8 in the volume, described in Phillipps's *Catalogue* as 'De Solvendis Decimis' although written in the vernacular, in fact consists of two separate papers on the topic of *diezmos*.

[3]   On the significance of this episode in relations between Crown and Papacy, see Azcona (1960: 110–32).

the Church to the later involvement of Papacy and monarchy; the virtues of the 1482 concordat are extolled, and he argues that the king must continue to seek papal Bulls of confirmation for candidates (f. 31v). In examining historical cases involving various Spanish dioceses and problematic or disputed appointments of bishops, whether the problems arose from divisions within the cathedral Chapters concerned, between Chapter and Crown, or involved the Papacy, the author employs a range of sources including printed chorography and chronicle; sometimes the printed texts are quarried simply as convenient locations from which to cite earlier documents such as papal Bulls that they reprint, but elsewhere the texts of the chroniclers and historians may themselves be quoted verbatim and used, like the documents, as precedents to justify the course of action being recommended. His visualization of the consequences of attempting to extend royal involvement in the appointment of bishops reaches negative conclusions (ff. 30v–32v). The author considers, from his historical survey, that the Crown gained much from the concordat with Pope Sixtus IV arising from the dispute of 1482, in which the Reyes Católicos won confirmation of rights that would be unlikely to be conceded at the time of his writing, since their basis rested entirely on the concept of the Reconquest and the royal foundation and endowment of reconquered territory (ff. 29r–30v). As a result, he argues, there is much to be gained from respecting the *status quo*. Without knowledge of the details of the argument being countered by the anonymous author, it is impossible to tell whether its motivation was political or economic, but both considerations underlay the tussle with the Papacy in the reign of Philip V. What is not clear from the text is whether this memorandum is responding to (or anticipating) an opinion or initiative coming from the Crown, or to an argument advanced (or expected to be advanced) by another source to the Crown for consideration. The general background, in either case, was what Richard Herr describes as 'a war of skirmishes between the Spanish court and Rome', which involved 'a complicated series of negotiations' from 1713 until the agreement of a concordat with Fernando VI in 1753 (Herr 1958: 12–13). The memorandum of 1718 seems to belong to a moment at which some kind of extreme assertion of the desirability of royal authority over ecclesiastical appointments either looked imminent or had recently been made.

This, however, is a matter more relevant to historians of relations between Crown and Papacy in the eighteenth century than to those of medieval Spain; what particularly interests the latter here is the use made of historical material in the arguments advanced by the anonymous author. The various cases cited constitute both examples of the problems, and precedents in so far as the author argues from them in favour of or against a particular potential policy, and uses them as statements of specific rights. An example of the use of both historical document and chronicle text for a single purpose is given by the author's examination of the implications of the description of a given bishop as 'electo' or 'confirmado', two terms which he traces in use in contexts such as the form of signature adopted by a bishop in a document, or the manner in which a prelate is described by a chronicler. Attention to detail at this level underlines the careful historical scholarship that informs this document. The organization of the material is systematic, with different dioceses examined separately to see if practice varied according to their status, within the generally chronological presentation of the material.

The anonymous author is widely read in Spanish history, and has located relevant material in twenty-six separate source works. These include post-medieval compilations which incorporate the texts of medieval documents or refer to episodes in the pre-Isabelline history of various dioceses, and they range from histories of particular cities or dioceses to general histories of Spain, in addition to ecclesiastical histories. His medieval sources include the *Siete Partidas*, and chronicles of Alfonso XI, Enrique II, and Juan II, plus Fernando del Pulgar's *Crónica de los Reyes Católicos*. His techniques in using his sources range from referring to the text (usually providing quite precise references) without quoting the material directly, to verbatim textual quotation of varying length (which is again usually provided with a precise source reference). The quoted material is generally marked by double inverted commas in the left-hand margin of each line of the quotation, although in some instances these are not continued to the end of the textual extract. Care has to be exercised, therefore, in determining the precise extent of quotation in the text, which may significantly exceed the sections marked by inverted commas.

This use of medieval evidence should alert us to the probable existence of a potentially useful body of textual material from chronicles quoted in policy memoranda and similar later manuscript contexts from the sixteenth to the eighteenth century, amongst which it may even be possible, in some instances (though not in the case of this particular memorandum, as will be seen), to isolate textual characteristics which cannot be identified with extant witnesses of the texts concerned, and thereby provide evidence for lost witnesses. This is, naturally, in addition to the more obvious potential significance of this corpus for the reception history of the works cited. The memorandum of course also illustrates an end-product of the kind of reading that often results in manuscripts and early printed editions of medieval chronicles attracting reader annotations of various kinds in the process of location and compilation of material from sources of this nature by the authors of such documents. In the present case, the source for the account of events involving Cuenca in 1482 is stated by the author to be the relevant chapter of the *Crónica de los Reyes Católicos* of Hernando del Pulgar: 'Con este suceso, fenecio Hernando del Pulgar la 2ª parte de la Chronica de los Reyes Catholicos, haciendo todo el Cap*itu*lo 122' (f. 24r), 'Este mismo Capitulo puso Antonio de Nebrixa en la version latina de Hernando del Pulgar; y en la Castellana, es el Cap*itu*lo 122. de la 2ª parte fol. 146' (f. 26r). This folio reference enables the edition used to be identified precisely as the 1565 Valladolid edition of Pulgar's chronicle, though the anonymous author had clearly also read the Latin version by Nebrija.[4] Interestingly, this very chapter was annotated by an early reader of a copy of the 1565 edition in the British Library (9180. h.13), who underlined some key phrases and added a marginal indexing note on the matter.[5] Whilst there is no evidence to connect the manuscript annotations in that specific copy with the production of the memorandum studied here, it is both unusual and informative (amongst the plethora of anonymous and undated marginalia encountered in extant copies of chronicles) to be able to match a case of reader annotation in a chronicle to an instance of the use of that very material in a quite separate text.

A problem that would be encountered in the use of such later works, however, is that composite manuscripts of the type represented by Phillipps MS 4140 and its fourteen erstwhile companion volumes have sometimes been divided into their component parts by the antiquarian book trade in order to sell these separately. Whilst numerous such composite volumes fortunately survive in libraries, thanks to such commercially motivated fragmentation the individual treatises which formerly constituted other similar volumes may now be encountered in isolation, robbed of that dimension of historical evidence provided by the manuscript context in which they formerly existed. Though this context of 'papeles varios' may itself have been that of a factitious collection of material from various sources, and hence arguably was merely a transient phase in the existence of such treatises, it was sometimes more coherent than a superficial examination would suggest, and its destruction has removed evidence for the intellectual world of the circles in which it was assembled. Although early catalogue entries may, in some cases, permit the recovery of something of that context, reassembling this evidence is rendered

---

4   Pulgar (1565) (but note that this edition is wrongly attributed on the title page to Antonio de Nebrija), hereafter referred to as *M* in the notes.

5   The marginal note is a visual location device, 'obispo de Cor[dob]a'; I refer to marginalia with this function as indexing notes, since their function is similar to that of a modern thumb-index. Here the sentences underlined in the British Library copy of the edition of 1565 (which are identified in the quotations below by underlining, even when the section of text containing the words thus marked is here quoted from the memorandum, in which, it must be borne in mind, these phrases are not underlined) have a similar function to the verbal note, that of a quick guide to the location of information (as opposed to other common annotation purposes such as its amplification, approbation, condemnation, confirmation, contradiction, extension, modification, source reference, etc.), but their selection (in the case of the first three sentences so marked) also constitutes an acute summary of the salient points of the royal position in the argument with Pope Sixtus.

more difficult by the imprecision of some cataloguing; Phillipps's own catalogue entry for this volume, for instance, gives the erroneous impression
that several of the works in it are in Latin, since some titles have been translated into Latin by the cataloguer; as stated above, moreover, one item in the
volume has also been overlooked entirely, probably because it was wrongly
identified as part of another treatise. In fact, its different ink (black instead of
orange-brown), larger paper size, distinct watermark, different mise-en-page,
and different hand, all distinguish it as a separate document.[6] Despite the
rather vague title given on the spine label, the thematic unity of MS Phillipps
4140 lies in the relation of all its component texts to questions of the reform
of Church governance and finance, and Church-state relations. The study
of the material contained in composite volumes such as this one is potentially rewarding, but it requires the kind of precise attention to physical detail
that would be applied automatically to the study of a medieval manuscript.
An unwarranted *a priori* assumption of codicological simplicity should not
lead us to neglect the information offered by the detailed examination even
of such post-medieval 'miscellanies', in our concentration upon the ideas
contained in the various texts of which they are made up, or on other aspects
such as the textual evidence they may offer for medieval studies.

The longest quotation in this memorandum is that concerning the crucial
events of 1482 involving the diocese of Cuenca, which the author clearly
viewed as a persuasive statement of an accommodation of conflicting interests which had his approval and therefore is quoted almost verbatim. It is
also textually one of the most interesting quotations in the memorandum. The
modern edition of Hernando del Pulgar's *Crónica de los Reyes Católicos* by
Juan de Mata Carriazo (1943), is based on Biblioteca Nacional, Madrid, MS
10862, a manuscript with significant differences from the early printed tradition; Carriazo records three printed editions in Spanish (1565, 1567, 1780),
and forty-three manuscripts (1943: I, lxx–lxxvii, cvi–cxliii), but there also
exist some manuscripts of it that have not been studied (one such was offered
for sale on an internet auction site in 2003). Carriazo offers preliminary
notes towards classing in families the witnesses known to him, but does not
offer a detailed study of the transmission of the text (1943: I, lxxviii–cxlvii);
nor does his editorial policy include an apparatus of variants. Any extensive textual citation of a medieval Spanish chronicle in a later text needs to
be examined to determine whether variant readings are merely the result of
error or adaptation by the author quoting the text, or constitute evidence of
a variant branch of the textual tradition of the chronicle concerned. In the

---

[6] The omission was not confined to Phillipps's *Catalogue*; the typed list of contents
provided with the manuscript by the New York bookseller H. P. Kraus when I purchased it also
overlooked this item.

case of our quotation from Pulgar, potentially this task would be complicated by the lack of previous study and the large number of extant witnesses, but for the fact that the author cites a specific chapter and folio number which can be precisely matched to those of the printed edition of 1565. Collation of the memorandum with the edition confirms that the quotation exhibits the textual characteristics of that edition in significant details, in which the latter differs from six other witnesses I have examined (Carriazo's edition accepted as reproducing BNM MS 18062; British Library MSS Egerton 304, Egerton 305, and Harley 4792; and the printed editions of 1567 and 1780).[7] It may, therefore, be taken as certain that where the memorandum quotation offers a reading different from that found in the edition of 1565, the differences are the result of the memorandum writer's adaptation or mechanical error in copying rather than derivation from some other variant branch of the tradition. (The only other possible explanation, derivation from a variant state of the printed edition, seems unlikely in the case of the longer substantive differences between the British Library copy consulted and the memorandum.) The quotation begins with a very faithful reproduction of the 1565 text (f. 24r):

> Con este suceso fenecio Hernando del Pulgar la 2ª parte de la Chronica de los Reyes Catholicos, haciendo todo el Capitulo 122, que aunque largo, deve copiarse aqui la maior parte de el: "Estando en aquella Villa (Medina del Campo)[8] entendieron en las provisiones de los Obispados, y Yglesias de sus Reinos, para que se hiciesen en Roma, a suplicacion suia, y no en otra manera. Y porque el Padre Santo havia proveido de la Yglesia de Cuenca, que era vaca, a vn Cardenal, su sobrino, natural de Genova (la qual provision el Rey, y la Reyna /24v/ no consintieron, por ser fecha a persona extrangera, y contra la suplicacion que ellos hauian fecho al Papa) acordaron de le suplicar, que le[9] pluguiese hacer aquella, y las otras provisiones de las Yglesias que vacasen en sus Reinos, a Personas naturales de ellos, por quien ellos suplicasen, y no a otros: lo qual con justa causa acostumbraron facer los Pontifices pasados, considerando que los Reyes sus Progenitores, con grandes trabajos, y derramamiento de sangre,[10] como Christianos[11] Principes, havian ganado la tierra de los Moros enemigos de nuestra Santa Fee Catholica, colocando en ella el nombre de nuestro

---

[7]   *Chronica de los muy Altos, y esclarecidos Reyes Catholicos Don Hernando y Doña Ysabel de gloriosa memoria* (Çaragoça: Juan Millan, M.D.LXVII) (British Library, two copies: G6440 and 593.f.14), ff. 95r–96v (Chapter CXXII); *Crónica de los Señores Reyes Católicos Don Fernando y doña Isabel de Castilla y de Aragon escrita por su cronista Hernando del Pulgar* (Valencia: Imprenta de Benito Monfort, MDCCLXXX), pp. 177–9 (Chapter CIV) (British Library, 09226/b.1).

[8]   (Medina del Campo)]: *om. M.*

[9]   le]: *om. M.*

[10]   de sangre]: de su sangre, *M.*

[11]   Christianos]: Christianissimos, *M.*

Redemptor Jesuchristo, y estirpando el nombre de Mahoma; <u>lo qual les</u>
<u>dava derecho de Patronazgo en todas las Yglesias</u> de sus Reinos, y Seño-
rios, para que deviesen ser provehidos a suplicacion suia, a personas sus
naturales, gratas, y fieles a ellos, y no a otros algunos, considerando la
poca noticia que los estrangeros tenian en las cosas de sus Reinos. Decian
asi mismo, que las Yglesias te/25r/nian muchas fortalezas, y algunas de ellas
fronteras de los Moros, donde era necesario poner guarda, para la defen-
sion de la tierra, y que era des servicio suio ponerlas en poder de personas,
que no heran naturales de sus Reinos: Por el Papa se alegaba, que era
Principe de la Ygles[i]a, y tenia livertad de proveer de las Yglesias, y de
toda la Christiandad, a quien el entendiese; y que la autoridad del Papa, y
el poderio que por Dios tenia en la Tierra, no era limitado, ni menos ligado
para proveer de sus Yglesias a voluntad de ningun Principe, salvo en la
manera que entendiese ser servicio de Dios, y bien de la Yglesia: y por esta
causa el Rey, y la Reyna embiaron diversas veces sus Embajadores a Roma,
por dar a entender al Papa, que ellos no querian poner limite a su poderio;
pero que era cosa razonable considerar las cosas suso alegadas, segun la
consideraron los Pontifices pasados en las provisiones que hicieron de las
Yglesias de sus Reynos: y por que estos Embajadores no pudieron haver
conclusion con el Papa; (segun lo hauian suplicado) el Rey, y la Reina, /25v/
embiaron mandar a todos sus naturales que estavan en Corte Romana, que
saliesen de ella: Esto ficieron con proposito de convocar los Principes de
la christiandad a facer Concilio, asi sobre esto, como por otras cosas que
entendian proponer, cumplideras al servicio de Dios, y bien de su universal
Yglesia:

The 1565 edition, at this point (f. 147r), contains a sentence giving the
reaction of the Spaniards at Rome to this order, which is omitted by the
memorandum: 'Los naturales de Castilla y Aragon, recelando que el Rey
y la Reyna les embargarian las temporalidades que tenian en sus reynos,
obedecieron sus mandamientos, y salieron de la corte de Roma.' Thereafter,
in the memorandum there is some adaptation and considerable compression
in the treatment of the source, with the omission of some matter rather more
relevant to the minutiae of the diplomacy of 1482 than to the central question
of rights over the appointment of bishops (f. 25v):

Estando las cosas en este estado, (prosigue) que[12] el Papa embio por su
Eembaxador a los Reyes[13] a Dominico Centurion,[14] vn cavallero Genoves,[15]

---

[12] (prosigue) que]: *om. M.* (*Verba dicendi* added in memorandum.)
[13] embio por su Embaxador a los Reyes]: embio al Rey y a la Reyna por su embaxador
con sus breues credenciales, *M.*
[14] a Dominico Centurion]: a vno que se llamaua Domen Nego Centurion, *M.*
[15] vn cavallero Genoves]: hombre lego natural de la ciudad de Genoua, *M.*

para conferir en esta materia,[16] y que llegado a Medina del Campo,[17] los Reyes, no solo le negaron la audiencia, pero le mandaron salir de sus dominios,[18] extrañandole, que en tan mala coyuntura, hubiese aceptado aquella comision:[19]

Here, Pulgar's text contains a description of the reaction of the papal ambassador to this expression of royal outrage (f. 147v), which is passed over by the memorandum:

Aquel embaxador, vista la indignacion del Rey y de la Reyna como auia aceptado en las razones que le embiaron dezir: y considerando que era lego, y que ellos eran Reyes tan poderosos: embioles dezir, Que el renunciaua de su propria autoridad el preuilegio y seguridad que tenia como embaxador del Papa, y no queria gozar del: y que si les pluguiesse, el queria[20] ser su natural, y queria ser juzgado por ellos, y sometido a su imperio en todo lo que les pluguiesse hazer de su persona y de sus bienes.

The memorandum thereafter continues the text of the chronicle with some adaptation; apparent *nonsequiturs* in the text of both memorandum and chronicle are caused by the fact that here the 1565 edition itself follows a variant in the textual tradition (one dominant in the printed texts) that omits

---

[16] para conferir ... materia]: *om. M.*

[17] y que ... Campo]: Y como este llego a la villa de Medina, embio dezir al Rey e a la Reyna como venia a ellos como embaxador del papa, para los communicar algunas cosas sobre aquella materia que por estonces se tractaua. El Rey y la Reyna sabida la venida de aquel embaxador: embiaronle dezir, que el papa se auia mas duramente en sus cosas, que en las de ningun otro principe de la Christiandad, seyendo ellos y los Reyes sus predecessores mas obedientes a la silla Apostolica que ninguno otro Rey Catholico: y que auida esta consideracion, ellos entendian buscar los remedios que segun derecho deuian y podian, para se remediar de los agrauios que el Padre Sancto les fazia, *M.*

[18] los Reyes ... dominios]: Y que le mandauan que saliesse fuera de sus reynos, y no curasse de proueer ninguna embaxada de parte del Papa, porque eran auisados que todo lo que de su parte les querian explicar, era en derogacion de su preheminencia real. Y embiaronle dezir, que ellos le dauan seguridad de su persona y de los suyos que con el venian en todos sus reynos e señorios, por guardar el preuilegio e immunidad, de que los mensajeros y embaxadores deuen gozar, especialmente viniendo por parte del sumo Pontifice, *M.*

[19] Extrañandole ... comision]: pero que se marauillauan del, estando las cosas en el estado en que estauan, como auia aceptado aquel cargo, *M.*

[20] This instance of underlining, spread over two lines in the edition thus annotated, is a good illustration of a common enough tendency for it not to mark all of a phrase (or to mark grammatically incomplete or even incoherent sections, often because it ends at line breaks rather than following the syntax in a text). The key element being singled out here is presumably 'embaxador del Papa'.

the brief imprisonment of the ambassador and the fact that the Cardinal's intervention is intended to secure his release (ff. 25v–26r):[21]

> Pero que[22] la respuesta humilde del[23] Embaxador templo la indignacion Real,[24] interponiendose la autoridad grande del Cardenal don Pedro Gonzalez de Mendoza;[25] suplico (prosigue la Chronica)[26] al Rey, y a la Reyna, que se hiciesen[27] con el benignamente, y que tornasen a ablar en la /26r/ Concordia con el Papa, la qual, mediante el Cardenal, se hizo, para que de las Yglesias principales de todos sus Reinos, el Papa proveyase[28] a suplicacion del Rey, y de la Reyna, a personas de[29] sus naturales, que fuesen dignas, y capaces para las haver: y el Papa revoco la provision que hauia echo de la Yglesia de Cuenca al Cardenal de San Jorge su sobrino, y proveio de ella a don Alphonso de Burgos, capellan maior de la Reyna, obispo que era de Cordova, por quien hauia suplicado &ca." Este mismo Capitulo puso Antonio de Nebrixa en la version latina de Hernando del Pulgar; y en la Castellana, es el Capitulo 122 de la 2ª parte fol. 146. Garivay en el t. 2 lib. 18 cap. 21 de su Compendio historial: Mariana en la Historia de España t. 2 lib. 24 cap. 16: Salazar de Mendoza chronica del gran Cardenal lib. 1 cap. 52: Gil Gonzalez en el theatro ecclesiastico. t. 4 Yglesia de Osma pag. 61: Y Salgado de Regia protectione t. 2 3ª pte cap. 10 p. 150 desde el no. 227.

The textual differences between these two versions may be divided into various categories. Ignoring instances in which the author of the memorandum has intercalated links of the type 'Prosigue' and 'prosigue la Chronica', it is necessary to arrange the other differences in a hierarchy of textual significance. In general terms, a fundamental distinction must be made between mechanical error and conscious adaptation. In the former category should be placed, for example, readings explicable as omission by eyeskip (often in effect single-word homoeoteleuton when successive words end, or begin,

---

[21] Compare Carriazo (1943: 455): 'E mandáronlo llevar preso a la fortaleza de Medina, en la qual estouo algunos días; durante los quales el cardenal de España ynterçedió por él, e suplicó al Rey e a la Reyna, & fablóse en la concordia con el Papa'; MS Egerton 304 offers a text closely related to that in Carriazo, narrating the imprisonment but omitting 'de España', and supplying 'que lo soltasen' before '& fablóse'.

[22] pero que]: om. M.

[23] del]: de aquel, M.

[24] Real]: que el Rey y la Reyna auian concebido, M.

[25] Interponiendose ... Mendoza; suplico]: Y despues de algunos dias el Cardenal de España, intercedio por el: y suplico, M.

[26] (prosigue la Chronica)]: om. M. (Verba dicendi added in memorandum.)

[27] hiciesen]: ouiessen, M.

[28] proveyase]: proueyesse, M.

[29] de]: om. M.

with the same letter, as in the omission of 'su' before 'sangre'). Unless a coherent and compelling case for intentional adaptation can be advanced to account for textual differences in such instances, mechanical omission should be preferred as a sufficient explanation. Where individual readings cannot be readily explained in terms of identifiable causes of error, they may in theory arise from unconscious substitution, deliberate adaptation, or derivation from a variant exemplar (which itself may, of course, also have contained readings identifiable as arising from mechanical processes of copying, but the latter alone are insufficient evidence to suggest the existence of such an exemplar). In the present case, there is a tendency in the memorandum to abbreviate, visible most obviously in the dramatic reduction of the account of the arrival of the papal ambassador Dominico Centurion and of the exchanges between him and the Catholic Monarchs, which is not easily explained as arising from mechanical error but can be seen in terms of its marginal relevance to the principal matter in hand. This tendency can also be seen in minor verbal economies such as the compression in the memorandum of the royal expression of astonishment. Into this category may also be placed minor omissions not otherwise explicable by mechanical processes or alternative solutions of syntax; examples might be the replacement of 'el Rey & la Reyna' by 'los Reyes' or 'real' (missing the point of the deliberately reiterative binary expression in Pulgar, perhaps understandably since such constant and forceful emphasis on this duality was no longer a political imperative in 1718). Different readings not readily explained by any of the above factors may be attributed to stylistic preference or unconscious substitution, but (although this is not an issue here since the specific edition used by the author is known) could also conceivably arise from the use of a variant exemplar. The importance of producing full variorum editions of even the better-known medieval chronicles is clear: only such editions offer the possibility of identifying the branch, or ideally the precise manuscript, from which texts such as the quotation in our memorandum derive. This is an important process, for the identification of a specific manuscript as the source of a particular author may be an important clue to the milieu in which that author was working and the libraries to which he had access. The absence of such an *apparatus criticus* is one of the principal disadvantages of the otherwise useful editions in the Colección de Crónicas Españolas by Juan de Mata Carriazo.

The debate over appointment to vacant sees in the eighteenth century thus opens a new line of enquiry for medieval chronicle studies in so far as it suggests that some of the numerous memoranda (and indeed other political papers) of Hapsburg and Bourbon Spain may offer an unexpected opportunity to obtain information about the history of the transmission of these texts, as well as prompting some reflections upon the process of recording and editing the latter. Although such memoranda as that examined here are not normally considered essential reading for medievalists, it is clear that this kind of material may contain significant textual extracts, and that such extracts should be regarded as having, potentially, an importance similar to that of any other primary witness of a chronicle text; even when, as in the present case, they constitute secondary witnesses because their precise exemplars can be identified, they retain their significance as testimony to the reception of the source text. There is, for obvious reasons, currently no prospect of producing a general catalogue of such later quotations, and isolated serendipitous discoveries by scholars engaged upon research into papers of this kind, to whose courtesy and professional generosity appeal must be made, are likely to be important early contributors to revealing the extent and potential of this material. Ultimately, it is to be hoped that the attention and treatment traditionally accorded to early quotations from and references to works such as the *Libro de buen amor* and *Celestina* will be extended to late quotations from medieval chronicles.

List of Works Cited

Azcona, Tarsicio, 1960. *La elección y reforma del episcopado español en tiempo de los Reyes Católicos* (Madrid: CSIC, Instituto 'P. Enrique Flórez')

Carriazo, Juan de Mata (ed.), 1943. *Crónica de los Reyes Católicos por su secretario Fernando del Pulgar. Versión inédita*, 2 vols, Colección de Crónicas Españolas, V–VI (Madrid: Espasa Calpe)

Geddes, Michael, 1715. *The Life of Don Álvaro de Luna, Prime Favourite and First Minister to Don John II, King of Castile: Giving an Account of his Rise and Fall*, in *Several Tracts Against Popery: Together with The Life of Don Álvaro de Luna* (London: Printed by E. J. for B. Barker & C. King, 1715), pp. 227–370

Herr, Richard, 1958. *The Eighteenth-Century Revolution in Spain* (Princeton: Princeton University Press)

Munby, A. N. L. (ed.), 2001. *The Phillipps Manuscripts. Catalogus librorum manuscriptorum in Bibliotheca D. Thomae Phillipps, Bt. Impressum Typis Medio-Montanis 1837–1871* ([London:] Orskey-Johnson) [1st edn 1968]

Nebrija, Antonio de, 1565: see Pulgar 1565

Pulgar, Fernando del, *alias* Nebrija, Antonio de, 1565. *Chronica de los muy altos y esclarecidos reyes Catholicos don Fernando y doña Ysabel de gloriosa memoria* (Valladolid: en casa de Sebastián Martínez)

——, 1567. *Chronica de los muy Altos, y esclarecidos Reyes Catholicos Don Hernando y Doña Ysabel de gloriosa memoria* (Çaragoça: Juan Millán)

——, 1780. *Crónica de los Señores Reyes Católicos Don Fernando y doña Isabel de Castilla y de Aragon* (Valencia: Imprenta de Benito Monfort)

Round, Nicholas, 1986. *The Greatest Man Uncrowned: A Study of the Fall of Don Alvaro de Luna* (London: Tamesis)

'El omne con bondad ... acrecenta las riquezas': Juan Manuel and Money

JOHN ENGLAND

In an article which combines characteristically sharp textual analysis with wide-ranging elucidation of social and cultural context and astute observations on human behaviour, Nick Round showed how Juan Ruiz, Archpriest of Hita, used the *nummus* tradition in the *Libro de buen amor* to satirize the power of money and its ability to distort human conduct and eternal truths.[1] The development of a monetary economy had been relatively slow in medieval Castile, but by the first half of the fourteenth century the process of change was well underway.[2] It seems appropriate, then, in this volume to use Nick Round's study as the starting point for an analysis of Juan Manuel's response to these changes. Juan Ruiz and Juan Manuel, in this as in many other respects, provide fertile ground for a 'compare and contrast' approach. On the one hand they were both producing texts at approximately the same time, within the same society and the same set of historical circumstances, in the same language, and with interests in similar areas of humanity (the tensions between physical existence in this life and spiritual existence in the next). On the other hand, Juan Ruiz was a cleric, whereas Juan Manuel was a layman; and Juan Ruiz only produced one text (as far as we know), whereas Juan Manuel produced many; Juan Ruiz's text is enigmatic, ironical

---

[1]   See Round (1997) for the analysis of the *Libro de buen amor*. With Juan Ruiz nothing is ever simple, and the reader has to take into account the fact that the *nummus* passage is spoken by Don Amor, an unreliable witness, in terms which indicate that the powers of love and money are very similar; compare, for example, stanzas 490–1 and 155–9.

   It has been normal practice for colleagues in Sheffield to ask Nick Round to comment on first drafts of material for publication, and to receive the benefit of his kindness, wisdom and encyclopedic knowledge; on this occasion, for obvious reasons, it has not been possible to consult him. The defects of this chapter thus bear ironic witness to one aspect of his scholarly achievements.

[2]   Liu (2003) places Juan Ruiz's views within the context of late medieval economic theory and practice; I am grateful for the author's generosity in sending me a copy of his paper.

and humorous, whereas Juan Manuel's texts are predominantly transparent
and serious in tone. My analysis of the proper role of money as defined by
a powerful secular figure aims to complement Nick Round's analysis of one
view from within the clergy, and help us to understand better the diversity of
views held on such matters in fourteenth-century Castile.

It is possible to arrive at a rounded picture of Juan Manuel's views on many
topics, because of the range of texts which he produced: eight full-length
texts survive, in diverse genres, as well as a number of letters.[3] He is also the
subject matter of other texts, as in some of the letters reproduced by Giménez
Soler, and in the *Crónica de Alfonso XI* and the *Poema de Alfonso XI*. Analysis
of all these texts can provide us with an understanding of Juan Manuel's
views and his alleged conduct with regard to, among other topics: poverty vs.
wealth; status and wealth; trade and the income of those earning their living
through trade; clashes between monarchs and aristocrats over income; debt
and borrowing; begging; property and money; how to acquire money; money
and deception; and officials responsible for financial matters. Some of his
comments make it clear that he thought seriously about very practical issues,
such as the risks involved in having a *despensero* who has responsibility for
large sums of money, but does not earn much himself (*Estados*, Ch. XCVII,
407–8), or the foolishness of taking advice on how to acquire money from
someone who is poor (*Lucanor*, 85). It is not surprising that he gave thought
to such practical issues, as the correspondence published by Giménez Soler
shows that money matters were frequently to the fore in his life. He was not
afraid to defend his financial interests, as, for example, when he reminds
James II of Aragon in 1313 that he is still owed money as part of the dowry
from his marriage to Costanza (letter CCLXXIV, 432); James II claimed that
he had other more pressing financial matters to attend to (conduct which is
justifiable according to *exemplo* VIII of *El Conde Lucanor*), part payment
was not made until 1321 (letter CCCLXXIII, 500), and in 1336 Juan Manuel
was still trying to obtain the remainder (letter DXXXIV, 619). Another letter
shows him trying to recover money owed to his sister (letter CV, 307). He
was prepared to pawn goods (letter CCCXLII, 475), to ask to borrow galleys
(letter CCCXLV, 478), and to seek loans to acquire land (letter CCXLI, 408).
In a different type of text (*Ordenanzas dadas a la Villa de Peñafiel*), he issued
regulations concerning commerce, fraud and the supply of loans by Jews;
whilst according to the *Crónica de Alfonso XI* he was (along with others)
involved in disputes with the Crown over the distribution of income and the
right to mint money (Valdeón Baruque 1977: 184–5). Kinkade is probably

---

[3]   The full-length texts are edited in Blecua (1982–83), which is the edition used for all
texts except *El Conde Lucanor*, for which I use Serés (1994). The letters and the *Ordenanzas
dadas a la Villa de Peñafiel* are in Giménez Soler (1932).

correct in his speculation that Juan Manuel took control of municipal government in Peñafiel largely to boost his income (1990: 108).

It is clear from his literary texts that Juan Manuel regarded money as an integral part of human society, which could be a force for good, and indeed was something which a nobleman like him needed to acquire if he was to fulfil his role in life; it was also his duty to help those for whom he was responsible to prosper (*Ordenanzas*, 655). A substantial section of the *Libro de los estados* is given over to the duties of officials responsible for looking after the financial affairs of the powerful, on the assumption that the acquisition and enhancement of personal wealth is a proper concern (Part I, Chs XCIII–XCVII). A man in a position of power needed to exercise his responsibility in acquiring money to look after himself, his vassals, his friends and, more specifically, in order to provide security by investing in the strengthening of fortifications:

> Et por ende vos digo que vna de las cosas que cunplen a los grandes sennores es que aya buenas rendas et que ponga buen recabdo en ellas, et las acresçiente et las adelante quanto pudiere con derecho et sin pecado. Ca [por] las rendas se acrescientan los averes, et por el aver se mantienen los sennores et las fortalezas et los amigos et los vasallos. Ca ninguna destas cosas non se puede mantener luenga mente sin ellas.
>
> (*Libro enfenido*, 174)

The *Ordenanzas dadas a la Villa de Peñafiel* confirm that Juan Manuel did indeed invest his own money in providing security for the town (Giménez Soler 1932: 655). If the nobleman was to fight a war (as sometimes he must, and Juan Manuel did), he needed money (*Libro enfenido*, 176); great achievements depend on having the necessary resources.

Assumptions such as this inform all his writings, whether the subject is dealt with in general terms or is the focus of an analysis of the behaviour of specific (fictional) characters. In the *Libro de los estados* Julio uses an extended metaphor, derived from the *Bocados de oro* (Devoto 1972: 266), comparing different types of empire with the different ages of man; the healthiest empire is that which is continually increasing its wealth:

> mas el emperio o regno que es moço es aquel en que [el] enperador o rey a mas de renda de quanto se despiende, ca con lo que finca puede conbrar et labrar et acresçentar sus rendas con derecho, et fazer toda su vida con grant prevision, tan bien en las viandas que ha mester para su despensa commo en las cosas que oviere a dar, commo en todas las cosas que oviere de conprar para su vestir del et su conpanna, et las otras cosas quel convienen para onra et apostamiento de su casa et de su estado.
>
> (Part I, Ch. LXXX, 360)

Indeed, the emperor's wife also needs an adequate income for her to be able to fulfil her role effectively:

> Otrosi, deue guardar el enperador que su muger que aya rentas çiertas con que pueda mantener su casa muy onrada mente, et que sea muy abastada de pannos et de joyas et de capiellas et de todas las cosas que pertenesçen a su estado. Et demas de lo que a mester para lo que es dicho, conuiene que aya mas renda para lo poder dar por amor de Dios, et fazer otras cosas muchas quel pertenesçen, que non se pueden nin deuen escusar.
>
> (Part I, Ch. LXVI, 321)

For both the emperor and his wife, there is a need to maintain status and to have sufficient funds for making gifts; and there is an assumption often stated that land and money go together ('sabra acresçentar su tierra et sus rendas con derecho' [Part I, Ch. LVII, 301]). In the case of the fictional characters of *El Conde Lucanor*, the needs are more varied and pressing, but similar principles apply. Lucanor himself experiences periods of financial hardship, which put him under severe personal pressure:

> Pero algunas vegadas me contesce de estar tan afincado de pobreza, que me paresce que querría tanto la muerte commo la vida. (*Ex.* X, 50)

The young man in *Ex.* XXXV does not have sufficient wealth to fulfil his responsibilities (148), and his decision to marry in order to escape poverty is to be applauded. Those who become poor are extremely vulnerable (*Ex.* XLV), and it is normal human behaviour to wish to escape poverty (*Ex.* VII). Money is needed not only for one's own benefit, but in order to benefit others (e.g. Patronio's conclusion to *Ex.* X, 51), and so even when the nobleman is wealthy ('loado a Dios, yo só assaz rico' [*Ex.* XXIII, 94]), it is Patronio's emphatic advice that he should seek constantly to increase his wealth (96). And in his concluding remarks to *Ex.* XXV he makes it clear that a good man will increase his wealth to the benefit of his family, his vassals and society at large, and refers to examples of people who were not as successful as they should have been, and who, as a consequence, lost their wealth, to the detriment of all who depended on them (109).

Within Juan Manuel's world-view, money is not only necessary for a successful life on this earth, but must also be used to enhance one's chances of salvation. A repeated theme of his works is the importance of giving, and of giving in the right spirit, to the point where the amount given represents a genuine sacrifice:

Otrosi, el que da limosna tal que non siente menos lo que da, yo non digo que tal limosna sea mal, mas digo que seria mejor si diese tanto por amor de Dios fasta que sintiese alguna mengua.

(Libro de los estados, Part I, Ch. LX, 310)

Similar statements occur in the *Libro enfenido* (e.g. 153, 176), and the theme is examined at greater length in the *Libro del cauallero et del escudero* (Ch. XIX, 47), as well as in story XL of *El Conde Lucanor*, in which Patronio sets out clear conditions for alms-giving to be effective:

Et más, para que la limosna sea buena, conviene que aya en ella cinco cosas: la una, que se faga de lo que omne oviere de buena parte; la otra, que la faga estando en verdadera penitencia; la otra que sienta omne alguna mengua por lo que da et que sea cosa de que se duela omne; la otra que la faga en su vida; la otra que la faga omne simplemente por Dios, et non por vana gloria nin por ufana del mundo. (163)

The conditions for giving are strict, but it is obvious that, in order to give, one must first have something to give; Juan Manuel therefore opposed the Franciscan attitude to poverty, repeating the argument that Christ possessed money (*Libro de los estados*, Part II, Ch. XL, 478).

In Juan Manuel's view, then, it is desirable for men of his social class to accumulate money if they are to fulfil their social responsibilities to others and their spiritual responsibilities to themselves. We can see the connections between his works and his actions both in the donations he made (e.g. Giménez Soler 1932: letter CCCXVI, 461), and in the gratitude which he felt towards Sancho IV for the latter's generous gift to him (*Libro de las armas*, 135). Much of what he has to say about financial transactions appears to be based on the experience of one who has given much thought to the matter, as can be seen in story XXXVI of *El Conde Lucanor*. The merchant at the centre of the story understands the concept of value for money, and remembers for twenty years the piece of advice which he purchased for the considerable price of one *dobla*, precisely because it was expensive; remembering and acting on that advice twenty years later prevents him killing his loyal wife and only son, and therefore proves to be an excellent investment, saving him from execution for murder, and eternal damnation.

Despite the essential nature of money and its potential for good, however, more often than not, and especially in the fictional world of Part I of *El Conde Lucanor*, it is misused as a force for evil. The key distinction for Juan Manuel here, as with other forms of human behaviour, lies in the motives underlying one's actions, in this case both in the acquisition of money and in the spending of it.[4] Whilst, as we have seen, the acquisition of money is not wrong, and indeed is essential for most people, it is wrong to acquire money for its own sake, thinking only of life on this earth:

> Et los omnes todos passan en el mundo en tres maneras: la una es que algunos ponen todo su talante et su entendimiento en las cosas del mundo, commo en riquezas et en onras et en deleytes et en conplir sus voluntades en cualquier manera que pueden, non catando en ál sinon a esto.
>
> (*El Conde Lucanor*, Part V, 280)

Such behaviour, strongly criticized here in general terms, is exemplified in Part I through characters such as the *lonbardo* of *Ex.* XIIII, 64–6. The count has been advised to accumulate as much wealth as he can, but Patronio deems such advice to be only partially correct:

> commo quier que a los grandes señores vos cunple de aver algún tesoro para muchas cosas, et señaladamente por que non dexedes por mengua de aver de fazer lo que vos cunpliera; et pero, non entendades que este tesoro devedes ayuntar en guisa que pongades tanto el talante en ayuntar grand tesoro por que dexedes de fazer lo que devedes a vuestras gentes et para guarda de vuestra onra et de vuestro estado [...]. (64)

The narrative of the *exemplo* vividly illustrates this point, which Patronio then develops in his conclusion:

> commo quier que el tesoro, commo desuso es dicho, es bueno, guardad dos cosas: la una, en que el tesoro que ayuntáredes que sea de buena parte; la otra, que non pongades tanto el coraçon en el tesoro por que fagades ninguna cosa que vos non caya de fazer, nin dexedes nada de vuestra onra nin de lo que devedes fazer por ayuntar grand tesoro de buenas obras, por que ayades la gracia de Dios et buena fama de gentes. (66)

The points made by Patronio here are constants in Juan Manuel's texts: money should be acquired through fair means, and it must not be acquired for its own sake, but for the positive use to which it can be put. The opposition *tesoro verdadero/tesoro fallecedero* of the verses at the end of *Ex.* XIIII (66), also occurs in an amplified form in the *Libro de los estados*, where it is made clear that the Pope must not only cherish the spiritual treasures of which he is custodian, but must also exercise great care in the acquisition and distribution of material wealth:

---

[4] Le Goff gives a brief analysis of the increasing focus of theologians from the twelfth century onwards on the examination of motives behind an action (1990: 11–12).

Otrosi, en el segundo tesoro, que son las rendas et los lugares et todas las cosas tenporales que a el papa, puede mucho desmesresçer s[i] non obrare en ello commo deue; ca tan bien puede desmeresçer en ganando las riquezas commo en partiendo las. (Part II, Ch. XXXVIII, 475)

In his advice to his son he re-affirms the importance of acquiring money honourably (*Libro enfenido*, 174), going on to define *tesoro* as consisting of *aver monedado, pannos, oro* and *plata* (175). The archetypical example of wealth earned dishonourably is the *treynta dineros de oro* for which Judas sold Christ (*ibid.*), an example also used in the *Libro de los estados* (Part II, Ch. VIII, 444), and any money earned illicitly should not be kept for personal gain, but used for the benefit of the Church or society:

Et asi, los dineros que los sennores han de callonnas o de algunos fechos de fuerças o de alguna manera que non sean derecha mente ganados, non deue[n] del[l]os fazer tesoro, mas deue[n] los poner en fazer eglesias et monesterios, o, a lo menos, los muros de las fortalezas de las villas o de lugares. (*Libro enfenido*, 175)

He goes on to explain in some detail that the monies collected from fines are tainted by the criminal act from which they arise, and must therefore be used for the common good (175–6).

In the light of all this, it seems reasonable to assume that Juan Manuel would not have been impressed by Alfonso XI's explanation to the Archbishop of Toledo in 1336 that his men had been collecting from the Archbishop's vassals money which rightly belonged to the Archbishop, to help him finance his conflicts with, amongst others, Juan Manuel (Giménez Soler 1932: letter DXLVII, 630). And his principles are applied with rigour even to those who fight against the Moors, driven by the desire for money:

commo quier que todos los que van contra los moros fazen bien, pero non deuedes creer que todos los que mueren en la guerra de los moros son martires nin sanctos; ca los que alla van robando et forçando las mugeres et faziendo muchos pecados et muy malos et mueren en aquella guerra, nin avn los que van sola mente por ganar algo de los moros o por dineros que les den o por ganar fama del mundo, et non por entencion derecha et defendimiento de la ley et de la tierra de los christianos, estos, avn que mueran, Dios, que sabe todas las cosas, sabe lo que a de seer destos tales. (*Libro de los estados*, Part I, Ch. LXXVI, 348–9)

Wrongful acquisition of money is not the only problem, however; there are still dangers in how wealth is used, and even if it is given away, the spirit in which it is given is crucial. Avarice can, and does, surface at any one of the three points in the cycle: acquisition, possession, distribution. Human nature makes it difficult for man not to love wealth for its own sake:

> Dixo una ves el dicho omne sancto que mas se deleytaua el quando traya la mano a la su gata por el lomo, que sant Gregorio, que era papa, en todas sus riquezas. (*Libro de los estados*, Part I, Ch. LV, 297)

The rich and the powerful have constantly to examine their motives when spending their money. The emperor, for example, has to purchase the exterior symbols of his high status in order to fulfil his social responsibilities, but must also show moderation and resist the temptation to take undue pleasure in his wealth, if he is to fulfil his spiritual responsibilities:

> Otrosi, deue guisar que ande sienpre vestido de pan[n]os mejores et mas preçiados que las otras gentes de su corte, et eso mismo deue fazer en las vestias et en sus ensellamientos. Pero si quisiere, alguna vegada, bien puede fazer que estas cosas sean de menos preçio, por que tomen ende enxienplo las gentes para non despender lo suyo en lo que con razon pueden escusar. [...] Pero en todas estas cosas non deue tomar plazer nin deleyte desordenado. Et deue se acordar que todo esto es falleçedero et que poco le a de durar. (*Libro de los estados*, Part I, Ch. LXII, 316)

The best use which can be made of wealth is to spend it in ways which enhance one's status and reputation, and at the same time have potential spiritual benefits. For example, Al-Hakam II of Córdoba, according to *Ex.* XLI of *El Conde Lucanor*, responded to criticisms that his achievements had been trivial by providing the means to complete the construction of the Great Mosque in the city; this is held up by Patronio as a model of behaviour for the count, who has been similarly ridiculed for his negligible achievements. But as can be seen in *Ex.* XL, the intention behind such actions is always crucial: the good works promised by the Seneschal of Carcassone were futile, because they were driven by selfish motives. The dangers inherent in acquiring money, enjoying the pleasures it can bring, and even in doing good works for the wrong reasons, are a recurrent concern of Juan Manuel as he attempts to provide a coherent code of conduct from the perspective of the rich and powerful.[5]

The final aspect to be analysed in this study is the question of fraud and deception; this is an important theme in Part I of *El Conde Lucanor*, and places the focus on the intended victim and the potential for disastrous personal and social consequences if the fraud is successful. It can be assumed (and often goes without saying) that the fraudsters, even if successful, are

---

5   For the broader context to this, see Macpherson (1970–71).

doing themselves great spiritual harm: 'Non se ayunta el aver de torticería, et si se ayunta, non dura' (*El Conde Lucanor*, Part II, 231).

The presence of so many stories of this type in *El Conde Lucanor* is probably best explained in part because they provide the basis for strong narratives, in part because Juan Manuel had witnessed or had been the victim of deception, and in part because it is quite simply a constant of human society, which the organized legal codes normally legislate against, as in the case of the *Ordenanzas dadas a la Villa de Peñafiel*.[6] Probably the two best known examples are stories XX and XXXII, in each of which a king is defrauded of large sums of money. In neither case are we informed directly that the victim has learned his lesson, but we are told that the count acted successfully on Patronio's advice, and we, as readers, are meant to do the same: if we are to be successful in this life we must be careful not only of what we do unto others, but also of what others may try to do unto us. The desire for money is such that the world is full of confidence-tricksters, and gullibility on the victim's part can often be regarded as resulting from negligence.[7]

---

[6] The boundaries between fact and fiction in this aspect of human conduct are difficult to establish. One of the best known examples of financial fraud in medieval Castilian literature is the (presumably fictional) deception of Rachel and Vidas by El Cid; the similarities to the following (presumably factual) account of a confidence trick contained in a newspaper in Valladolid in February 1787 are striking:

> En el año pasado se apareció en esta Ciudad un D. Nicolás Martinez, que se decia natural de Viana del Bollo, hombre astuto y embaucador de profesion, que llegó á persuadir á un gran numero de Personas de todas clases, se hallaba comisionado por el Ministerio para el remedio y socorro de varios Conventos de Religiosas de esta Ciudad. Por lo que no solamente estafó algunas cantidades à sujetos particulares, sino que alucinando con su labia à la R. Priora del Convento de *Corpus*, le sacó 12 533. rs. propios de dicha Casa, dexandole en custodia un caxoncito de pino, clavado con tachuelas, en que dixo habia 5. libras de perlas finas, 70. aderezos de diamantes, y 160. reloxes exquisitos. Hizo fuga el embustero, y abierto el caxon delante del Sr. Don Pedro Sanchez Yebra, Alcalde del Crimen, y Juez de Vagos, se hallaron dos resmas de mal papel solamente. Fué perseguido desde luego este hombre, y por las requisitorias, que á todas partes habia remitido el Sr. Yebra, se logrò su prision en Andalucia por el Excmo. Sr. Conde de Oreilly: no se hallaron dineros, ni bienes: y consultada su causa á S. Mag. ha sido sentenciado á los Presidios de Africa por 4 años, dexando por unica paga a los acredores el desengaño y escarmiento.
>
> (Beristain 1978 I: 46)

Juan Manuel would have approved of El Cid's actions (deception carried out for good reason), and as in the 1787 incident, he often left the victims in his stories poorer but wiser. A further illustration of fiction and reality mirroring each other is provided by Juan Manuel's story of a fraudulent alchemist (*Ex*. XX), and the employment by General Franco and his co-conspirators of a Hindu alchemist, who produced no gold and fled under suspicion of being a British agent (Preston 1999: 27).

[7] Diz sees in *Ex*. XX the suspicions of the late medieval aristocrat when confronted by the early manifestations of capitalism (1984: 84–8); Juan Manuel's version certainly has a different

And we must be particularly on our guard against combining our own desire for money with gullibility, as this can lead to severe cases of self-deception such as that of Doña Truhana in *Ex.* VII. Dealings with one's fellow human beings become particularly difficult where deceptions are concerned, as the underlying truth is difficult to discover, and motives are all: the confidence-trickster of *Ex.* XX is given a large sum of money in order to undertake a journey, without revealing his true intentions; the bridegroom of *Ex.* XXV does exactly the same, but because his character has been properly assessed in advance, he handsomely repays the trust placed in him.

The differences between Juan Ruiz and Juan Manuel on the subject of money are quite marked: the cleric uses traditional material to satirize the power of money, whereas the aristocratic layman accepts the presence of money in human society and seeks to establish rules on how to prevent it being disruptive. In this, for once, they conform with the expectations we might have of the clerical and the secular writer, whereas in many other respects they do not; for example, the *Libro de buen amor* extols the delights of sexual love, whereas Juan Manuel is reticent on such matters. In stanzas 490–510 of the *Libro de buen amor* Juan Ruiz presents a vehement criticism of the power of money, and in the remainder of the work there is little to support a more positive view. Juan Manuel, too, is aware of the power of money and of its dangers, but he accepts it as a social reality, as a necessity with the potential for good, provided it is acquired for the right motives and used in the correct way. He treats the subject with due seriousness and accommodates it into his demanding but clear conditions for living a life successful both on this earth and as preparation for the next. He recommends caution, and his views were largely shaped by traditional analyses of social and economic structures which were in the process of disappearing, but he did make strenuous efforts to incorporate money into the models of behaviour that he describes. For Juan Manuel both money and the lack of money were serious matters; poverty for a character in the *Libro de buen amor* might represent no more than an obstacle in the seduction of women (e.g. stanza 636), but for many of Juan Manuel's characters it has the potential for preventing them fulfilling their social responsibilities and achieving their spiritual ambitions. In the prologue to the *Libro enfenido*, which contains the fruits of a lifetime's experience and reflection, he writes that many people are uncertain over the relative importance of *el aver* and *el saber*; he goes on to observe that the answer is clear, and that knowledge and wisdom are more important than wealth and possessions. But his is not the reaction of an

---

focus from Al-Jawberi's earlier Arabic version, in which the confidence-trickster is praised for risking his money in a venture which proves successful (see Marsan 1974: 617–18).

intellectual with little interest in material possessions; rather, the first reason
he gives for valuing *el saber* highly is as follows:

> Et muchos dubdan qual es mejor, el saber o el aver; et çierta mente esto es
> ligero de indagar; ca çierto es que el saber puede guardar el aver, et el aver
> non guardar el saber. (*Libro enfenido*, 146)

The prologue centres on *el saber*, and he does give a series of theological
reasons for affirming its importance; but within Juan Manuel's world-view it
is also crucial because it empowers the individual in the proper acquisition,
possession and sharing of wealth.

List of Works Cited

Beristain, José Mariano, 1978. *Diario Pinciano. Primer periódico de Valladolid
(1787–88)*, facs. ed. and intro. Celso Almuiña Fernández (Valladolid: Grupo
Pinciano con la colaboración de Caja de Ahorros Provincial de Valladolid))
Blecua, José Manuel (ed.), 1982–83. Don Juan Manuel, *Obras completas*, 2 vols
(Madrid: Gredos)
Devoto, Daniel, 1972. *Introducción al estudio de don Juan Manuel y en partic-
ular de «El Conde Lucanor»* (Madrid: Castalia)
Diz, Marta Ana, 1984. *Patronio y Lucanor: la lectura inteligente «en el tiempo
que es turbio»* (Potomac, MD: Scripta Humanistica)
Giménez Soler, Andrés, 1932. *Don Juan Manuel: biografía y estudio crítico*
(Zaragoza: Academia Española)
Gybbon-Monypenny, G. B. (ed.), 1989. Arcipreste de Hita, *Libro de buen amor*
(Madrid: Castalia)
Kinkade, Richard P., 1990. '"Guardandoles en justiçia": Juan Manuel's Social
Contract with the Town of Peñafiel in the Year 1345', *Anuario Medieval*, 2:
102–23
Le Goff, Jacques, 1990. *Your Money or Your Life. Economy and Religion in the
Middle Ages*, trans. Patricia Ranum (New York: Zone Books)
Liu, Benjamin, 2003. '"De la propiedat que el dinero ha": Economics of Good
Life' [Unpublished conference paper]
Macpherson, Ian, 1970–71. '*Dios y el mundo*: The Didacticism of *El Conde
Lucanor*', *Romance Philology*, 24: 26–38
Marsan, Rameline E., 1974. *Itinéraire espagnol du conte médiéval (VIII–XV
siècles)* (Paris: Klinksieck)
Preston, Paul, 1999. *¡Comrades! Portraits from the Spanish Civil War* (London:
HarperCollins)
Round, Nicholas, 1997. 'Juan Ruiz and Some Versions of *Nummus*', in *The
Medieval Mind: Hispanic Essays in Honour of Alan Deyermond*, ed. Ian
Macpherson and Ralph Penny (London: Tamesis), pp. 381–400

Serés, Guillermo (ed.), 1994. Don Juan Manuel, *El Conde Lucanor* (Barcelona: Crítica).

Valdeón Baruque, Julio, 1977. 'Las tensiones sociales en Castilla en tiempos de don Juan Manuel', in *Juan Manuel Studies*, ed. Ian Macpherson (London: Tamesis), pp. 181–92

THE NINETEENTH-CENTURY NOVEL

From Socartes to Madrid: The Continuity between *Marianela* and *El doctor Centeno*

GEOFFREY RIBBANS

The traditional division of Galdós's novels into his early novels ('de la primera época') and those of his 'segunda o tercera manera' has been the subject of much discussion.[1] While some scholars such as Richard Cardwell seek a sweeping 'total view' that is sceptical about the validity of the distinction, the majority of critics believe there is reason to accept some differentiation. At the same time it has been convincingly argued, on the one hand, that *La familia de León Roch* (1879) is a transitional work, and on the other, that *La desheredada* (1881), habitually considered as the work initiating the second manner, has some transitional characteristics, being, in Eamonn Rodgers's words, 'still constrained within the context of his reformist, Krausist-enlightenment outlook' (1993: 77).[2]

Across the divide, however, there is an evident link between *Marianela* (1878) and *El doctor Centeno* (1883) that has been frequently noted but has attracted little detailed investigation. Yet, as José-Carlos Mainer points out in his cogent discussion in the Introduction to his edition of *El doctor Centeno* (2002: 9–10), Felipe's story is explicitly anticipated at the end of the narration in the standard edition of *Marianela*.

> Despidámonos para siempre de esta tumba, de la cual se ha hablado en *The Times*. Volvamos los ojos hacia otro lado; busquemos a otro ser, rebusquémosle, porque es tan chico que apenas se ve; es un insecto imperceptible,

---

[1] The two essential texts revealing Galdós's intentions are his letter to Pereda announcing his 'gran proyecto', conceived 'hace tiempo' (4 March 1879, ed. Bravo Villasante 1970–71: 32), a novel that will require a year and a half's work, and his letter to Giner de los Ríos in which he speaks of the 'segunda o tercera manera' (14 April 1882). For a good discussion see Enrique Miralles (Introduction to his edition of *La desheredada*, 1992: ix–xxv).

[2] See Martha Krow-Lucal's valuable study of the importance of recurring characters; for her *La desheredada* brings 'el comienzo de una nueva etapa pero no un rechazo de su obra anterior' (1978: 177).

> más pequeño sobre la faz de la tierra que el *philloxera* en la breve exten-
> sión de la viña. Al fin le vemos; allí está, pequeño, mezquino, atomístico.
> Pero tiene alientos y logrará ser grande. Oíd su historia, que no carece de
> interés.
>
> Pues señor ...
>
> Pero no, este libro no le corresponde. Acoged bien el de Marianela, y a
> su debido tiempo se os dará el de Celipín. (242)[3]

This ending gives rise to a puzzle: why did Galdós not follow up immediately with the sequel he promised in this extremely unequivocal declaration of intent, instead of writing three other novels first? Jacques Beyrie, in
particular, draws attention to the problem:

> Pourquoi ce long délai de cinq ans, chez un homme qui nous avait habitués
> à mettre ses projets à exécution avec beaucoup plus de célérité? Question
> importante, susceptible de projeter une nouvelle lumière sur le problème
> de la mutation réalisée par le romancier. (1980: II, 325)

The answer to this question may indeed shed light on wider issues concerning
the relationship between all the novels written in the crucial developmental
stage between 1878 and 1883.

There are several important aspects to this relationship. One concerns the
use of imaginary locations, set in 'la geografía moral de España' (*Gloria*,
515). The place in which *Marianela* is set, Socartes, situated in the Cantab-
rian area, is rather more specific than the other two imaginary settings, Orbajosa and Ficóbriga. Linked though it is with nearby Ficóbriga, Socartes seems
to have been inspired by a more modern, less ideological, reality: the zinc
mines at Reocín.[4] Although after *Marianela* the use of imaginary locations is
abandoned, it is remarkable how constantly the narrator of *El doctor Centeno*
refers back, as we shall see, to his character's origins in Socartes.

Incidentally, Galdós's change of technique in this respect is of greater
significance than has habitually been acknowledged. The choosing of a non-
identifiable location with an imaginary name and some symbolic significance, reveals a much more abstract, universalizing and idealistic criterion
than placing the narrative within an urban reality like Madrid's, with very

---

[3] Felipe Centeno is referred to in a variety of ways: Celipín, Felipín and the ironic terms
'El doctor Centeno', 'El doctorcillo', 'Aristóteles', etc. I use the form Felipe throughout this
essay.

[4] During the excursion through Cantabria that gave rise to his *Cuarenta leguas por
Cantabria* (1879), Galdós visited the mines at Reocín. He mentions the place in passing,
describing the effect of the surrounding mountains as 'sublime y guerrero' (1216). Galdós
revived the Ficóbriga location in the play *La de San Quintín* (1894). By this time he was again
more concerned to provide a symbolic setting than a realistic one.

specific references to recognizable streets and buildings.[5] In the latter technique the Tainian criteria of *milieu* and *moment*, as well as *race*, can be firmly established. Time as well as space is accorded a more concrete role, for the temporal vagueness of the early novels is replaced by a firm chronology of action, encompassing in the process external events set in time, that is to say history, as it has evolved or is evolving.

In this respect *La familia de León Roch* is a halfway house.[6] It is set largely in Madrid, though a long stretch at the beginning is located in the Basque bathing resort of Ugoibea (Part I, Chs I–VII). Apart from a description of a bullfight (Part II, Ch. I, 843–5), there is little topographical detail, not even concerning the three dwellings where most of the action takes place: the Tellerías's apartment, in an unspecified location; the house of León himself, who chose to live as far as possible from his in-laws, 'en lo más apartado de la zona del Este' (802); and the Fúcars's residence in outlying Suertebella. The timing too is unspecific; the action presumably takes place over three to four years in the late 1860s or early 1870s, but there is no trace of the momentous political events that occur during these years. The socio-political environment is thus quite different from that of the novels following *La desheredada*.

A second aspect linking *Marianela* and *El doctor Centeno*, and one that has escaped critical attention, concerns chronology. The degree of immediate follow-up Galdós adopts from the one narration to the other is striking; he has deliberately chosen to develop Felipe's story from the precise moment of Marianela's death, alleging in typical fashion that accurate historical research has authenticated it. The grandiose tombstone gratuitously provided the orphan girl by Florentina gives the date of her death as '12 de Octubre de 186 ...' (241), incongruously and ironically linking her with the spirit of enterprise and adventure represented by the discovery of America. The later novel dates the appearance of Felipe Centeno at the Observatory in the southern industrial development of Madrid at precisely 10 February 1863.[7] By these means it is made clear retrospectively that Marianela died in 1862.[8]

---

5   There is little doubt that this development is influenced by Naturalism, but this is too large a subject to pursue here.

6   The case of the incomplete novel, *Rosalía*, ably reconstituted and commented on by Alan Smith, and dating from about 1872, should be noted. Although *Rosalía* has its base in Castro Urdiales, most of its action takes place in Madrid, with frequent references to historical events during the interim period following the 1868 Revolution.

7   Mainer indicates that on that day, a Tuesday, *La Iberia*, the progressive newspaper edited by Calvo Asensio, 'editorizaba contra el gobierno O'Donnell', noting the 'tranquilidad completa en el país' (2002: 96, n. 2). Yet O'Donnell's long Unión liberal government is about to fall. Cienfuegos has a copy of the newspaper in his hand (100), and the narrator emphasizes that it is a February issue.

8   Mainer, in his edition of *El doctor Centeno*, misses this connection, wrongly dating the novel, like *León Roch*, as 'a mediados de los años 70' (2002: 11, and 100, n. 5).

With notable precision Felipe informs Alejandro Miquis that he has taken seven weeks and two days to walk from Socartes. The intervening time of about ten weeks he has spent as *la tía Soplada*'s unpaid servant, a period that included more than a month ('mes y días' [108]) attending school, and for an unspecified time doing odd jobs and sleeping rough in porches and sheds. It is a plausible chronology constructed with obvious care to account for the seventeen weeks since Felipe left his home.

As previously noted, abundant references to Socartes are provided, starting with Miquis's utter ignorance of the place and his mocking attitude towards it (106, 110); Felipe's parents are referred to in passing (106). Even the source of the famous cigar that made Felipe ill is linked with Socartes, for it was given to him by an artillery sergeant from that imaginary location, Mateo del Olmo, who had been his sister Pepina's fiancé. Marianela, or Nela, herself is also alluded to fleetingly: 'Si la Nela me viera ...' (150). Discouraged by his lack of scholarly success in Polo's school, Felipe refers very specifically to his earlier domestic situation: 'no estaba en su lugar', he declares, 'sino en Socartes, rodeado de sus iguales, las piedras, y de sus dignos prójimos, las mulas' (157). Galdós is clearly at pains to emphasize the continuity with the Socartes story, while tacitly insinuating that it has been superseded.

These two points – the insistence on references to Socartes and the strict chronology adopted in the second novel – even raise the intriguing possibility that Galdós may have sketched out some preparatory material for *El doctor Centeno* earlier than has been assumed, before the start of the 'segunda manera' with *La desheredada*. This tentative suggestion might conceivably account for the novel's peculiar structure, and the doubts, which have so intrigued critics, both about its unity and about who – Felipe himself, Pedro Polo or Alejandro Miquis – is its protagonist.[9] While the opening of the novel is clearly tied to *Marianela*, the subsequent development of the stories of both Polo and Miquis takes us a long way beyond the unfolding of Felipe's aspirations announced in the previous work. The existence of a preliminary draft might even provide an explanation as to why a younger member of the Miquis family, Augusto, should appear as a mature adult in *La desheredada* before his elder brother Alejandro has lived and died in 1863–64 in a novel apparently written later. The contrast between the two brothers, the pragmatic Augusto and the imaginative Alejandro, in his way as unrealistic as Isidora, is one of several striking presentations of the conflict between fantasy and pragmatism.[10]

---

[9] A strong case for its unity is made by Germán Gullón, who rightly sees Felipe as 'el prisma humano a través del cual se filtran los hechos que ocurren en la novela' (1970–71: 580).

[10] It is worth noting that the Miquis comes from Don Quixote country, El Toboso/Tomel-

A hypothetical earlier version might also shed some light on another anomaly concerning Felipe: his presence in *La familia de León Roch*, which is otherwise out of sequence in his career. By the time he appears in Part III of the novel, published in early 1879, had Galdós already concluded that the boy's broader ambitions were not viable? This might account for a certain discrepancy of tone between the last paragraphs of *Marianela* and the somewhat burlesque approach displayed in *El doctor Centeno*. At all events, by the early 1870s, Felipe is more mature, perhaps around twenty years old. He identifies himself to Luis Gonzaga, María Egipciaca's fanatical twin brother, in the most sparing of terms as 'Felipe Centeno ... De Socartes' (830), and is described as '[u]n lacayín con pechera estrecha de botones, la carilla alegre y vivaracha, la cabeza trasquilada, los pies ágiles y las manos rojas llenas de verrugas' (830). Having taken Felipe into his service, León Roch comments that 'he tenido cariño a ese muchacho por su aplicación, su deseo de instruirse y el fondo de bondad que se le descubre en medio de sus puerilidades' (846). Lively, well-intentioned and a bit juvenile, Felipe is still attracted by book-learning: 'siempre que aquí venía se quedaba extasiado delante de mis libros' (846), but by now is clearly confirmed in his function as a reliable if somewhat volatile retainer. When he is dismissed by María Egipciaca because he did not go to confession, his retort, 'Señora, déjeme en paz; yo no quiero nada con cuervos' (846), may perhaps be seen as anticipating his experience with Pedro Polo in the earlier discourse time but later narrative time of *El doctor Centeno*. Felipe's dismissal is, moreover, the event that causes León to take a more decisive stand against María's religious fanaticism.

Whether or not any such earlier sketch of the novel exists (and one must admit that this is sheer speculation), it is undeniably true that the close chronological link with *Marianela* entails an important consequence, namely, that *El doctor Centeno* becomes the earliest in discourse time of all the *novelas contemporáneas* and coincides with the young Benito's earliest recollections of Madrid. It is highly significant, moreover, that the date 1863 proceeding from *Marianela* determines the chronology of the two novels that immediately follow, *Tormento* (1867–68) and *La de Bringas* (1868), since the three novels together form a loose trilogy. The concern with the aftermath of the September Revolution of 1868 so notably displayed in *La desheredada* is thus disrupted for a time, but in ample compensation the novelist is enabled to fill in the chronological gaps between 1863 and that crucial 'glorious' revolution. Galdós accordingly takes on board such a significant early historical occurrence as the unexpected fall, on 27 February 1863, just after *El doctor*

loso, like Isidora, and also from an impoverished background. They too have *chiflado* antecedents (Doña Isabel Godoy) and, curiously, all three brothers, including Constantino, from *Lo prohibido*, have been given heroic classical names.

Centeno opens, of O'Donnell's long Unión Liberal ministry, opening the way
to Narváez's return to power; and the sudden death of Pedro Calvo Asensio,
the dynamic editor of *La Iberia*, on 18 September of the same year. This
last occurrence is fully integrated into the fictional action. The sententious
and politically naïve concierge of the Observatory, Don Florencio Morales y
Temprado, is acquainted with Calvo Asensio since both characters, the real
and the fictional, are natives of Mota del Marqués. Felipe witnessed the grandiose funeral given for the Progressive leader by climbing up a lamp-post,
thus delaying his task of delivering a vital letter to Alejandro's aunt, Doña
Isabel Godoy. These events are followed, in *Tormento*, by the continuous
growth of political tension as the revolution approaches. In *La de Bringas*,
the increasing momentum of Prim's conspiracies culminates finally in the
'Glorious Revolution'.[11] Henceforth the *novelas contemporáneas* are set in
the post-revolutionary period.

Let us now look more closely at how Felipe is presented in *Marianela*,
particularly regarding his relationship with Marianela's story.[12] Far from
being an idyll or 'lyrical interlude',[13] the novel serves to highlight first of
all the dismal failure of Spain's social structure to offer care of any mean-
ingful sort for an ill-formed, stunted and neglected orphan like Marianela;
the overall problem described by Golfín is exemplified in her.[14] Nobody in
the Aldeacorba community has bothered to do anything for her. She has early
come to have a deep-rooted and reiterated fatalistic conviction that she is
no use for anything, compounded by the open declaration of characters like
Sofía and Señana that she would be better dead. Her attractive human qualities, shown in her spontaneous song and dance, her primitive rejoicing in
nature, her simple religious notions and her generosity, remain undeveloped
and unfulfilled. When the one function, acting as a guide to the blind Pablo,
that gives meaning to her life and opens out the remote possibility, in which
she scarcely believes, of his loving her, is taken from her, nothing is left.
Geraldine Scanlon is surely right in emphasizing that 'ultimately, Nela is a
victim of the class system' (1988: 48), and that everything is too late for her

---

[11] For the integration of these and other historical events into the fictional structure see
Ribbans (1993a, Chapters 4, 5, 6).

[12] I am not concerned in this study with possible biographical references, or the various
literary influences, such as the *Bildungsroman*, that have been traced in the novel by Pattison
and others.

[13] The fallacy of this approach is well demonstrated by Jones (1961: 515) and Caudet
(intro. to *Marianela*, 2004: 13–15).

[14] Golfín singles out ignorance, lack of dignity and the sense of being abandoned ('desem-
parados'), as the major handicaps the poor suffer (144).

(46).[15] For Felipe, on the other hand, the hope is afforded, at this stage, of breaking through the barriers of poverty and ignorance to a better future.

The thirteen-year-old boy is deeply conditioned by the mining industry. The presence of the mines is felt from the very beginning of the novel; they are grandiose, awesome and menacing: a giant distortion of human features that is at once a sign of inexorable progress and a monster that needs to be curbed.[16] The brutalizing effect on the miners and the all-pervading dust that covers the inhabitants are reflected in the constant image of stone. It is an image that directly impinges on Felipe and is most evidently worked out in the description of his family in Chapter IV under the significant title 'La familia de piedra'. Without being the most downtrodden of the community, the Centeno family clearly demonstrates the degradation of values produced by the mines. Sinforoso Centeno, the charge-hand (*capataz*) responsible for the mules used for transport, has a pathetically restricted notion of learning, while his wife Señana incorporates in her mental makeup a complete lack of ambition for her children and the devouring avarice of country people obsessed by the fear of poverty, whom the narrator describes with unexpected vehemence as 'la bestia más innoble que puede imaginarse' (99). In the Centeno household where Marianela, nominally taken in as a work of charity, is deprived of every kindness and is rated in consideration below the household pets, the cat and the thrush, Felipe, alone among his siblings, is desperate to escape. His urge to break away from his parents' stifling acquiescence in the status quo is an aspect of the theme of self-help (Scanlon 1988: 54), with a hint of the 'survival of the fittest' motif later elaborated by Herbert Spencer. This aspiration is insolubly linked to education.

Significantly, the image of stone, with its absolute rigidity, is related with blindness, which shuts out visual experience just as completely. Thus, Marianela's noble but unrefined concept of philosophy is inevitably 'petrificado' (167), and she remains immutably one of the 'ciegos del espíritu' (229), as Pablo had been physically. Pablo, for his part, is significantly described in terms of stone, as sculptured and cold: 'aquel rostro de Antinoo ciego poseía la fría serenidad de mármol' (109). Contrasting with the images of stone and blindness are images from the natural world of beauty and imagination (stars, flowers) associated with Marianela, but the figure that stands out is of flight. Birds represent freedom, ambition, the potentiality to rise above the oppressive circumstances of earth-bound life. Nela declares: 'Estaba pensando que por qué no nos daría Dios a nosotros las personas alas para volar como los

---

15 Caudet comments forthrightly and correctly that '[e]l matrimonio de Pablo y de Nela es imposible porque Nela es pobre' (intro. to *Marianela*, 2004: 43).

16 In his thoughtful assessment of degrees of charity in *Marianela*, Peter Bly (1972) is categorical in viewing the novel as an outright condemnation of the mining industry.

pájaros' (120). The blind Pablo is, according to his father, 'un valiente pájaro con las alas rotas' (155), but he will have his wings – his sight – restored. Soaring imagery also characterizes the Golfín brothers: Nela tells Felipe that '[d]on Teodoro y don Carlos eran como los pájaros que andan solos por el mundo' (162). 'Pájaros, a volar' (179), Don Francisco says to his son, Florentina and Nela, as he sends them off on their last walk together, and, as they fly off to the country, Florentina imitates the birds' flight (180). While Pablo and Florentina are airborne, there is no further prospect of flying for Marianela.

The stories of Felipe and Marianela are closely intertwined. Marianela has supported Felipe's endeavour to get away by providing him with minimal finance heroically amassed. His departure coincides with Marianela's fateful moment of decision once Pablo has recovered his sight. She abandons her half-hearted plans to join Felipe and though she will not tell him where she intends to go, she has decided on suicide: to join her mother in the Trascava, a move that, despite her rescue by Golfín, presages her death. Felipe, for his part, promises not to forget Socartes, and the narrator declares that '[l]a Geología había perdido una piedra, y la sociedad había ganado un hombre' (202). El doctor Centeno will work out what sort of man he turns out to be.

Felipe finds a living model in Teodoro Golfín, who succeeded, with the opportune support of employers and patrons,[17] in working himself up in society to become a distinguished doctor and ophthalmologist and, at the same time, to provide resources for his brother to become a mining engineer.[18] I have no doubt that in Galdós's presentation scientific advances, in both medicine and industry, are deemed positive and necessary, but they come at a heavy social price. Teodoro presents himself as 'una especie de Colón, el Colón del trabajo, una especie de Hernán Cortés; yo había descubierto en mí un Nuevo Mundo, y, después de descubrirlo, lo había conquistado' (151). His sort of exploration and conquest, encompassed in his motto 'Adelante, siempre adelante …' (71–3), is enterprising and courageous, without the defects of cupidity, ruthlessness and cruelty associated with the conquistadores. His work-ethic forms part of the ideal of rewarding merit that Jo Labanyi has perceptively traced in La desheredada and that is equally apparent in the two novels we are concerned with: 'the point Galdós is making is that wealth is not a right, but must be earned. He is putting the case for a genuine meritocracy' (1979: 53). By contrast, the dazzling new life Golfín offers Pablo, in Chapter XX, significantly entitled 'El nuevo mundo', takes him in a different, more conventional direction. The New World parallel Pablo embraces leads

---

[17] Caudet argues very reasonably that the Golfín brothers '[s]on producto ellos … de la mente utópica del narrador y no de la realidad' (intro. to Marianela, 2004: 42).

[18] It is not fortuitous that both Pepe Rey and León Roch studied at the Instituto de Minas.

him to Florentina, not Nela (220), and in doing so he joins the static patriarchal world of his father Don Francisco and his uncle Don Manuel.

Aspiring to be a physician like Golfín, Felipe has already acquired, ironically, the nickname of 'el doctor Centeno', and been given a chapter heading
(XII: 'El doctor Celipín') with this title. His understandable aims appear
at this stage more than a little naïve, with hints of over-reaching ambition
('todas las ciencias las he de aprender' [163]), and presumptions of opulence
('[v]erás tú qué fino y galán voy a ser' [163]), which provokes from Marianela
a cautionary note: 'No pienses todavía en esas cosas de remontarte mucho
... Vete poquito a poquito' (163). It is a counsel that will resonate right up
to *El doctor Centeno*. At the end of the narrative, however, no limits are as
yet imposed on his potential attainments: 'tiene aliento y logrará ser grande'
(242).

In the novel to which his name is given Felipe continues, as Peter Bly
notes (1986: 162), to be associated with a minute insect. From 'tan chico
que apenas se ve ... un insecto imperceptible ... pequeño, mezquino, atom-
ístico' (*Marianela*, 242), he is compared with 'la primera mosca que pasa o
con el silencioso, común e incoloro insectillo' (*El doctor Centeno*, 93). Now,
however, his prospects of success are immediately put in doubt.[19] Although
dubbed a hero, he is satirized from the start, in a narrative characterized
by a sustained tone of humorous exaggeration that veers towards hyperbole
(Nimetz 1968: 24): what Mainer calls '[l]a huella de la parodia' (48). As Hazel
Gold has indicated (1989: 228),[20] his climbing the hill up to the Conservatory
is in striking and ironic contrast with Rastignac's arrogant ascent to the Père
Lachaise cemetery to challenge Paris at the close of *Le Père Goriot*.[21] At the
end, Gold concludes, 'what the reader encounters is not a Balzacian hymn to
life but a monument to waste and death' (229), while Scanlon (1978), rightly
discerns 'obsolescent values' as a salient characteristic of the novel.

The paramount theme of education is made explicit in the first two chapter
headings: 'I: Introducción a la pedagogía'; 'II: Pedagogía'.[22] It is clear from
the outset that educational facilities and opportunities are woefully inadequate. In marked contrast with Golfín's extraordinarily fortunate experience,

---

19 Scanlon perceptively comments that '*El doctor Centeno* (1883) gives a much more realistic account of the difficulties facing a poor boy who wished to acquire an education. This is far
from the novel of the self-made man which Galdós seems to promise at the end of *Marianela*'
(1988: 56).

20 A modified version is included in her book of 1993.

21 One of the lodgers in Doña Virginia's pension, Arias Ortiz, is an avid collector of
Balzac's novels. Miquis possesses a copy of *Le Père Goriot* (282).

22 See Gloria Moreno Castillo (1977), who suggests that by permeating virtually every
aspect of the novel, education in the widest sense including its opposite pole, educational
cultural failure, gives the novel its unity.

Felipe is saddled with conspicuously inadequate teachers and masters. Pedro Polo is a capricious autocrat, and his female relations, his mother Claudia and his sister Marcelina, are over-demanding. Polo's pedagogic criteria emphasizing learning by rote and coercion are perniciously out-dated and his methods, relying on corporal punishment and deprivation of meals, are cruel and ineffective. A self-made man like Golfín, Pedro Polo Cortés is identified, as his name and Extremaduran provenance imply, with Hernán Cortés: 'era de Medellín; por lo tanto, tenía con el conquistador de México la doble conexión del apellido y de la cuna' (137), but, unlike the ophthalmologist, he is associated, not with the enterprise of the conquistadores but with their rigidity and harshness. The one proclaimed 'maestro de escuela', José Ido, is, though well-intentioned, hopelessly inadequate, and he commands no respect.

Felipe, for his part, has a long way to go. His amusing use of the suffix *des-* in all his utterances 'neatly serves', as Gold observes, 'to undo the meaning of his words' and denotes an element of self-destruction (232). He is completely out of his depth in Polo's school (157); its arid subjects, arithmetic, grammar, religious history, Christian doctrine, mean nothing to him, and as he learns nothing he loses, not unlike Nela, all confidence in himself. He is successful in learning to read, and reaches out towards geography, but his desire to learn practical subjects is unfulfilled.[23]

It remains unclear whether or not in more advantageous circumstances he would have done better. As it is, he takes refuge in his friendship with the picaresque Juanito del Socorro and in wandering the streets and playing at bullfights.

He is no more fortunate in his second master, for Miquis's good qualities of kindness and generosity are marred by his unbridled imagination and financial indiscipline. As a consequence we have not one but two flawed heroes. At a still formative stage between childhood and maturity, Felipe lacks suitable guidance. Under Miquis's spell he dreams of becoming a poet. Like Lazarillo, he paradoxically supports his master, descending to mendacity to do so, but rapidly squanders what money he acquires. His studies continue in a desultory fashion, but are not exactly fostered by the fact that he is used for odd tasks by all the inhabitants of Doña Virginia's pension. He has access to the student-lodgers' books and Cienfuegos's biological specimens, but cannot make head or tail of them. The culmination of his medical aspirations comes when he attempts to apply poorly assimilated medical notions from Moreno Rubio's examination of his master to diagnose the ailments of Rosa Ido's cat and in conducting an autopsy on the dead animal. These amusing incidents

---

[23] A sympathetic account of Felipe's struggles to obtain an education is given by Denah Lida (1967).

show unlimited enthusiasm, but reveal the complete lack of coherent and methodical knowledge Felipe had been able to acquire. He is evidently not cut out to be a Teodoro Golfín, though he has other gifts like generosity, imagination and loyalty. Gold makes a convincing case that the novel has a circular structure, with the result that '[a]t [the] novel's conclusion [Felipe] appears transformed on the inside (compassionate, better educated, realistic) but unchanged without (young, unsituated and disempowered)' (Gold 1989: 236). He is an example therefore of limited but real progress, of someone who, unlike Golfín, does not advance beyond the bounds of realistic expectations. All this is expressed, as Willem has expounded with exemplary clarity, through narrative techniques of internalized viewpoints such as present-tense narration, filtered description, free indirect thought, so as to present a multifaceted vision of an evolving personality (1998: 100–13).

No less significant was the decision Galdós made in *El doctor Centeno* to separate radically 'discourse time' from 'narrative time' by a much emphasized period of twenty years, making the latter, exceptionally, rigorously contemporaneous.[24] To bridge this lengthy gap his narrator adopts a familiar conspiratorial tone, bringing his readers into the same circle as the characters and himself and no doubt reflecting, in a note of *Ubi sunt* reminiscent of Jorge Manrique, his own experiences as a student at this period: 'Acuérdate, lectorcillo, de cuando tú y yo y otras personas de cuenta vivíamos en casa de doña Virginia' (263). Among the repercussions this twenty-year time-gap has is that it converts Doña Virginia's boarding house in Part II into a sort of nurturing ground for several of the young students and others who will become the staple background characters for subsequent novels. Though some have disappeared, Zalamero, Cienfuegos, Leopoldo Montes, 'el señor de los prismas', as well as the ubiquitous Federico Ruiz and Basilio Andrés de la Caña, survive for future deployment. Felipe, incidentally, who would be in his early thirties by 1883, is nowhere to be seen in this role-call.

During this twenty-year period the country had passed through the whole gamut of the *sexenio revolucionario* and the Restoration. Whatever progress may have been made in some directions, little or nothing had been accomplished in the crucial area of educational reform, paramount in this novel. Hence the importance of the elaborate prank played on Jesús Delgado, the former educational official driven crazy by the faulty system, with the result that he wrote, and replied to, incessant letters to himself. A sample offered declared prophetically that no change could be envisaged for a long time: 'Pasarán años; será preciso que todo el régimen del Estado varíe' (311). The burlesque letter composed by the unruly students contains the following statement:

24 For a perceptive discussion of this important distinction, see Willem (1998: 107–9).

Usted [...] no ha apreciado el veloz paso del tiempo. *¡Han transcurrido
veinte años sin que usted se dé cuenta de ello!* Ya no existen aquellos ruti-
narios moldes que se oponían a la *Educación completa.* Todo ha variado,
egregio hierofante: la sociedad ha vencido su letal modorra, y despabi-
ladísima aguarda las ideas del legislador de la enseñanza. (314)

The irony of these sentiments is transparent. The changes produced in the
intervening period, however revolutionary in intent, were more superficial
than profound and the new stability of the *turno pacífico* established by the
Restoration hardly offered a society free from lethargy. In public education, in
particular, it had been marked less by any official reforms than by notorious
measures of intolerance like Orovio's attempt to impose a loyalty oath on
university professors, even though these measures were revoked by Sagasta's
government in 1881. Felipe accordingly would have scarcely better chances
of advancement through public education twenty years later.

Parallel with the theme of Felipe's education is the important functional
role he assumes as a 'narrative filter' (Willem 1998: 103), who casts indirect
and ambiguous light on the relationship between Polo and Amparo (Ribbans
1993b). This focalizing function will be continued in *Tormento*, set four years
later, where Felipe also plays the crucial role of saving Amparo's life on his
own initiative by substituting a harmless tranquillizer for the poison she has
ordered from the pharmacy. In other respects he has become a foil to José de
Ido, Galdós's quintessential service figure. Continuity with the earlier novel
is established by the resumption of the dramatic dialogue between the two
characters that concluded *El doctor Centeno*. While Ido has abandoned his
unproductive career as a schoolmaster to become rather more prosperous
as a hack-writer, Felipe has settled down, after a short period of unsatisfactory employment, in the position of loyal and trustworthy servant to
Agustín Caballero. He is enabled to continue his studies, but his high hopes
for success in the world as a doctor have faded. Marianela's caution about
excessive aspirations has been fulfilled. He is destined to be a manservant
not a professional: the same role as he plays in *La familia de León Roch*. He
does not appear in later novels.

This brings us to *León Roch* (1879) itself, *La desheredada* (1881) and
El amigo Manso (1882), the three novels that have been leapfrogged in the
jump from *Marianela* to *El doctor Centeno*. Apart from Felipe's presence in
the first, which we have already discussed, other specific themes crisscross
between them. As James Whiston has elucidated, *León Roch* is also related
with one of the *episodios*: *El voluntario realista*, written, very rapidly, just
after *Marianela*, between February and March 1878, and in the same year
as *La familia de León Roch*. Both the *episodio* and the novel bear a close
relationship to Gumersindo de Azcárate's Krausist document *Minuta de un*

testamento (1876).[25] Not only do they share with the *Minuta* a concern with the major themes of freedom and conscience, but Galdós also seems to have been anxious to follow through in greater depth a specific educational theme: the very paternalistic notion of the educated man attempting to mould an apparently unformed woman according to his own wishes: an aspiration that Catherine Jagoe, very pertinently, associates with the Pygmalion myth (1992). The fact that Federico Cimarra derides León's decision 'de casarse para ser "maestro de escuela" ' demonstrates the link between the two educational objectives (796).

Máximo Manso is a teacher with similar objectives. In what amounts to a similar refutation of the tenets of Azcárate's *Minuta*, he sets out to apply, with spectacular lack of success, pedagogic guidance with a distinctly personal slant, to an apparently docile female pupil who nonetheless has a mind and an agenda of her own.

Meanwhile, in *La desheredada*, Galdós has made a number of crucial innovations. In particular, he supplies constant historical information intertwined with fictional incidents and makes functional use of specific space like the asylum of Leganés and the Museo del Prado (Gold 1993: 130; Mercer 2003: 66–9). At the same time he gives the novel a conspicuous dramatic structure, providing a list of characters for each book and making extensive use of dialogue. It is also a practice adopted to bridge the gap between *El doctor Centeno* and *Tormento*. These innovations apart, there are significant relationships with both earlier and later novels.

Isidora shares one dominant theme deriving from *Marianela*: her ambition to rise in social status. Isidora's aspirations, however, are not based on the personal striving of a Teodoro Golfín or a Felipe Centeno, but on the false expectation of a supposed aristocratic lineage independent of merit. Her antecedents proceed moreover from a different source: the last of the early *episodios*, *Un faccioso más*, written little more than a year before, in which an equally *chiflado* Captain Rufete appears as a collaborator of Aviraneta's. He is referred to in Isidora's confidences to Canencia as Isidora's grandfather and Tomás's father (25; see Ribbans 1994–95). Mariano is another socially deprived figure, in whom a lethal combination of lack of education or effective mentoring and obsessive ambition has disastrous results, which curiously recall the 'dos sendas' that, according to Golfín in *Marianela*, confront the desperately underprivileged: 'la del presidio, la de la gloria' (147).

The broad theme of education remains then prominently in evidence in *La desheredada*. In this context both the *dedicatoria* and the *moraleja* take on an exceptional importance. The dedication refers – in somewhat dismissive tones, to be sure – to

25 On this subject see López-Morillas (1956) and Lida (1967).

*algunas dolencias sociales, nacidas de la falta de nutrición y del poco uso
que se viene haciendo de los beneficios reconstituyentes llamados* Arit-
mética, Lógica, Moral y Sentido Común.[26]

These *dolencias sociales* range from the problem of deprivation, so endemic
in these novels, to certain shortcomings that might be remedied by education
(Arithmetic, Logic) and others that are individual qualities, either of principle
(Morals) or of practicality (Common Sense). To whom, asks Galdós, does
one turn to achieve these goals? Not to the unfortunate patients or victims
themselves, who can do little about it, nor to false prophets: the 'curanderos'
equated with 'filósofos' (Manso, or the more abstract sort of *krausista* no
doubt) or the 'droguistas'-cum-'políticos', who traffic in narcotics not realities, but – back to basics – to the true physicians, the scandalously neglected
'maestros de escuela'.

The injunction of the final 'moraleja' relates to the frequent use of images
of flight we have discussed. Addressing at the same time character and reader,
the narrator admonishes that in any flight of fantasy or ambition: 'Si sentís
anhelo de llegar a una difícil y escabrosa altura' (490) (something that applies
very precisely to Felipe at the beginning of *El doctor Centeno* as well as to
Isidora), one should refrain from using false wings; if you cannot grow them
(a difficult task), be willing to take to the stairs. Felipe was disposed to do
this, Isidora was not. The 'sentido común' of the dedication is clearly relevant
here. Not only *La desheredada*, but in some degree all the novels we have
been discussing, come under the umbrella of the two maxims that encom-
pass that novel. The gradual shift towards new approaches thus embraces all
the narratives from *Marianela* to *Tormento*. While I personally would not
deny that *La desheredada* represents a new start, the process of elaborating
earlier ideas, as Cardwell indicated, is much more complex than has been
recognized.

What I find impressive is Galdós's capacity to keep promising projects on
hold, archiving or hoarding them for later development. As well as the ideological confrontation and the clash of science and tradition in the so-called
thesis novels, such themes include the problem of social deprivation and
concepts of charity to alleviate it; the ambition to succeed, including work
and self-improvement as positive forces; the role of education within this and
other contexts; the conflict of illusion and reality. Even the programme set
out so methodically as early as 1870 in the *Observaciones sobre la novela
contemporánea en España* (in *Ensayos de crítica literaria*, ed. Bonet 1990:

[26] The dedication is not in the manuscript (Ribbans 1992–93: 71). Nor are the lists of
characters mentioned earlier, which were largely overlooked until Enrique Miralles restored
them in his 1992 edition.

105–20), took an astonishingly long time to be applied, especially in its exaltation of the evolving middle classes, implicitly of Madrid. Undoubtedly, the enormous task of completing the two series of *episodios nacionales*, which had become so burdensome to their creator by the end, was a gigantic distraction that impeded implementation of these issues.[27] Part of this unfinished business was the story of Felipe Centeno. *Marianela*, as Cyril Jones pointed out long ago, has a rich heritage (1961: 519).

List of Works Cited

Beyrie, Jacques, 1980. *Galdós et son mythe*, 3 vols (Lille: Université de Lille III)

Bly, Peter A., 1972. 'Egotism and Charity in *Marianela*', *Anales Galdosianos*, 7: 49–66

——, 1986. *Vision and the Visual Arts in Galdós* (Liverpool: Francis Cairns Publications)

Cardwell, R. A., 1971. 'Galdós' Early Novels and the *Segunda Manera*: A Case for a Total View', *Renaissance and Modern Studies*, 15: 44–62

Gold, Hazel, 1989. 'Looking for the Doctor in the House: Critical Expectations and Novelistic Structure in Galdós' *El doctor Centeno*'. *Philological Quarterly*, 68: 219–60

——, 1993. *The Reframing of Realism. Galdós and the Discourses of the Nineteenth-Century Novel* (Durham: Duke University Press)

Gullón, Germán, 1970–71. 'Unidad de *El doctor Centeno*', *Cuadernos Hispanoamericanos*, 250–2: 579–85

Jagoe, Catherine, 1992. 'Krausism and the Pygmalion Motif in Galdós's *La familia de León Roch*', *Romance Quarterly*, 39: 41–52

Jones, C. A., 1961. 'Galdós's *Marianela* and the Approach to Reality', *MLR*, 56: 515–19

Krow-Lucal, Mart[h]a G., 1978. '*Un faccioso más y León Roch*: fin y nuevo comienzo', in *Actas del Segundo Congreso Internacional de Estudios Galdosianos*, 2 vols (Las Palmas: Cabildo Insular de Gran Canaria), I, pp. 170–80

Labanyi, J. M., 1979. 'The Political Significance of *La desheredada*', *Anales Galdosianos*, 14: 51–8

Lida, Denah, 1967. 'Sobre el "krausismo" de Galdós', *Anales Galdosianos*, 2: 1–27

López-Morillas, Juan, 1956. *El krausismo español* (Mexico: Fondo de Cultura Económica)

---

[27] 'El mes que viene sale el tomo de *Los apostólicos* [...] este libro y esta colección me tiene ya refrita la sangre y el día que concluyan me parecerá que vuelvo a la vida' (Letter to Pereda, 20 June 1879, ed. Bravo Villasante 1970–71: 32).

Mercer, Leigh, 2003. 'Appreciating Women: Art and Bourgeois Legitimization in the Nineteenth-Century Spanish Novel', *Cincinnati Romance Review*, 22: 60–74

Moreno Castillo, Gloria, 1977. 'La unidad de tema en *El doctor Centeno*', in *Actas del Primer Congreso Internacional de Estudios Galdosianos* (Las Palmas: Cabildo Insular de Gran Canaria), pp. 382–96

Nimetz, Michael, 1968. *Humor in Galdós. A Study of the 'Novelas contemporáneas'* (New Haven, CT: Yale University Press)

Pattison, Walter T., 1954. *Benito Pérez Galdós and the Creative Process* (Minneapolis: University of Minnesota Press)

Pérez Galdós, Benito, 1970. *Gloria* [1877] and *La familia de León Roch* [1879], in *Novelas*, I, ed. Federico Carlos Sainz de Robles (Madrid: Aguilar)

——, 2004. *Marianela* [1878], ed. Francisco Caudet, 2nd edn (Madrid: Cátedra)

——, 2002. *El doctor Centeno* [1883], ed. José-Carlos Mainer (Madrid: Editorial Biblioteca Nueva)

——, 1992. *La desheredada* [1881], ed. Enrique Miralles (Barcelona: Planeta)

——, 2002. *Tormento* [1884], ed. Francisco Caudet (Madrid: Akal)

——, 1973. *Cuarenta leguas por Cantabria* [1879], in *Novelas y Miscelánea*, ed. Federico Carlos Sainz de Robles (Madrid: Aguilar)

——, 1970–71. 'Veintiocho cartas de Galdós a Pereda', ed. Carmen Bravo Villasante, *Cuadernos Hispanoamericanos*, 250–2: 9–51

——, 1990. *Ensayos de crítica literaria*, ed. Laureano Bonet, revised and amplified edn (Barcelona: NeXos, Ediciones Península)

Ribbans, Geoffrey, 1992–93. '*La desheredada*, novela por entregas: apuntes sobre su primera aparición', *Anales Galdosianos*, 27–8: 70–5

——, 1993a. *History and Fiction in Galdós' Narratives* (Oxford: Clarendon Press)

——, 1993b. '"Amparando/Desemparando a Amparo": Some Reflections on *El doctor Centeno* and *Tormento*,' *Revista Canadiense de Estudios Hispánicos*, 17: 495–524

——, 1994–95. 'Unas apostillas más a Rufete y Canencia', *Anales Galdosianos*, 29–30: 101–3

Rodgers, Eamonn, 1993. *From Enlightenment to Realism. The Novels of Galdós, 1880–1887* (Dublin: Jack Hade)

Scanlon, Geraldine M., 1978. '*El doctor Centeno*: A Study in Obsolescent Values', *Bulletin of Hispanic Studies*, 55: 245–53

——, 1988. *Pérez Galdós, 'Marianela'* (London: Grant & Cutler)

Whiston, James, 1985. '*Un voluntario realista*: The First Part of a Reply to Azcárate's *Minuta de un testamento*', *Anales Galdosianos*, 20.2: 129–40

Willem, Linda M., 1998. *Galdós's 'Segunda Manera'*, North Carolina Studies in the Romance Languages and Literatures (Chapel Hill)

The Recovery of the Knight: Myth and Regeneration in Galdós's *El caballero encantado*

EAMONN RODGERS

For several decades after its publication in 1909, Galdós's *El caballero encantado* was dismissed by critics as a 'curioso capricho' (Gamero y de Laiglesia 1934: 368), or as evidence of 'a decline in creative energy' (Eoff 1954: 16).[1] By the 1970s, the novel was being taken more seriously as a reflection of the political and social context of the time of its composition, notably by Julio Rodríguez-Puértolas, who associates the work with post-1898 regenerationist literature, with the political events of 1909 (notably the Morocco expedition and the Semana Trágica) and with the concerns which led Galdós to assume leadership of the Conjunción Republicano-Socialista in the same year. Clericalism and *caciquismo* are, he argues, clearly portrayed as the scourges of national life, especially in the countryside, where tenants, constantly ground down by high rents and low yields, become the virtual slaves of grasping landowners. Hunger, disease and lack of education create a vicious cycle in which the rural population, inhibited by fear from exercising even the ineffective political rights granted by parliament, becomes permanently imprisoned.[2]

Few critics would quarrel with this view. There is no shortage of evidence, both in the novel itself and in Galdós's other writings in the years around 1900, of his increasing interest in the plight of the rural poor, a concern which he shares with regenerationist writers such as Joaquín Costa. Nevertheless, a predominantly socio-political reading prompts a number of questions. The remedy for the ills of rural Spain proposed by the protagonists

---

[1] See also Hinterhäuser (1963: 44) and Schraibman (1966: *passim*). An early exception to this general trend is Antonio Regalado García, who recognized the importance of 'la vida intrahistórica' reflected in the novel (1966: 489).

[2] See Rodríguez-Puértolas (1972: 117–32); Rodríguez-Puértolas (ed.) (1979: 13–72). All references to the novel are to this edition, and will be incorporated in the main text of the paper.

at the end of the novel (draining the malarial marshes around Boñices, and providing twenty thousand schools) is unencumbered by any clear practical measures for achieving these goals. The echoes of the violent events of 1909, the Semana Trágica and the Moroccan War, are so faint as to be virtually non-existent.[3] Though it is true that Galdós's political writings and speeches in the period 1907–10 were frequently inflammatory (Berkowitz 1948: 391–2), by the spring of 1910, he had moved towards a more moderate position, and soon left the Conjunción to form the Partido Reformista (Dendle 1986: 33–44). Some of this moderation is reflected in a speech by the mythical figure of La Madre, who personifies Spain in all its historic diversity. Responding to a particularly impassioned diatribe by the aged Celedonia, who urges her audience to take violent action against their landlords, she says, 'Modérate un poco, Celedonia, que no debemos ir tan aprisa en la enmienda de los males que afligen al mundo. Contra la usura y la avaricia ya dijeron los Santos Padres más de lo que pudiéramos decir tú y yo' (251).

This leads into a quasi-comic scene in which the various people present vie with each other to provide relevant quotations from the Church Fathers, a discussion which is abruptly terminated for rather mundane reasons:

> Llevaba camino el maestro de agotar su archivo de refranes; pero viendo que las migas empezaban a pasar de la sartén a las bocas, cortó discretamente su perorata [...] porque todos acudían al olor del pan frito con chorizo, y a ello atendían más que a las divinas y profanas sentencias sobre lo mío y lo tuyo. (252)

What this passage illustrates is that Galdós's characteristic touches of humour and irony prevent the novel from taking on the tenor of a political tract.[4] In fairness, it must be said that few critics interpret *El caballero encantado* in this reductionist way, but, in my view, they often pay insufficient attention to the implications of tone, juxtaposition, context and the various ironic devices, of varying degrees of subtlety, whereby Galdós encourages the reader to maintain a certain detachment. In evaluating the views expressed by a character, for example, we need to take into account the various hints whereby the narrator enables us to assess the clarity and reliability of the character's judgement. This is so even where Galdós is known to have shared the character's standpoint. For example, the long lament by Don Alquiborontifosio about the state of education, and the deplorable condition of the

---

[3] La Madre's assertion that she has sent the heraldic lion of Spain to the Atlas mountains 'para que se reponga con los aires nativos' could be a tenuous reference to the Moroccan War, but it is presented with Galdós's characteristically light touch (145).

[4] 'Galdós ignoró aquí los planteamientos sociales ya operantes en el tiempo de la composición' (Ynduráin 1977: 348).

teaching profession (286–7), is modified a little later by the insertion of a
reference to his 'chochez infantil' (288).[5]

This ironic detachment places *El caballero encantado* within the main-
stream of Galdós's fiction. In other respects, too, it displays continuity with
some of his most deeply held attitudes and preoccupations. As early as 1870,
when he published his 'Observaciones sobre la novela contemporánea en
España' in the *Revista de España*, he welcomed the fact that the aristocracy
'ayuda a impulsar [...] el movimiento de la civilización'. If it is failing to live
up to its historic mission, it is because it has lost 'la primitiva caballerosidad
castellana' (Bonet 1972: 120). Although throughout the 1880s and 1890s
Galdós concentrated on portraying the life of the middle classes and the
upper bourgeoisie, and often presented the aristocracy as effete, extravagant
and debt-ridden, he never totally repudiated the notion that they had the
potential to exercise a beneficial influence in society, as 'guía y ejemplo de
las [clases] inferiores' (Ghiraldo 1923–33, I: 125). This was because, for all
their current decadence, they were, or at least ought to have been, the reposi-
tories of the chivalric and patriotic values represented by their ancestors,
those heroic figures who had in the past made Spain the most powerful nation
in Europe, especially during the sixteenth century: 'Si los héroes de tiempos
pasados levantaran la cabeza y vieran el bombo que se da hoy a mediocres
hazañas, se reirían de nosotros' (Ghiraldo 1923–33, VII: 76).

Galdós, of course, is too much of a realist to propose a return to the
rigid hierarchical social structure and religious conformity of Hapsburg
Spain, which would have been repugnant to his liberal convictions. It was
this dislike of authoritarianism which also caused him to reject the notion
of an 'iron surgeon' proposed by Costa. He did, nevertheless, believe that an
elite characterized by innate intelligence, taste and a deep sense of tradition
could be a force for energizing and reforming society, preferably independently of the institutions of the state.[6] This is, admittedly, a minor current in
Galdós's writing during the central part of his literary career, but it begins to
become more prominent in the 1890s, when his faith in the reforming enterprise of bourgeois liberalism has been significantly weakened. In an essay
of 1893, he concludes gloomily that the century-long struggle to realize the
ideals of political and intellectual freedom has exhausted itself without radically regenerating the national character. Despite structural advances such as
universal suffrage, there is not only a lack of social well-being or justice, but

---

5   Nevertheless, Peter Bly's assertion that 'the supposed victims of these social injustices
[i.e., the state of agriculture and primary education] are in part responsible for their fate through
their own actions and attitudes' seems unduly severe (1979: 20).

6   This notion has significant points of contact with the Krausist concept of the *minoría
rectora*. See López-Morillas (1982: 73–87).

also moral confusion and mediocrity: 'desasosiego alarmante', 'desencanto político', 'el predominio del vulgo ilustrado', which emasculates the energies of 'grandes hombres' (Ghiraldo 1923–33, II: 185–6 and 194–5).

Exceptional men, therefore, are not to be looked for in the middle classes. It is significant that in *El caballero encantado* the middle classes only appear as avaricious and flint-hearted *caciques* or brutal local government bureaucrats such as Galo Zurdo. Nor do the aristocracy or the working class, as at present constituted, offer much immediate prospect for the regeneration of the country. It is here, nevertheless, that hope for the future is to be sought. Provided that the aristocracy abandon its effete lifestyle, become more modest and practical, and recognize the essential community and interdependency of the whole nation, it will be ready to assume the responsibilities of leadership, and thereby provide the working class with improved educational opportunities and economic well-being.

This is the main issue which Galdós explores through his depiction of the moral reformation of Carlos de Tarsis. His self-indulgent and irresponsible behaviour is emphasized in the opening chapters in order to highlight the radical nature of his later conversion, but it is also made clear from an early stage that he has the potential for reformation. Despite his 'ansia de satisfacer todos los goces de la vida', he is credited with 'las virtudes caballerescas, y, además, la gracia, el ingenio, el don de simpatía' (76). He has enough common sense to know that the trappings of the military order into which he is admitted are 'degenerado simbolismo de cosas que fueron grandes', and 'profanación de tumbas, traslado burlesco del antaño glorioso' (78). Besides, 'Anhelaba, sí, reformar su vida, pero no con ideas y elementos tan distantes de la realidad' (78–9). In the dramatized scene with Bálsamo, Becerro and Ramirito in Chapter 3, Tarsis displays his awareness of the unjust socio-economic system, which enables people like himself to live a life of idleness on the backs of the impoverished peasantry: 'La agricultura, digo, [...] es y será siempre servidumbre. Ellos esclavos y nosotros señores, acabaremos lo mismo, por consunción, por gangrena de inutilidad' (98).

Tarsis has to confront the reality of this situation when, by virtue of the magic spell operated by the eccentric antiquarian Becerro (an agent of La Madre), he suddenly finds himself with a changed identity, as an agricultural labourer called Gil, ploughing what had once been his fields, and, by a further irony, employed by a tenant whom he had earlier oppressed with demands for increased rent. Gradually, the memory of his former identity reawakens, something which is essential to his reformation, as it keeps alive in his mind the full extent of the shortcomings for which he is being punished by the magical reversal in his fortunes. The duality in his identity during his enchantment also means that his growth towards self-knowledge and repentance is not a smooth linear process, for his Tarsis side influences his behaviour as Gil, frequently for the worse.[7] He is still, for example, a womanizer: he willingly allows himself to be seduced by Usebia, his employer's wife, and when he goes to a neighbouring village for provisions, 'ponía en juego todas sus artes de seducción para proporcionarse una conquistilla' (158). His aristocratic arrogance displays itself in sudden outbursts of rage, even physical violence, in his lethal confrontation with Galo Zurdo (257–8), and his frustrated attack on the Civil Guard Regino (302). But not all Tarsis's characteristics are negative. When Regino first reveals his attraction towards Tarsis's beloved Cintia (who has also been enchanted, under the guise of a rural schoolteacher, Pascuala), Tarsis-Gil leaves him in no doubt as to his own prior claim. Regino's response, and Tarsis-Gil's acceptance of it, are presented without any of the ironic undertones which are present in large swathes of the novel:

> Quedó triunfante la honradez generosa, la cual no tardó en recibir aliento de las virtudes nativas que fortalecían su ser. [...] Estrecháronse con fuerte apretón las manos el guardia y Gil, con lo que el primero dio fe de su hidalguía y el segundo de su gratitud, correspondiéndose ambos en nobleza y caballerosidad. (216–17)

Nobility and generosity are not, however, the preserve of the aristocracy. At several points throughout the novel, Tarsis–Gil is the recipient of unstinting hospitality from people who have very little, but who share it unquestioningly: for example, the travelling performers whom he meets for the second time in Chapter 22 (295). Galdós clearly has deep respect for the dignity and stoic endurance of people like Gil's first employer, José Caminero, 'honradísimo trabajador, esclavo del áspero terruño y de la inclemente comarca en que había nacido' (119). This sympathy for the rural poor, however, is a comparatively recent development in Galdós's thinking. For much of his career, he had tended to regard the rural population as brutal, ignorant and superstitious, a 'conjunto de candor y barbarie'.[8]

Gradually, however, Galdós's attitude began to change. By about 1900, he had come to a deeper realization of the interdependence between the urban population and the people of the countryside, whose labour provided the cities with food and other products. In 1904, he wrote in terms that are especially relevant to the issues explored in *El caballero encantado*, not least

---

7   See Ynduráin (1977: 340): 'pugna la antigua personalidad por manifestarse en la nueva encarnación'.

8   See his 1871 essay 'Ramón de la Cruz y su época', in Sainz de Robles (1968: 1488). The same pessimistic view underlies his depiction of the inhabitants of Orbajosa in *Doña Perfecta*, and of Socartes in *Marianela*: 'todo [...] se revuelve en su alma con supersticiones y cálculos groseros' (Pérez Galdós 1960 edn: 46).

because of the underlying note of paternalism reflected in the reference to 'inferior' classes, and his own identification with the ruling elite implied by his use of the first person plural:

> A las ciudades vienen las saneadas rentas que permiten al terrateniente urbanizado gustar todos los beneficios de la civilización [...]. En el campo se queda el trabajo penoso, abrumador, y con él la miseria, el hambre y la desnudez, la ignorancia, que algunos llaman barbarie faltando al respeto que merecen las clases inferiores de la nación, las cuales, por ser alma y sangre nuestra, tienen derecho, por lo menos, a que les saquemos de ese estado anfibio, medianero entre animales y personas.[9]

Furthermore, his long-standing impatience with the social posturing of the urban bourgeoisie was reinforced and complemented by his recognition that rural life represented 'la España real, [...] la raza despojada de todo artificio y de las vanas retóricas cortesanas' (Sainz de Robles 1964, II: 1255). It is this encounter with 'la España real' that constitutes the centrepiece of Tarsis–Gil's reformation. Solidarity with the downtrodden is undoubtedly an important element of this process, but it also operates at the much deeper level of what Unamuno was to call *intrahistoria*. Though Galdós did not use the term, there is a little-noticed passage at the end of his 1897 inaugural Academy discourse which expresses essentially the same concept. Historiography, especially the literary history of the Golden Age, '[deja] en la penumbra las profundísimas emociones que agitan el alma social', and ignores 'el verdadero sentir y pensar de los pueblos' (Bonet 1972: 181).

Tarsis–Gil's re-education is a matter not simply of recognizing the injustice of the existing socio-economic structure of Spain, important as this preoccupation is, but of acquiring an awareness of shared identity with its people, an identity which has immeasurably deep roots in the antiquity and the physical reality of the Peninsula. As Stephen Gilman observed, the novel is 'a portrait of Spain's millennia of historical experience presented as a spiritual antidote to the *mal du siècle* of national old age' (1986: 45). This is the justification for that feature of the novel which has proved disconcerting to many critics, its mythic and fantastic framework, for the historical and cultural vision is so ample in its scope that it would be intractable by any other literary means: as the novelist himself declared, the 'forma fantástica' permitted him to say 'con la envoltura de una ficción lo que de otra manera sería imposible' (quoted in Bly 1991: 93). Galdós prevents the treatment of this vast perspective from becoming too diffuse by providing a relatively compact format, a novel of some 270 pages (in the Cátedra edition), which

---

[9] '¿Más paciencia?', in Sainz de Robles (1968, VI: 1499).

focuses on the bizarre experiences of Tarsis and Cintia over a limited period. At the same time, however, he keeps the larger dimension constantly in view by invoking literary and mythic paradigms which would be recognizable by an educated Spanish reader.

The antiquarian Becerro, for example, is explicitly connected with the fifteenth-century humanist, alchemist and suspected necromancer Enrique de Villena, whose biography he is writing (103, 144).[10] This is the first of a series of associations which extends to embrace virtually the whole of the Spanish experience, from the novels of chivalry, via the medieval ballads and epic poems, to Roman and pre-Roman history. It is in the novels of chivalry that Becerro 'llegó a sorprender el intríngulis magnético de las *Urgandas* y *Merlines* y el dinamismo prodigioso de *Madanfabul*, de *Famongomadán* y otros apreciables gigantes' (143–4). When he is appointed to a minor post at the site of the Numancia excavations, he spends his nights ecstatically invoking images of the distant past suggested by the ancient ruins:

> ¡Oh ensueño; oh, dulce embriaguez de los enigmas atávicos! Ya que no venís a mí, hermanas pelásgicas, etruscas o fenicias; ya que no quiere Dios que yo penetre el misterio de vuestro origen, dejadme que busque y husmee vuestras huellas; y a estas piedras dormidas preguntaré si sois hijas de Atlas o Héspero, si os trajo Gargoris, rey de los Curetos, para que fuerais fundamento y troquel de la civilización hispánica. (203–4)

Becerro's antiquarianism is taken to such extreme lengths as to be thoroughly comic. In the scene above, he imagines himself taking on the identity of the heraldic lion of Spain, and he has earlier provided an absurd derivation for Tarsis's surname: 'su primer apellido venía en línea directa de Tarsis, hijo de Túbal, nieto de Japhet y biznieto del patriarca y curda Noé' (82). But it should be noted that the name Tarsis and the title Marqués de Mudarra were conferred on the protagonist by the narrator at the beginning of the novel, where the ironic and comic overtones, while still detectable, are comparatively muted. The name Tarsis, despite Becerro's implausible explanation, is possibly to be identified with a historic place, the Phoenician Kingdom of Tartessos, which in the seventh and sixth centuries BC was centred on the Guadalquivir valley. It is as if the narrator, through Becerro, is underlining the antiquity and nobility of Tarsis–Gil's heritage. As a descendant of Mudarra, he combines in his person the Ibero-Roman and Arab strands in Spanish identity, which are also highlighted by La Madre (235–6).[11] Furthermore, the

---

10 As noted by Rodríguez-Puértolas (1979: 105 n. 21).

11 Galdós was one of the very few writers to take seriously the Arabic and Islamic elements in Hispanic culture. We have to wait until Juan Goytisolo's *Reivindicación del conde don Julián* (1970) for a comparable recognition of this inheritance.

novel is replete with other references to the antiquity of the landscape and the various tribes who have inhabited it.

This emphasis on antiquity is sometimes used to suggest the endemic and historic nature of *caciquismo*, as, for example, in the choice of the archaic name Gaytán, and the reference to the obsolete *onza* as a unit of currency (127). At other times, however, it has more positive and even heroic associations. La Madre, while lamenting the disappearance of epic heroes like Fernán González, proclaims that 'aún dura y perdurará por siglos, en uno y otro mundo, la lengua que en vuestros días y en vuestros labios empezó a remusgar, y al fin quedó hecha, *sicut tuba*, trompeta de nuestra energía' (150). The ancient nomadic existence of shepherds is extolled by Sancho because 'con ser tan antiguo como el roncar, no se ha encontrado cosa más arrimada a lo natural que esta vida nuestra' (134).

Sancho and his companions, Mingo, Rodrigacho and Blas, provide one of many links with literary and cultural paradigms from the Spanish past, for they spring straight from one of the *Églogas* of Juan del Encina (156).[12] Another possible model is Quevedo: the brusque reversal in Tarsis's fortunes recalls that suffered by the various figures in *La hora de todos*, and Tarsis's revelatory journey, undertaken under the guidance of a tutor (La Madre), is reminiscent of episodes in the *Sueños*, especially 'El mundo por de dentro'.[13] The most significant paradigm of all, however, is incontrovertibly Cervantes, 'el príncipe, por no decir el rey, de mis ingenios', as La Madre describes him (318). Rodríguez-Puértolas lists several unmistakably Cervantine echoes, including, among others, the obvious theme of enchantment, the references to the flocks of sheep as armies (133), and Becerro's encounter with the prostitutes at the inn (298–9).[14] To these we can add: the chapter-headings, which imitate the style of those of *Don Quijote*; the fact that La Madre, despite being totally different from Dulcinea, can be identified with a figure from Tarsis's 'real-life' experience, significantly called la Duquesa de Cervantes (152); the parallels between Tarsis–Gil's imprisonment (279), and the capture of Don Quijote by the priest and the barber, and his confinement in the cage (*Don Quijote* [henceforth *DQ*], Part 1, Chs 46–7); the similarities between the episode of the enchanted boat (*DQ*, Part 2, Ch. 29) and Tarsis–Gil's rescue from drowning in the Tagus by 'dos hombres o monstruos marinos' (324);[15] and the figure of La Madre herself, plausibly modelled on

[12] As Regalado García (1966: 488), Rodríguez-Puértolas (1979: 31) and Ynduráin (1977: 347) have pointed out.

[13] See my 'Galdós y Quevedo, modernizadores de mitos antiguos' (Rodgers 1988: 105–20).

[14] Rodríguez-Puértolas (1979: 30).

[15] 'Cuando España y los españoles entren en contacto con la profundidad de la historia – representada por el viejo Tajo – se producirá el cambio radical, volverá el antiguo esplendor'

the allegorical personage España in Cervantes's *El cerco de Numancia*, where she is addressed as 'Madre querida, España' (Cervantes 1970 edn: 176–7).

The most important of these references, however, is undoubtedly to the Cueva de Montesinos (*DQ*, Part 2, Chs 22–3). Becerro's house, where Tarsis's enchantment begins, is explicitly called a 'cueva' (111). Becerro's assertion that he can do without food (106) echoes Don Quijote's statement that he felt no hunger in the cave, and that the enchanted people he saw there had no need to eat (*DQ*, 709).[16] Like the Scholar Cousin who guides Don Quijote to the entrance to the cave, Becerro is full of garrulous and useless erudition. Just as Don Quijote awakes in an 'ameno y deleitoso prado' (*DQ*, 702), so Tarsis finds himself on 'un suelo de césped, rodeado de robustas encinas' (114). The dancing 'amazonas' of Chapter 5 recall the 'labradoras que por aquellos amenísimos campos iban saltando y brincando como cabras' (*DQ*, 709). The castle made of glass (*DQ*, 703), whose heroic inhabitants lie under a spell cast by Merlin, is paralleled by the glass fish-tank under the Tagus, a 'cristalino palacio' (337), which Tarsis–Gil shares with other enchanted notabilities, and which is explicitly compared to the Cueva (327).[17] One of the most significant similarities of all is the idea of *dis*enchantment, which is the overall outcome of Tarsis–Gil's experience, as he abandons his former frivolous lifestyle. As E. C. Riley has pointed out, Don Quijote emerges from the Cueva in a very melancholic frame of mind, which 'may well be taken as an early symptom of disillusionment. [...] The only person in any way disenchanted as a result of his "mission" to the otherworld will be Don Quijote himself' (1982).

The episode of the Cueva ends in farce when one of the 'labradoras' approaches Don Quijote to ask for money, and instead of thanking him, 'hizo una cabriola, que se levantó dos varas de medir en el aire (*DQ*, 712). There is a similarly farcical atmosphere at the beginning of Tarsis's enchantment, when the 'amazonas', having performed a stately dance, end by tossing him in the air with savage whoops, and throwing him down a steep embankment (a possible reminiscence of Sancho being tossed in a blanket in *Don Quijote*, Part 1, Ch. 17). This sudden descent into incongruity is characteristic of dream-states, and Riley argued convincingly that the Cueva de Montesinos episode, though its exact nature is highly debatable, makes most sense as a dream (1982: 111). This is not to say that the parallel between the two

---

(Villegas 1976: 22). Villegas's reading is persuasive and illuminating, but in my view he pays insufficient attention to the specifically literary-historical associations which largely structure the novel.

16 Page references, incorporated into the main text, are to Riquer's edition of *Don Quijote*.

17 As Sylvia López has aptly observed, Tarsis is reborn after taking on 'a primitive, pre-natal existence as a fish' (2002: 791).

novels is exact in every detail. Though there are definite points at which Don Quijote falls asleep at the beginning of the dream-sequence and wakes up at the end, it is not clear whether Tarsis–Gil is awake or dreaming during his enchantment. This seems a deliberate tactic on Galdós's part, as locating Tarsis–Gil's experience exclusively within a dream-world would have diminished the elements of social realism in Gil's observation of rural life, which are necessary to Galdós's critical presentation of *caciquisimo*.

Nevertheless, Galdós tantalizingly keeps before our minds the possibility that Tarsis–Gil may be dreaming: 'si no le engañaban sus ojos, si no era un durmiente que se paseaba por los espacios del ensueño, lo que vio era una mujer' (136). On his release from enchantment, a friend who has undergone a similar fate tells him, 'esto no es más que un despertar, un abrir de ojos, que nos pone delante el mundo que desapareció al cerrarlos por cansancio ... o del sueño' (337–8). This procedure enables Galdós to exploit the most significant connection with the Cueva de Montesinos. It is a common experience that figures who appear in dreams replicate one or more figures from the waking life of the dreamer, usually transformed in bizarre ways, and combining familiar and unfamiliar characteristics.[18] When Tarsis–Gil sees La Madre for the first time, he has the impression that he has met her before, possibly in some aristocratic salon in Madrid (115). On the first occasion when she speaks to him directly, she expresses herself 'con el llano y gentil lenguaje que emplear podría cualquier señora viva de la más ilustre clase social' (136).

La Madre is portrayed predominantly as a mythic figure, appearing most frequently as a stately and beautiful matron, but also taking on the appearance of a frail old woman. This protean quality is, however, constrained by repeated reference to actual figures from Tarsis's 'normal' life, the Duquesa de Cervantes and the Duquesa de Mio Cid. The fact that these names have large historic resonances does not preclude their being attached to typical members of the modern aristocracy. When Tarsis emerges from his enchantment, and returns to Madrid in the company of his friend Pepe Azlor, the identification of La Madre with the Duquesa de Mio Cid, to whom Pepe is actually related, is strengthened, but without her losing any of her mythic significance as representative of the spirit of the nation: 'Viaja de continuo, y las ruedas de su automóvil se saben de memoria todo el mapa de España. Su *chauffeur* es un espíritu genial, engendrado por el tiempo en las entrañas de la Historia ...' (339).

That Tarsis's experience of enchantment is connected with his 'real' life is confirmed when, on a visit to the home of the Duquesa de Ruy-Díaz, he sees other figures who recall those he encountered during his peregrina-

---

[18] See Riley's discussion of 'duplicated dream-figures' (1982: 114).

tions through various parts of Spain: one of the aristocratic ladies has the features of Tarsis's peasant lover Usebia, and Don Alquiborontifosio appears in the person of 'un académico melenudo y cegato' (341). If this connection were lacking, then the story of Tarsis's reformation would lose much of its point, and the novel would simply be a work of fantasy. But the duplication of dream-figures ensures that the moral maturity Tarsis has gained from his experience, that 'ciencia compendiosa del vivir patrio' (340), will be lived out in his customary milieu, with a new awareness of 'la síntesis social, [la] armonía compendiosa entre todas las ramas del árbol de la patria' (342). There is undoubtedly a touch of ironic detachment in the references at this point to Tarsis's 'imaginación exaltada', but this does not detract from his discovery of the value of community solidarity, an ideal which Galdós frequently upheld in other writings.

To read *El caballero encantado* merely as an exercise in fantasy, an attack on *caciquismo*, an advocacy of socialist revolution or 'an ironic view of *Regeneracionistas*' (Bly 1991) (though it has elements of all these), is to overlook the larger mythic and historical dimensions of the novel: 'tradición inmutable y revolución continua' are inseparably bound up with each other (300). Galdós makes no attempt, in constructing the ending, to conceal the idealistic and possibly impractical nature of the plan of regeneration proposed by Tarsis and Cintia: will even her increased wealth be enough to drain the marshes of Boñices and found twenty thousand schools? The novel is not a detailed blueprint for the revitalization of rural Spain, but an optimistic vision of a possible remote future:

> TARSIS. —[...] he soñado que vivimos en un mundo patriarcal, habitado por seres inocentes que no viven más que para compartir con amorosa equidad los frutos de la tierra ...[19]
> LA MADRE. (*Graciosa*) —Hijo, te has anticipado a la Historia dando un brinco de cien años o más, para caer en un porvenir que yo misma no sé cómo ha de ser. [...] Hoy, por desgracia, mis hijos viven más en sus querellas locas que en las leyes de amor. (153)[20]

Even if my interpretation of the novel is correct, it is likely to be uncongenial to the majority of critics of Galdós, who place most emphasis on his political radicalism, for, as I have suggested repeatedly in this essay, Galdós's reforming vision in *El caballero encantado* is unmistakably paternalist: the

---

19 The same vision is outlined by Pedro Polo in *Tormento* (1884).

20 'What is presented is not a revolution but the dream of a revolution, which in spite of its portion of nightmare is essentially theatrical and comic' (Gilman 1986: 46).

vision of the future is of 'un mundo patriarcal'.[21] Tarsis has been singled out
for conversion by La Madre because he has potential leadership qualities
which are deeply rooted in the history and ethos of his class, and which can
benefit the oppressed and long-suffering masses he has encountered in his
journeyings:

> La Madre impone su corrección a los hijos bien dotados de inteligencia, y
> que sufren de pereza mental o de relajación de la voluntad. En la naturaleza
> corregida de estos elementos útiles, espera cimentar la paz y el bienestar
> de sus reinos futuros. (343–4)

List of Works Cited

Berkowitz, H. Chonon, 1948. *Galdós, Spanish Liberal Crusader* (Madison:
University of Wisconsin Press)

Bly, Peter, 1979. 'Sex, Egotism and Social Regeneration in Galdós' *El caballero
encantado*', *Hispania*, 62.1 (March): 20–9

——, 1991. '*El caballero encantado*: Galdós's Ironic View of "Regeneracionistas"', in *Galdós' House of Fiction*, ed. A. H. Clarke and E. J. Rodgers (Oxford:
Dolphin Book Company), pp. 85–97

Bonet, Laureano (ed.), 1972. Benito Pérez Galdós, *Ensayos de crítica literaria*
(Barcelona: Ediciones Península)

Cervantes Saavedra, Miguel de, 1970. *Obras completas*, 16th edn (Madrid:
Aguilar)

Dendle, Brian J., 1986. 'Galdós in Context: The Republican Years, 1907–1914',
Anales Galdosianos, 21: 33–44.

Eoff, Sherman H., 1954. *The Novels of Galdós: The Concept of Life as Dynamic
Process* (St Louis: Washington University Studies)

Gamero y de Laiglesia, Emilio, 1934. *Galdós y su obra*, II: *Las novelas* (Madrid:
Blass)

Ghiraldo, Alberto (ed.), 1923–33. Benito Pérez Galdós, *Obras inéditas*, 10 vols
(Madrid: Renacimiento)

Gilman, Stephen, 1986. '*El caballero encantado*: Revolution and Dream', *Anales
Galdosianos*, 21: 45–52

Hinterhäuser, Hans, 1963. *Los Episodios Nacionales de Benito Pérez Galdós*
(Madrid: Gredos)

---

[21] *Pace* Ynduráin, there is more to this ending than the establishment of 'una armonía en
que se redujeran tan inicuas diferencias' (1977: 345), for the existing social hierarchy remains
essentially in place. The inherent conservatism of the vision proffered in the novel is also
reflected in the place Galdós implicitly assigns to women. As Sylvia López has shrewdly
remarked, 'While neither Madre nor Cintia are confined to the home [...] neither one occupies
a position in the political or business arenas, which Carlos did and can continue to do because
he is a man' (2002: 792).

López, Sylvia, 2002. 'From Monstrous to Mythical: The Mother Figure in Galdós's *Casandra* and *El caballero encantado*', *Hispania*, 85.4 (December): 784–94

López-Morillas, Juan, 1982. 'F. Giner de los Ríos y las minorías rectoras', in *Essays on Narrative Fiction in the Iberian Peninsula in Honour of Frank Pierce*, ed. R. B. Tate (Oxford: Dolphin Book Company), pp. 73–87

Pérez Galdós, Benito, 1960 edn. *Marianela* (Madrid: Hernando)

Regalado García, Antonio, 1966. *Benito Pérez Galdós y la novela histórica española: 1868–1912* (Madrid: Ínsula)

Riley, E. C., 1982. 'Metamorphosis, Myth and Dream in the Cave of Montesinos', in *Essays on Narrative Fiction in the Iberian Peninsula in Honour of Frank Pierce*, ed. R. B. Tate (Oxford: Dolphin Book Company), pp. 105–19. [Reissued in Spanish in 2001 as Chapter 5 of Edward C. Riley, *La rara invención: Estudios sobre Cervantes y su posteridad literaria* (Barcelona: Crítica)]

Riquer, Martín de (ed.), 1958. *Don Quijote de la Mancha*, 2 vols (Barcelona: Editorial Juventud)

Rodgers, Eamonn, 1988. 'Galdós y Quevedo, modernizadores de mitos antiguos', in *Les Mythes et leur expression au XIXe siècle dans le monde hispanique et ibéro-américain*, ed. Claude Dumas (Lille: Université de Lille III, Presses Universitaires de Lille), pp. 105–20

Rodríguez-Puértolas, Julio, 1972. 'Galdós y *El caballero encantado*', *Anales Galdosianos*, 7: 117–32

——(ed.), 1979. Benito Pérez Galdós, *El caballero encantado* (Madrid: Ediciones Cátedra)

Sainz de Robles, Federico, 1964–68. Benito Pérez Galdós, *Obras completas* (Madrid: Aguilar)

Schraibman, José, 1966. 'Galdós y el "estilo de la vejez" ', *Homenaje a Rodríguez Moñino*, 2 vols (Madrid: Castalia)

Villegas, Juan, 1976. 'Intepretación mítica de *El caballero encantado* de Galdós', *Papeles de Son Armadans*, 82, no. 244 (July): 11–24

Ynduráin, Francisco, 1977. 'Sobre *El caballero encantado*', in *Actas del Primer Congreso Internacional de Estudios Galdosianos* (Madrid: Editora Nacional), pp. 336–50

Regeneración and Philosophy
in the *Torquemada* Novels

RHIAN DAVIES

Although critics often note that Galdós's works depict Spain in a state of decadence, few have drawn attention to the direct connection between the *Torquemada* novels and *regeneración*.[1] This is not altogether surprising since neither the term itself nor its derivatives feature in any of the novels. The closest references relate to 'reformas', which can be seen as representing the practical attempts at *regeneración* (frequently termed *regeneracionismo*), although the author does refer to its antithesis, in the form of 'decadencia' or 'degeneración'.[2] However, as I have noted elsewhere, it was not uncommon for writers to avoid the direct use of the term *regeneración* in the period, even where their proposals were connected with the aim of regenerating Spain (Davies 2000). Like the general editor and contributors of *La España Moderna* [*LEM*], the review for which *Torquemada en la hoguera* [*TH*] (1889) was written,[3] Galdós avoided the use of the term *regeneración* as his

---

[1] Peter Earle, for example, notes that the *Torquemada* novels present us with 'una España decadente y poco consciente de su propio ser' (1967: 30). The following abbreviations have been used in this chapter: *LEM* – *La España Moderna*; *TH* – *Torquemada en la hoguera*; *TP* – *Torquemada en el purgatorio*; *TC* – *Torquemada en la cruz*; *TSP* – *Torquemada y San Pedro*. All page references relate to the first editions of these novels. In the case of *TH* this is the edition published by *La Guirnalda* in 1889.

[2] See, for instance, Gamborena's speech in *TSP*: 'La voluntad humana degenera visiblemente, como árbol que se hace arbusto, y de arbusto, planta de tiesto' (I, 11: 90).

[3] See Davies (2002). It was the success of this novel, which was praised by Narcís Oller and Pereda, that provided Galdós with the incentive to explore the theme of *regeneración* in greater detail by producing three more novels based on the Spanish moneylender. A letter (dated 19 June 1901) from Joaquín Costa reveals Galdós's interest in *regeneración*: 'Sí, señor; es imposible, como V. dice, que el país sea indefinidamente testigo y víctima callada del mal que padece; tiene V. razón, así no se puede seguir; pero sigue, y la malla no se rompe, ni se romperá como no se pongan á ello ustedes mismos, los que lo ven y denuncian y tiene detrás millares de corazones y de brazos que les oyen ..., y que les aguardan' (quoted in Ortega 1964: 418).

aim was to adopt a detached, critical attitude towards the subject, and thereby promote a kind of *regeneración* that was far more constructive and profound than the series of empty proposals linked to a 'fiebre regeneradora'.[4]

The few critics who consider the direct connection between *regeneración* and the *Torquemada* novels fail to highlight the complexity of the issues involved. Patrick Dust's article, 'Regeneration as Destiny in *TH*', is restricted to a consideration of the spiritual concerns of the novel, suggesting that the middle class's decadence highlights the need for spiritual regeneration. Dust adopts a somewhat moralistic reading of the novel, regarding Bailón as 'a striking symbol of a spiritual past which carried within itself the seeds of a possible salvation', and arguing that the character has been 'so corrupted by the passion for material gain that his type no longer offers any escape from the impasse of decadence' (1981: 100). By contrast, he claims that Valentín's spirituality has not been corrupted and, had he not died, this young boy could have saved Torquemada, who, for Dust, represents decadent materialism.

This interpretation is unconvincing. It is, for example, difficult to equate Valentín with uncorrupted spirituality when he is described as 'monstruo' and 'Anticristo', and at other times, acts like a typical child of his age, playing pranks on his neighbours. By applying such radically different terms to the same character, Galdós is proposing that everybody has different perceptions and is entitled to them. As a consequence, the work is far from being a moralistic tract. From the very beginning, it is evident that *TH* is not a novel that can be taken at face value. The opening paragraphs suggest that it will be a didactic work, that we will witness the punishment of a man who has persecuted his fellow men and will suffer as a consequence. However, several warning notes are sounded and the reader begins to wonder if the tone of this work, which Pierre Ullman has compared to that of a 'romance de ciego', is after all a parody of such a 'romance' and should not be taken seriously (1965). As the novel develops, we note that the contrast between good and evil is not clear-cut and that negative and positive terms sometimes become interchangeable. Thus Valentín can be both 'ángel' and 'monstruo'.

The connection between *regeneración* and *TH*, and, indeed, all the *Torquemada* novels, is also more profound than Dust suggests. By the end of the century, the concept was multi-dimensional and could be applied to four main areas: politics, practical concerns, philosophy and literature. All of these areas feature in the *Torquemada* novels, which, as well as dealing with themes of universal, timeless significance, can be read as a commentary on the specific issue of Spain and *regeneración* some time before the subject became a topic of major interest. Since I do not have sufficient space to examine all facets of

---

[4] Dorado writes of 'la fiebre regeneradora que nos ha cogido de la noche á la mañana' (1898: 40).

the concept here, I shall limit myself to the philosophical concerns, an area of particular interest to Nicholas Round.[5]

While the implied need for political and practical *regeneración* forms the background to the action, ideological concerns lie at the heart of the *Torquemada* novels. Through Torquemada we are compelled to reflect upon mankind's ability to confront issues such as destiny, providential plans and historical inevitability, which are considered simultaneously from a specifically Spanish and a universal perspective and acquire both psychological and historical dimensions. The novels also examine the extent of man's free will, in particular his power to change his destiny through class intermarriage, educational and other philosophies, and through suicide.

Some nineteenth-century thinkers deemed Spain's decadence to be a consequence of deterministic forces. Situating themselves within the 'raza latina', a decadent race faced with the wrath of the mighty Anglo-Saxons, they feared that their country was doomed to extinction. Although this line of thought appealed to those seeking some appearance of order amidst the complexity and confusion of nineteenth-century life, it was manifestly pessimistic, implying as it did that Spaniards had no control over their destiny and should resign themselves to inevitable decadence.

Decadence permeates the *Torquemada* novels, both in the characters' fundamental characteristics and in their evolution. National decadence is alluded to through the presentation of degenerate racial habits. We read that Torquemada 'tiene la avaricia metida en los huesos' (*TP* I, 5: 36), and the priest, Gamborena, refers to his other inbuilt characteristics, including his selfishness and his hard-heartedness; such qualities, along with 'pereza', 'cólera', 'tristeza', 'vanidad' and 'orgullo', were perceived to be typical Spanish faults of the period. Lucas Mallada, for instance, defined 'pereza' as 'el fondo sombrío de nuestro modo de ser, que nos impide marchar a paso más rápido por el camino de la perfección' (1890: 33). More importantly, Rafael del Águila suffers from 'el maldito orgullo de raza' (*TC* I, 5: 176). The fact that this 'orgullo' ultimately leads to his death might prompt us to ask whether it represents a national flaw, one which could lead to Spain's downfall. However, these references remain implicit and there are no suggestions as to how such qualities might be eradicated.

The fact that Don Francisco's namesake was Tomás de Torquemada, Inquisitor General of Spain (1483–98), is noteworthy since some psycho-

---

[5] In this connection, see Nicholas Round's list of publications and especially the articles 'Time and Torquemada: Three Notes on Galdosian Chronology' (1971), 'Galdós Rewrites Galdós: The Deaths of Children and the Dying Century' (2003), and his virtuoso contribution to the Sheffield Galdós Lecture series, '"What is the Stars?": Galdós and the Measures of Mankind' (2004).

logical determinists, whilst trying to define the supposedly inherent characteristics of the Spanish race, expressed the belief that the true national character was essentially 'inquisitorial'. In *LEM*, Hipólito González Rebollar claimed, in this vein, that '[e]n España no hay espíritu social, no hay sed de justicia, no hay solidaridad voluntaria' (1904: 111).[6] Galdós, however, does not exploit the possibilities he raises, and there is little to suggest that he believes in fundamental and unchanging national characteristics. Once again, the power of the association comes from what might be inferred, rather than what is said.

In more general, evolutionary terms (as Dust has noted), *TH* alludes to the possibility of biological determinism and the influence of heredity, together with the notion that evolution has yielded superior beings.

> En honor del tacaño debe decirse que, si se conceptuaba reproducido físicamente en aquel pedazo de su propia naturaleza, sentía la superioridad del hijo, y por eso se congratulaba más de haberle dado el ser. (*TH* II: 15)

This theory is undermined later since Torquemada's second son is, to all intents and purposes, the antithesis of his half-brother and a striking example of biological degeneration.

Furthermore, if we draw a connection between Valentín I and the theories relating to the 'genio' in the period,[7] a sinister note is introduced, as it becomes evident that the process of degeneration commenced from the birth of the first son. The Italian criminologist Lombroso argued that the 'genio' was the product of the degeneration of the species (Araujo 1900), and many of its negative features – hinted at in terms such as 'fenómeno' or 'monstruo' and the characteristically large head – are associated with Torquemada's first son.[8] In this context, Valentín I bears little resemblance to Dust's uncorrupted child who could have been Torquemada's saviour, and it becomes apparent

---

6 See also Edmundo González Blanco, who referred to Unamuno's theory that 'no perdió España la Inquisición, sino que España se la hizo, sacándola de sus entrañas de su espíritu inquisitorial' (1902: 92). Likewise, Dorado wrote '[e]l Estado (oficial) es el más feroz de los inquisidores, el más intolerante, el más cruel y tiránico, el de miras y espíritu más estrecho' (1908: 125).

7 See Araujo (1903b and 1905).

8 Valentín I had 'la cabeza más grande de lo regular, con alguna deformidad en el cráneo' (*TH* I: 9; see also *TH* II: 19). It may, in addition, be possible to link the claim that the intense mental work of the *hombre de genio* could lead to hallucinations and obsesiones (Araujo 1903a: 167), to the obsessive ramblings of the sick Valentín, desperately trying to decipher some mathematical equation. Valentín II is also referred to as '[un] fenómeno' (e.g. *TSP* II, 3: 148).

that Torquemada's hereditary traits have yielded an inferior being.[9] Further-more, it was believed that 'niños precoces', on growing up, inevitably disap-point.[10]

Surprisingly, we are presented with Augusta's suggestion that the deformed Valentín II, like Víctor Hugo, could turn out to be a truly talented child.[11] To the cynical reader, this seems unlikely at a time when the child is more like an animal than a human. We are also aware that Augusta is trying to encourage Fidela to be optimistic about her own son's future and thus she, herself, might not be convinced of the possibility. However, we are obliged to accept that all is not as it first seems. Presented with a variety of interpretations, we are less likely to attempt to favour one theory over another. If we do, we may later discover that the ground moves beneath our feet. Some, for instance, claim that Torquemada's epilepsy is passed down to his eldest son and is indicative of negative hereditary traits. However, the medical term is never mentioned and it is not clear if we are expected to make this connection.

Likewise, the novels appear to adhere to naturalist theories, particularly as the environment exerts a strong influence over Torquemada. Yet such ideas are undermined when we discover that the protagonist thrives in the bustling, polluted, city of Madrid but is extremely unhappy in the fresher air of Hernani in the north of Spain. In this sense the *Torquemada* novels are closer to anti-naturalism, obliquely exposing flaws in naturalist thought. It is as if Galdós wanted his readers to muse on such ideas but not to regard his work as a treatise in support of one particular theory. He recognized that life was more complex and less clear-cut than some of his contemporaries tended to assume.

The theme of determinism brings us to the issue of providential plans. On the one hand, Gamborena is convinced that he has a predestined role in life, that his character and temperament were made for fighting. On the other hand, characters such as Rufina and Rafael are simultaneously terrified by the idea that God exacts punishment, yet desperate to embrace the notion of

---

[9] Heredity was considered to be an influential factor in the product of the 'genio', often leading to physical ailments such as rheumatism, hypochondria and epilepsy. (See Araujo 1903b: 173–6.)

[10] 'La precocidad en las criaturas es un bien engañoso, una ilusión que el tiempo desvanece. Fíjate en la realidad. Esos chicos que al año y medio hablan y picotean, que á los dos años discurren y te dicen cosas muy sabias, luégo dan el cambiazo y se vuelven tontos' (Araujo 1904: 165).

[11] 'Era como el tuyo, y los padres ponían el grito en el cielo ... Luégo vino el desarrollo, la crisis, el segundo nacimiento, como si dijéramos, y aquella cabezota resultó llena con todo el genio de la poesía' (*TSP* I, 8: 62). Likewise, Araujo wrote in *LEM*, '[n]iños que parecían fenómenos, resultaron después hombres de extraordinario talento' (1904: 165).

predestination if it can offer them comfort and a reassuring sense of order amidst the confusion they are experiencing.[12]

In most cases, the characters exhibit a perverted belief in divine intervention, an obsessive self-interest, and a merely superficial understanding of religion. When Rafael runs away from home, for example, the facile nature of his faith is exposed when he assumes that God will provide him with some coffee or hot chocolate for breakfast (TC II, 12: 244). Materialism plays a far more significant role in the characters' lives than religion, and idolatry is a recurring theme: 'Las dos hembras sentían por el ciego un amor que la compasión elevaba á idolatría. Él les pagaba en igual moneda' (TC II, 5: 173). The literal and figurative dimensions of 'pagar' here highlight the fact that monetary concerns have not only replaced religious values but have become a metaphor of almost universal application.

The idea of providential plans strikes a disturbing note in TH, which revolves around the protagonist's horror at the possibility that he has offended God and that his son's illness is a punishment for his own wrong-doings. However, retributive justice here is ambiguous. It is not Torquemada, the executioner, but his son who suffers and dies – although seeing his child suffer might be a worse punishment for the parent than suffering himself. Nor should it be forgotten that Valentín is not entirely innocent: as noted above, he is a 'monstruo', and can be mischievous as well as angelic. Moreover, even if we cling to this notion of justice, the fact that Torquemada abandons the attempt to avoid divine punishment by reforming his character implies that his lesson has not been learnt and that no good has come from his child's death.

At the same time, we cannot wholly despise Torquemada. Despite his association with the eponymous executioner, it could be argued that his alleged victims are to blame for their own predicaments, and that he himself is a victim, since he is manipulated by the likes of Don Juan.[13] Of course, such interpretations can be traced to Torquemada himself, as some of these justifications appear in free indirect discourse. Nonetheless, many will identify with Torquemada's plight as a helpless parent, and perceive Valentín's death as cruel and incomprehensible, as evidence of the powerlessness of humankind in the face of mortality, and as challenging the notion of a benign and divine Providence. This idea is developed in the later Torquemada novels, as the protagonist once more confronts the pointlessness of premature death: first, that of his wife and, later, his own.

---

12 Rufina is terrified that God will punish her wicked father: '[Dios] está mirando donde se cometen injusticias para levantar el palo' (TC I, 7: 56). Likewise, Rafael believes that their father was punished for offending God (TC II, 11: 235–6).

13 '[Torquemada] ponía la cuerda al cuello [de Don Juan] y tiraba muy fuerte, sin conseguir sacarle ni los intereses vencidos' (TH VI: 68–9).

Ranged against determinist thinkers in the nineteenth century were those who argued that the nation's problems were primarily historical. Some argued that the Inquisition had isolated Spain from Europe and condemned the country to decadence. Unamuno drew on the natural imagery of the regenerative processes of plants, to claim that '[la Inquisición] [i]mpidió que brotara aquí la riquísima floración de los países reformados donde brotaban y rebrotaban sectas y más sectas, diferenciándose en opulentísima multiformidad' (1895: 39).

In the *Torquemada* novels, however, Galdós does not suggest that the whole Spanish race is inquisitorial in this sense. The references to the notion, which are rarer in later novels, serve primarily to highlight the question of retributive justice and the fact that materialistic values were so prominent in nineteenth-century Spanish life that they were effectively a new religion. In this context it was apt that the new Inquisitor should be a moneylender.[14]

It is also possible to relate the *Torquemada* novels to other theories of historical processes. We could, for instance, consider Torquemada's trajectory in the light of Manuel Sales Ferré's suggestion (1903) that countries progressed from 'salvajismo', to 'barbarie', arriving finally at 'civilización'. Unamuno also employed the term 'barbarismo' to indicate the initial stages of *regeneración*: 'la invasion de los *bárbaros* fué el principio de la regeneración de la cultura europea ahogada bajo la senilidad del imperio decadente' (1895: 29). Given such associations, it is notable that, in *TH*, the protagonist is described as 'salvaje' when Valentín dies (9: 106), the term 'barbaridad' is used frequently in *Torquemada en la cruz* [*TC*] and, thanks to Cruz del Águila, Torquemada undergoes a process of 'civilization' in *Torquemada en el purgatorio* [*TP*], where he is described as '[el] salvaje convertido en persona' (I, 3: 134). However, this process is not entirely successful since the changes which occur are artificial and a 'salvaje bebé' is born in *Torquemada y San Pedro* [*TSP*] (I, 13: 107). Once again, we seem to be going backwards, not forwards.

The issue of decadence is thus repeatedly foregrounded; but were there any solutions? Could anything be done to counteract what appeared, in both psychological and historical terms, to be a perpetually problematic and regressive process? One way in which the characters actively try to take control of their destiny is by exploring the opportunities offered by inter-marriage and cross-breeding. Mockery is made of the characters' genealogy since Torquemada is able to marry the aristocratic Fidela and purchase a title despite his working-class origins. Yet, perhaps surprisingly, the picture of the married couple is not entirely pessimistic. Fidela apparently benefits from the

---

[14] '[N]o pudo [Torquemada] eximirse de la influencia de esta segunda mitad del siglo XIX, que casi ha hecho una religión de las materialidades decorosas de la existencia' (*TH* II: 11).

union: 'su nuevo estado era una liberación, un feliz término de la opresora miseria y humillante obscuridad de aquellos años maldecidos' (*TP* I, 2: 14). Many are surprised that she accepts her new role as Torquemada's loyal wife with a degree of quiet resignation, affectionately calling him 'Tor', and she is extremely enthusiastic about her role as mother to Valentín II. However, it is clear that the comforts Fidela enjoys are not of the spiritual kind and serve largely to mask the emptiness of her marriage. She is described as 'anémica' and 'enclenque' and the narrator employs images that hint at her imminent death:

> no le permitía ver los vacíos que aquel matrimonio pudiera determinar en su alma, vacíos que incipientes existían ya, como las cavernas pulmonares del tuberculoso, que apenas hacen padecer cuando empiezan á formarse.
>
> (*TP* I, 2: 15)

In returning to a childlike state she could be seen as suffering from a condition not dissimilar to Rafael's blindness. She is merely blocking out the reality that repels her.

As far as the continuity of the genealogical line is concerned, this instance of cross-breeding is disastrous and reflects the decadence of the aristocracy in the period. Their son is deformed and there is no true heir to carry on either the Águila or the Torquemada family name. The narrator disapproves of the union, referring negatively to the tendency towards uniformity in the period, and the marriage has a devastating effect upon Rafael.

The debate as to whether inferior human types could be improved by education receives less scathing treatment. The attitude of criminologists of the period depended largely on whether they believed that evil was innate in criminals, possibly through the influence of heredity. Those who subscribed to this view sometimes argued that the evil inner qualities of a person were reflected in their external appearance. If evil could not be eradicated, the only solution was to eliminate the evil-doers, either by execution or by deportation (Vida 1893, Lombroso 1893a and 1893b). Others, however, argued that criminals could exercise their free will and reform their characters through education (Ferri 1893 and Lubbock 1897: 164).

To an extent, the issue of education *versus* free will is questioned through the curious case of Valentín II. The characters abandon all hope in him and view his education as impossible: after Fidela's death we read, 'nadie creía en Valentinico' (*TSP* II, 3: 147). However, this pessimism contrasts with the facts, as we later learn that his nursemaid has been able to teach him to talk.[15] Does Galdós, therefore, hope that the reader will retain some hope

---

15 'En lo único que adelantó algo [Valentinico] fué en el lenguaje, pues al fin la niñera

in the benefits of education? Furthermore, is he trying to highlight the fact that the main problem is precisely a general lack of faith? Fidela evidently hoped to make up for others' despair and the use of religious terminology stressed the spiritual depth of her love: 'Fidela, al menos, *tenía fe* en que el hijo despertase á la razón' (*TSP* II, 3: 147; my italics). However, she herself wondered whether the only solution to Valentinico's problems would be his death (*TSP* I, 10).

The character whose education is most central to the novels is, of course, Torquemada. He initially undergoes a process of practical education but the concern to improve his appearance and language in accordance with his newfound social status diminishes in importance as he approaches death, and (in line with her new spiritual dimension) Cruz's education of the protagonist changes tack. She is no longer preoccupied with the practical *regeneración* of the 'Palacio de las Gravelinas' but with 'la salvación de su alma' so that Torquemada may enter 'la mansión de los justos' (*TSP* II, 4: 253). Likewise, the doctors withdraw and place Torquemada's life in the hands of the priest Gamborena, who resolves to fight like a lion for his soul.

If we regard Torquemada as representative of the *pueblo*, which, for many, held the key to Spain's future, his education is crucial to the country's future.[16] Although he is successfully educated in social terms, and gains respect for his more refined appearance, manners, and speech, Torquemada's fundamental beliefs remain resistant to change. Hence he constantly protests when Cruz insists on spending his money, and reveals his rebellious nature in *TSP*, exclaiming to those who offer condolences following Fidela's death, '*Ataquemos*, digo, acatemos los designios ...' (*TSP* II, 9: 129). Thereafter, he returns to his roots and takes comfort in a working-class meal. To an extent, the circular effect achieved in *TH* is mirrored in the ending of *TSP*, where Torquemada dies uttering the word 'Conversión'.[17] Although it is deliberately left unclear whether Torquemada was referring to his religious repentance or to his plan to convert the national debt, we suspect that he has not repented. Thus Rafael's pessimism seems to be well-founded and we wonder whether it is futile to attempt to change (or regenerate) the character of an individual, or of a nation.[18]

le enseñó á articular muchas sílabas, y á pronunciar toscamente las palabras más fáciles del idioma' (*TSP* II, 6: 178).

[16] See, for example, Unamuno: 'Tenemos que europeizarnos y chapuzarnos en pueblo' (1895: 42).

[17] As Tía Roma anticipates, Torquemada does indeed revert to his wicked ways, swearing that he will abandon all religious belief in God, and sets up an altar to his dead son.

[18] Perhaps the novels can be viewed as an experiment to see whether the miser could be polished and to explore how he would react when exposed to high society. Leopoldo Alas highlighted the parallel between the *Torquemada* novels and Zola's works, describing the former as

However, it could also be inferred from this ambiguity that Torquemada has exerted his free will, and this possibility seems to be reinforced by the titles of the four novels. The first three indicate that Torquemada is subject to the desires of others and placed, albeit unwittingly, in particular predicaments by them: 'en la hoguera', 'en la cruz', 'en el purgatorio'. In each, Torquemada also falls under the influence of another character and his actions are largely the consequence of that influence. Bailón's words are constantly in his mind in the first novel; in the second, his marriage to Fidela is the fulfilment of the wishes of Doña Lupe and Donoso; his refurbishment of the 'Palacio' is carried out to satisfy Cruz, and so on. In the last novel, however, he meets his match, and the use of the conjunction (*Torquemada y San Pedro*) suggests that he is neither passive nor the sufferer of others' actions, but actively challenges the priest and has the audacity to stand up to him.

Rafael, for his part, does not rise to the challenges presented by change. Having no faith in intermarriage or education, his response to the family's fall from status is to cling to the past, ignoring his sisters' pleas. In *TP*, he commits the ultimate act of rebellion by taking his own life, thereby entering the category of *degenerados* as outlined by Rafael Salillas, who wrote the following in response to Nordau's work *Entartung* (*Degeneration*) (1892):

> La degeneración, según Sergi, comprende á los locos, á los suicidas, á los criminales, á las prostitutas, á los siervos y serviles, á los vagabundos y mendigos y á los parásitos. Mucho más recientemente Max Nordau califica de degenerados á los místicos, á los prerrafaelistas, á los simbolistas, á los tolstoístas, á los wagneristas, á los egotistas, á los diabólicos, á los decadentes y estáticos, á los ibsenistas y á los realistas. (1894: 76)

While many aspects of *degeneración* feature in the *Torquemada* novels, it is suicide which has the most dramatic and lasting impact upon their readers. Edmundo González-Blanco (1903), noted Durkheim's view that there were different kinds of suicide: one was *egoísta*, the result of apathy and scepticism, and another *anómica*, serving as a violent protest against life. In the climate of the time, the former understanding predominated and those who committed suicide were generally regarded as cowards. From this perspective, it was hardly surprising that there should be a marked tendency to commit suicide amongst members of the supposed 'razas inferiores' and 'degenerados'.[19]

'[h]istoria natural y social de un avaro plebeyo, bajo la restauración alfonsina'. (See Brownlow 1993: 296.)

[19] Schopenhauer, for his part, regarded the man who committed suicide as a false and incomplete pessimist, somebody who really wanted life, not pain. In this sense suicide was irrational. González Blanco also proposed that suicide was both immoral (because it was anti-religious) and anti-social. He notes a link between suicide and martyrdom since both involve

Rafael is not alone in contemplating suicide. In *TC* we are told that Torres had shot himself in Monte-Carlo (*TC* II, 12: 237), and that the Águilas's father would also have shot himself, had it not been for Donoso (*TC* II, 10: 218), while the three remaining Águilas consider a suicide pact (*TC* II, 6). On this occasion Rafael is 'acometido de un vértigo insano, entusiasmo suicida que no se manifestaba entonces en él por vez primera', which hints at his mental instability (*TC* II, 6: 185). It is possible that Galdós's own contempt is reflected in Fidela's horror, and she succeeds in preventing Rafael from killing himself at this point. When he throws himself out of the window at the end of *TP*, however, his death is reported in almost comic terms by the servant:

> —¡Por la ventana ... patio ... señorito ... pum!
> Bajaron todos ... Estrellado, muerto. (*TP* III, 12: 337)

A range of attitudes to Rafael's suicide are expressed by the novel's characters. It is probably in defence of her brother's actions that Fidela argues that people should be allowed to die when they want to (*TSP* I, 10). Her friend Augusta also states that suicide is acceptable if a woman or man goes to sleep and maintains the will of sleeping for centuries. Gamborena, by contrast, is horrified: accusing them of mocking the Catholic faith, which he regards as a vice characteristic of the time, he claims that the upper classes have lost their faith and calls for a return to religious simplicity, urging them to turn their thoughts to charity, worship and devotion (*TSP* I, 11).

Catholicism, however, does not provide many characters with the comfort or the assurance they are seeking. Galdós did not go as far as writers like Hispanus, who argued that Spain's decadence was due to 'la dominación asfixiante del catolicismo' (1903: 156), but he portrays Catholicism, as an institution, as being more concerned with show than true religious faith.[20] In *TH*, for instance, we read that Torquemada and Doña Silvia 'iban los dos á misa, por rutina; pero nada más' (III: 32); the moneylender disregards Christian customs by collecting the rent on Sundays and thinks that, by giving a

---

'la negación de la sensibilidad y la personalidad sensible', emerge from 'un sentimiento egoísta' and 'se propagan de modo epidémico' (González Blanco 1903: 87). It is notable that the author uses the image of an epidemic, one which was also applied to the *regeneradores* ('tal plaga de regeneradores') by P. Dorado in *LEM*, where he wrote: 'todo el mundo se considera llamado á redimir, con su sacrificio, á este pecador pueblo, harto pecador, sí, y hardo necesitado de algún Mesías que lo salve' (1898: 41).

[20] Mallada writes, '[d]igan lo que digan los preocupados y los escépticos, uno de los motives más eficaces del incremento en la inmoralidad pública es la pérdida de la fe religiosa'. He also highlights the problem of religious hypocrisy and the existence of 'católicos bullangueros' (1890: 200).

pearl to the Virgin, he can secure his sick son's life. In *TSP* he is infuriated by 'los cánticos de las niñas que iban allí cada lunes y cada mártes, con pretexto de religión, y en realidad para verse y codearse con sus novios' (*TSP* II, 6: 179). In the same novel the main purpose of Fidela's funeral is to create a fine impression and the Bishop and Donoso proudly proclaim, '[e]s una manifestación [...] una verdadera manifestación' (*TSP* II, 2: 139). The work of the Church is also questioned as Torquemada doubts whether it would be a good idea to take Cruz's advice and leave a third of his wealth to '*los de misa y olla*' (*TSP* III, 7: 282; original italics).

Dissatisfied with Catholicism and faced with the seemingly irrational events that befall him on earth, Torquemada ponders on religious phenomena. Reincarnation is raised in *TH* in relation to Bailón, who is convinced that, in a past life, he was a priest in Egypt. It is also discussed by Fidela in *TSP*, who believes that the dead come back to life and enjoy the freedom of coming and going as they please (*TSP* I, 14: 113). However, while insisting that 'no hay que burlarse de la conseja de las ánimas en pena' (*TSP* I, 14: 113), her use of the term *conseja* (fairy-tale) implicitly undermines this belief. Reincarnation is also fictionalized through Torquemada's conversations with the dead Valentín, who expresses his desire to live again. Although this wish is fulfilled in the birth of Valentín II, this newborn child (as noted) is 'un fenómeno'.[21]

The notion that salvation will come through a Messiah is obliquely referred to Valentín I in *TH*, where we read of 'el sin fin de ideas que tenía en aquel cerebrazo, y que en su día habían de iluminar toda la tierra' (*TH* II: 21); and it recurs in relation to the unborn Valentín II: 'Era la encarnación de un Dios, de un Altísimo nuevo, el Mesías de la ciencia de los números' (*TP* II, 9: 187). Once again, however, Galdós leaves the reader to choose between two conflicting interpretations: the statements can be read either as the observations of the narrator, or as free indirect discourse emanating from an obsessive and doting father.

Other philosophies present in the novels include pantheism and the 'Religion of Humanity'. An example of the first might be Bailón's idea that 'somos los átomos que forman el gran todo, somos parte mínima de Dios' (III: 32). He also tells Torquemada, 'Dios es la Humanidad', an idea derived from

---

21 Galdós may have responded to the suggestions of Narcís Oller, who, on 11 April 1889, wrote, '[l]o único que habría hecho yo en su lugar de Vd. es cambiar el tipo de Valentín. No sé si me equivoco pero creo que si le pinta Vd. estúpido ó si quiera desprovisto de ninguna calidad saliente había de resultar todavía más profunda la observación de Vd. y más patético el drama' (in Shoemaker 1964: 43).

Comte. It is adapted by Torquemada and amalgamated with his own ideas until he comes to the conclusion, '[h]e faltado á la Humanidad' (IV: 38).

To an extent, both these lines of thought could be related to the *krausista* quest for 'racionalismo armónico'. However, as is typical of Galdós (whose work *El amigo Manso* is arguably more of a critique of *krausismo* than an adherence to the philosophy), there is no explicit reference to the *krausistas*, and the philosophies are gently mocked through Bailón's ravings and Torquemada's confusion.

Rather than the harmony which the *krausistas* so ardently desired, Galdós presents a vision of hell on earth. This preoccupies Torquemada in *TSP* and is developed through the dehumanization of the characters, who, in their struggle for survival, are likened to animals. In *TC*, Cruz bemoans the bestial way in which her cousin and husband have treated the Águilas, and the unpolished Torquemada is referred to as 'bestia' and 'jabalí'.

Other non-Catholic features in *TH* include elements from Dante's Inferno (Brownlow 1993), and some Jewish references (Schyfter 1978), as well as allusions to superstitions. The tenants, for instance, exclaim: '¡D. Francisco con humanidad! Ahí tenéis por qué está saliendo todas las noches en el cielo esa estrella con rabo. Es que el mundo se va á acabar' (*TH* IV: 45). Tía Roma's description of what would happen if she accepted Torquemada's mattress is no less graphic.

> Si yo me durmiera ahí, á la hora de la muerte me saldrían por un lado y por otro unos sapos con la boca muy grande, unos culebrones asquerosos que se me enroscarían en el cuerpo, unos diablos muy feos con bigotazos y con orejas de murciélago, y me cogerían entre todos para llevarme arrastras á los infiernos. (*TH* VIII: 98–100)

The presence of divine or supernatural powers also exercises the characters of *TC*. On her deathbed, for example, Doña Lupe urges Torquemada, '[o]iga la santa palabra de su amiga, que ya le habla desde el otro mundo' (*TC* I, 1: 8), while Cruz wonders whether Rafael might be 'un ángel de Dios' (e.g. *TC* II, 5: 176).

A broader concern with the unknown is often raised in references to characters' dreams. For example, we read of Rafael's lucid dream (*TC* II, 12: 244), and wonder about the veracity of Torquemada's conversations with his dead son. Dreams were often described as one of Spain's 'vicios morales' (Macías Picavea 1979 edn: 161), and many claimed that Spaniards were overly influenced by the spirit of Don Quijote, preferring to live in a world of dream rather than of action: Mallada, for instance, laments that 'la patria de Don Quijote es un país de soñadores' (1890: 31). Dreams here often reveal characters' deeper feelings or fears: in *TSP* I, 12, Fidela dreams that Valentín tears out his eyes and plays with them, thereby conveying her extreme anxiety about her son and possibly her fear that he, like the blind Rafael, may ultimately destroy himself. They also raise more fundamental questions about life and death. In *TSP* Fidela wonders whether death is a dream, and, after her death, we are told that '[Fidela] dormía su sueño *largo, largo*' (*TSP* II, 1: 131).

I have suggested that Galdós outlines the need for philosophical regeneration by highlighting the characters' lack of spiritual depth and direction. He notes how religious concerns, in particular those relating to Catholicism, no longer form the centre of people's lives, whilst money and materialistic concerns are, by contrast, of paramount importance.

With the exception of Catholicism (which is portrayed as incapable of regenerating the nation) or marriage across classes (which is presented as an inadequate solution to the country's problems), the novels neither reject nor advocate any particular approach to spiritual regeneration. Instead, they present a range of quite different approaches to the subject, from the firm and constant Gamborena, who preaches humility and faith, to the self-destructive Rafael. In this way Galdós, not unlike the *krausistas*, highlights the importance of unity in diversity in spiritual matters, recognizing that these different philosophies have one feature in common: they are all a source of comfort to humankind. As Bailón tells Torquemada in *TH*, '[p]ara eso está la filosofía, ó, si se quiere, la religión: para hacer pecho á la adversidad. Pues si no fuera así, no podríamos vivir' (*TH* V: 52–3). Ironically, he succeeds only in confusing Torquemada.

Rather than expressing the pessimistic view that all such impulses to regenerate Spain are doomed to failure, however, the novels are forward-looking: they can be read as a critical commentary on the theories of 'degeneración' and *regeneración*, sometimes expressing stern condemnation, and sometimes gentle mockery of their weaknesses. In this oblique manner, Galdós shakes his readers' complacency and impresses upon them the need for *regeneración*. Like the question of *regeneración* itself, however, his analysis is sufficiently complex to allow for diverse interpretations and, like Unamuno, he wished to allow the reader to choose the necessary course of action: 'El lector sensato pondrá el método que falta y llenará los huecos' (Unamuno 1895: 45). Readers are thus neither frustrated nor overwhelmed by a picture of bleakness but are encouraged to be thoughtful, tolerant and sensitive, to maintain a constructive and open-minded attitude towards the philosophies discussed, and to consider a range of opinions before arriving at their own. Even when we suspect that Galdós's own views were opposed to those he describes (for example, in the case of heredity), any reservations are presented indirectly and the reader is left to assess their significance.

The openness of the *Torquemada* novels differ from the works of the *regeneracionistas*, many of which were consumed in negativity.[22] Galdós's prime aim was to engage with the concerns of his age and, to a large extent, his writing reflects the view offered by Rafael Altamira that:

> El primer signo de que un pueblo comienza á regenerarse ó siente á lo menos el deseo de hacerlo así, es que convierta su atención, en movimiento reflexivo y serio, al estudio de sus propias cualidades, para conocerse tal cual es y plantear, sobre este dato positivo, el problema de los remedios que deben allegar para aquel fin. (1892: 142)

The way in which Galdós explored these problems helped him to ensure that the *Torquemada* novels are constantly able to renew their appeal for readers of all backgrounds, beliefs, times, and ages.

List of Works Cited

Anon., 1890. 'Noticias', LEM, 20 (August): 215–23

Altamira, Rafael, 1892. 'El movimiento pedagógico en España', *LEM*, 48 (December): 142–62

——, 1899. 'Psicología del pueblo español', *LEM*, 111 (March): 5–59

Araujo, F., 1900. 'Revista de Revistas' ('Los hombres de genio'), *LEM*, 138 (June): 149–76 (pp. 159–65)

——, 1903a. 'Revista de Revistas' ('Cómo trabaja el hombre de genio': review of an article by Dr Regnault published in *La Revue*), *LEM*, 171 (March): 155–94 (pp. 167–71)

——, 1903b. 'Revista de Revistas' ('Las enfermedades del genio': review of an article by Dr Cavanés published in *La Revue*), *LEM*, 179 (November): 168–201 (pp. 173–6)

——, 1904. 'Revista de Revistas' ('Los niños precoces', review of an article published in *La Revue*), *LEM*, 187 (July): 165–202 (pp. 165–70)

——, 1905. 'Revista de Revistas' ('El genio': review of an article by Adolfo Padova published in the *Rivista d'Italia*), *LEM*, 196 (April): 176–201 (pp. 193–6)

Brownlow, Jeanne P., 1993. 'Epochal Allegory in Galdós' *Torquemada*: The Ur Text and the Episteme', *Publication of the Modern Language Association*, 108(2): 294–307

---

[22] This was noted in a review of *Los males de la patria* in *LEM*: 'es lástima que el Sr. Mallada se concrete á descubrir los males, callándose los remedios que, en su sentir y el nuestro, son tan necesarios' (*LEM*, 1890: 221), and by Juan Guixé in his *Problemas de España* (1912): 'el sentimiento, el tópico de Regeneración se convertía, por excesivo, en auto-denigración' (quoted in Tierno Galván 1977: 138).

While it falls outside the scope of this chapter, the openness discussed here also has a clear aesthetic function; the artistic dimension of the issues he explored was no less important to Galdós than the philosophical one.

Davies, Rhian, 2000. *'La España Moderna' and regeneración: A Cultural Review in Restoration Spain (1889–1914)* (Manchester: Cañada-Blanch Publications)

——, 2002. *Galdós y Lázaro: una breve y fructífera colaboración (1889–91)* (Madrid: Fundación Lázaro Galdiano & Ollero y Ramos)

Dorado Montero, Pedro, et al., 1896. 'Notas bibliográficas', *LEM*, 89 (May): 153–203 (pp. 159–60)

——, 1898. 'El discurso de apertura de los tribunales y la memoria del Fiscal del Supremo', *LEM*, 119 (November): 40–68

——, 1908. 'La inquisición política', *LEM*, 235 (July): 100–28

Dust, Patrick H., 1981. 'Regeneration as Destiny in *Torquemada en la hoguera*', in *La Chispa '81: Selected Proceedings*, ed. Gilbert Paolini (New Orleans: Tulane University), pp. 99–106

Earle, Peter G., 1967. 'Torquemada: hombre-masa', *Anales Galdosianos*, 2: 29–43

Ferri, Enrique, 1893. 'Educación, ambiente y criminalidad', *LEM*, 49 (January): 118–34

Ghiraldo, Alberto (ed.), 1923. Benito Pérez Galdós: *Obras inéditas*, 10 vols (Madrid: Renacimiento)

González Blanco, Edmundo, 1902. 'Psicología religiosa del pueblo español', *LEM*, 164 (August): 78–115

——, 1903. 'El suicidio en sus diversas formas', *LEM*, 176 (August): 54–87

González Rebollar, Hipólito, 1904. 'El pueblo español ante la reforma social', *LEM*, 182 (February): 86–113

Hispanus, 1903. 'Lecturas americanas', *LEM*, 176 (August): 135–58

Lombroso, César, 1893a, 'Aplicaciones judiciales y médicas de la antropología criminal', *LEM*, 51 (March): 106–19

——, 1893b. 'Aplicaciones judiciales y médicas de la antropología criminal', *LEM*, 53 (May): 78–124

Lubbock, John, 1897. 'El empleo de la vida', *LEM*, 101 (May): 137–76

Macías Picavea, Ricardo, 1979 edn. *El problema nacional* (Madrid: Instituto de Estudios de Administración [local])

Mallada, Lucas, 1890. *Los males de la patria y la futura revolución española: consideraciones generales acerca de sus causas y efectos* (Madrid: Tip. De Manuel Ginés Hernández)

Ortega, Soledad (ed.), 1964. *Cartas a Galdós* (Madrid: Revista de Occidente)

Pérez Galdós, Benito, 1889. Torquemada en la hoguera (Madrid: La Guirnalda)

——, 1893. Torquemada en la cruz (Madrid: La Guirnalda)

——, 1894. Torquemada en el purgatoris (Madrid: La Guirnalda)

——, 1895. Torquemada y San Pedro (Madrid: La Guirnalda)

Pero Pérez, el Licenciado, 1895. 'La Prensa internacional', *LEM*, 74 (February): 121–74

Rodríguez Martínez, J., 1899. *Los desastres y la regeneración de España: relatos e impresiones* (La Coruña: La Gutenberg)

Round, Nicholas G., 1971. 'Time and Torquemada: Three Notes on Galdosian Chronology', *Anales Galdosianos*, 6: 79–97

——, 2003. 'Galdós Rewrites Galdós: The Deaths of Children and the Dying Century', in *New Galdós Studies*, ed. N. G. Round (Woodbridge: Tamesis), pp. 125–39

——, 2004. ' "What is the Stars?": Galdós and the Measures of Mankind', The Seventh Annual Pérez Galdós Lecture (University of Sheffield)

Sales Ferré, Manuel, 1903. 'De la civilización y su medida', *LEM*, 180 (December): 35–53

Salillas, Rafael, 1894. 'La degeneración y el proceso Willié', *LEM*, 66 (June): 70–96

Sánchez Reyes, E. (ed.), 1953. 'Epistolario de Pereda y Menéndez y Pelayo', *Boletín de la Biblioteca de Menéndez y Pelayo*, 29: 207–391

Schyfter, Sara E., 1978. *The Jew in the Novels of Benito Pérez Galdós* (London: Tamesis)

Shoemaker, W. H., 1964. 'Una amistad literaria: la correspondencia epistolar entre Galdós y Narciso Oller', *Boletín de la Real Academia de Buenas Letras de Barcelona*, 30: 1–60

Tierno Galván, Enrique, 1977. *Idealismo y pragmatismo en el siglo XIX español* (Madrid: Tecnos)

Ullman, Pierre, 1965. 'The Exordium of Torquemada en la hoguera', *MLN*, 80: 258–60

Unamuno, Miguel de, 1895. 'En torno al casticismo', *LEM*, 78 (June): 26–46

Vida, Jerónimo, 1893. 'El proyecto de Código Penal para la República Argentina', *LEM*, 53 (May): 131–4

The Illusion of Realism:
Reflections on *El amigo Manso*

ARTHUR TERRY †

In 1897 Galdós was elected to the *Real Academia Española*. By then, he was in his mid-fifties and had been writing novels for the best part of thirty years. The speech he made on that occasion – one of his few critical statements – was called 'La sociedad presente como materia novelable'. On the face of it, what he has to say about the nature of the novel is disappointingly trite:

> Imagen de la vida es la Novela, y el arte de componerla estriba en reproducir los caracteres humanos, las pasiones, las debilidades, lo grande y lo pequeño, las almas y las fisionomías, todo lo espiritual y lo físico que nos constituye y nos rodea, y el lenguaje [...] y las viviendas [...] y la vestidura [...]: todo esto sin olvidar que debe existir perfecto fiel de balanza entre la exactitud y la belleza de la reproducción. (Bonet 1972: 175)

As I shall try to show, this is far from being an adequate description of Galdós's own novels. What makes the rest of his speech interesting, though, is something rather different: the sense that it is no longer possible to write fiction in the realist mode. Galdós himself is not quite so explicit as this; what he *does* claim is that Spanish society – the fictional material of his title – is losing its organic structure; the extremes of the social spectrum – the aristocracy and what he calls the 'pueblo' – are coming to be absorbed in a large amorphous middle-class which has lost its sense of direction and is uncertain of its own image. And with this goes the disappearance of human 'types', the kind of people who are defined by their social function and who, in turn, reflect the nature of society. Surprisingly, perhaps, Galdós's conclusion is fairly optimistic: the absence of 'types' will make individual characteristics stand out more sharply, and this will present a new kind of challenge to the novelist; and finally, he implies, we shall perhaps have to revise our notion of history as a sequence of important national events and to pay more attention to the ordinary life which escapes the history books, and which does not follow any simple pattern of cause and effect.

What gives the statement its urgency is Galdós's awareness that the conditions for writing fiction have changed, his sense that the novelist is no longer
able to create the illusion that he is describing a recognizable society, since
the identity of society itself is becoming blurred. This is one sense in which
one may use the word 'illusion' in the context of realist fiction: to suggest
that a novel is in some way a 'copy' of real life. It does not deny that fiction
is made of words, that the people and events it describes are imagined; on
the other hand, it assumes that reality itself is stable, and that language can
be trusted to give a true account of it. This, on the whole, is the view of
most nineteenth-century novelists working in the realist mode, though it is
not always accepted uncritically. As against this, there is the very different
sense in which the whole realist enterprise is said to be an illusion: the idea
that the actual premises of realism are false – that there is no such thing as
a stable reality and that language itself distorts, even when it seems most
transparent. So one of the most intelligent of contemporary French critics,
Gérard Genette, writes that 'the illusion of realism is to believe that what
one *names* is just as one names it' (1969: 247). This comes in a discussion
of Proust, who, in a famous passage, claims that what generally passes as
'realism' is superficial; it is a matter of 'lines and surfaces' and it avoids true
reality, which is concerned with 'essences' – something that language can
only reveal indirectly (1989 edn IV: 461, 468). So, if conventional 'realism'
is superficial, the notion of 'reality' on which it is based comes to be seen as
purely relative: what is 'lifelike' is so, only because it squares with a generally accepted 'way of life'. Or, as Stephen Heath puts it in his book on the
nouveau roman:

> [What is 'realistic'] may be described in the notion of the *vraisemblable* of
> a particular society, the generally received picture of what may be regarded
> as 'realistic'; such a *vraisemblable* being founded in our culture by, amongst
> other things, the novel itself. (1972: 20)

This means, of course, that realism always has ideological implications,
though to say this is one thing, and to suggest that no nineteenth-century
novelist is ever aware of such implications is quite another. In practice,
however, there are a great many varieties of realist novel; in Professor Stern's
phrase, there is no standard type which can be easily defined – only certain
'family likenesses' (1973: 28). 'Realism', therefore, is not so much a method
as a set of conventions which allow for a good deal of flexibility and which
may, on occasions, be challenged, even by those novelists who are usually
regarded as 'realists'.

If we come back to Galdós with some of these ideas in mind, a certain
pattern begins to emerge. For a start, if one of the tests of a realist writer is

his objectivity, Galdós's early novels of contemporary society hardly qualify. In an essay of 1870, he writes about the novelist's need to examine the social and religious questions of the day, though without suggesting solutions:

> Sabemos que no es el novelista el que ha de decidir directamente estas graves cuestiones, pero sí tiene la misión de reflejar esta turbación honda, esta lucha incesante de principios y hechos que constituye el maravilloso drama de la vida actual. (Quoted in Bonet 1972: 124)

Yet his early novels often *do* offer solutions, and the kind of social observation they contain is often distorted by the tendency to see human relationships in terms of issues and problems. Already, though, one begins to see some of the classic themes of the realist novel beginning to appear: the contrast between action and theory, the way behaviour is falsified by a kind of egotism based on superficial romantic attitudes, and the tendency for illusions to be undermined by the need for economic survival. Galdós's approach to these themes is not always as yet very sure: his ironic detachment sometimes amounts to a failure of imagination, and his use of parody – again, one of the basic realist modes – is occasionally too crude. Yet what in these early novels already points towards his best fiction is his growing awareness of social complexity and the corresponding need for a more pluralistic, less didactic, technique for putting this into words.

We can see something of what this entails in one of the best of the shorter novels, *El amigo Manso*, published in 1882. This is a first-person narrative told by Máximo Manso, a rather undistinguished professor of philosophy in his mid-thirties. The plot, like many of Galdós's plots, is basically a very simple one; it can be told in such a way as to make it sound like a romantic novelette, and it is quite possible that this was part of Galdós's intention. Manso himself is a rationalist, a man with a profound mistrust of the imagination, an educator rather than an individual thinker. In the course of the action, he acquires two protégés. One is a young girl, Irene, for whom he finds a post as governess in the household of his rich elder brother, who has recently returned from Cuba. Irene is attractive and educated, and Manso quickly comes to regard her as the perfect rational woman. The other protégé is Manuel Peña, the handsome, talented but rather bohemian son of a neighbour, the widow of a butcher, who now wants both herself and her son to rise in society. She therefore asks Manso to take Manuel in hand and to educate him: Manso soon finds that Manuel is not cut out to be an intellectual; on the other hand, he has a practical eye for a career, together with considerable gifts as an orator. And it is at this point that the two main strands of the plot start to come together. Both Manso and Manuel are called on to make speeches at a charity performance in a theatre; Manso's discreet speech is only politely received; Manuel's brilliant improvisation, by contrast, brings the house down, and a dazzling political future is predicted for him. And, significantly, Irene is present in the audience, and the fact that she is carried away by the general enthusiasm for Manuel leads Manso to suspect that she is not quite as rational as he had thought. It is this gradual revelation of Irene's true nature, hindered by Manso's reluctance to abandon his original image of her, which takes up the rest of the story. Briefly, she is caught between two men: Manso's married brother, who is trying to have an affair with her, and Manuel, with whom she is genuinely in love. Manso, who is too timid to confess his own love for Irene, only discovers the real situation near the end. All through the novel, other people have threatened to destroy his orderly, rational existence, and by this stage his whole life is in disarray. What he is made to realize in the end is that Irene is a very ordinary girl with conventional social ambitions, and it is a measure of the change which has taken place in him, that when he *does* discover this, he finds that he is more deeply in love with her than ever. Finally, he makes a desperate attempt to argue Manuel out of marrying Irene; when this fails, he finds himself in the paradoxical situation of having to plead for Manuel with his mother, who considers Irene beneath him. So it is largely thanks to Manso that the wedding takes place, and, once this happens, Manso himself falls mysteriously ill and dies.

Two things should be obvious from my summary of the plot: one is that Galdós uses the device of an unreliable narrator; the other is that a good deal of the story turns on an enigma which is only gradually resolved. The two things, in fact, are connected: Manso, because of his failings – in particular, his belief that all problems can be solved by deductive reasoning – persistently misreads the events which are taking place around him. This is especially ironical since he is shown as someone who prides himself on his ability to 'see things as they are'. But it is clear that what he takes to be his sense of reality comes from books, and precisely from the kind of books which have taught him to mistrust his imagination. Hardly surprisingly, he is contemptuous of novels – even, it is hinted at one point, the novels of Galdós – and one of the reasons for his timidity as a lover is that he cannot bring himself to use what he thinks of as the language of romantic fiction. Another sign of his rationality is what he calls his 'talent for generalization'. Here, for once, his self-analysis is correct, though in the end he is forced to recognize that his ability in this direction is double-edged: once the essential clue to the enigma has been given him, he can work out the rest, he says, 'as if he were reading a book'; on the other hand, it is his tendency to overleap the particular which has helped to create the mystery in the first place.

As for the enigma itself, this clearly has more than just a detective story interest, since it is the means by which Manso is led to a truer estimate of other people's identities. The actual presentation of the enigma, and the way it brings together the various plot sequences, have been analysed in great detail in a fine article by John Rutherford. One of the things Rutherford shows very clearly is the relation between the enigma and the narrative structure as a whole: '[T]he story is an extended question directed at the future – what will happen? The enigma is an extended solution directed at the past and the present – what is happening and what has happened?' (Rutherford 1975: 210), and he goes on to explain how the story concentrates the attention on Manso and the enigma on Irene. This is an important insight, I think, and it helps to focus something that most readers must have felt about this novel: that two basic rhythms are being played off against one another, and that one of them is working against the sense of linear progression.

Linear progression is generally assumed to be an essential feature of the realist novel, and the fact that it is possible to tell the story of *Manso* as a sequence of events and decisions seems to bear this out. Yet the presence of the enigma has the effect of retarding this sequence, and this process is compounded by the one major strategy I have so far left out of account. Though the device of a first-person narrator may suggest that the novel takes the form of a reminscence, this is not strictly so. In practice, most of the story is told just as it happens, or appears to happen, to Manso himself. Yet occasionally Manso will interrupt his account of a particular episode to say 'how well I remember this', or words to that effect. When this occurs, the result is disconcerting and, I would claim, deliberately so. On the one hand, it is as if the reader were being given a pointer ('what is happening now is more significant than it might seem at first sight'); on the other, it is as if Galdós had purposely broken the illusion of immediacy to introduce a more omniscient point of view while still remaining within the framework of the narrator. And what makes this possible is the most original stroke in the whole novel: the fact that Manso is deliberately presented as a fictional character.

The first words of the novel, in fact, are 'Yo no existo' (9), and in the rest of the opening chapter, this fiction is maintained: Manso explains that he has been brought into existence – a fictional existence, of course – as the result of a pact between himself and a novelist whom it is easy to identify with Galdós.[1] 'Vedme con apariencia humana', he says, and goes on:

> Es que alguien me evoca, y por no sé qué sutiles artes me pone como un forro corporal y hace de mí un remedo o una máscara de persona viviente, con todas las trazas y movimientos de ella. (10)

---

[1]   Page references throughout are to the Austral edition of *El amigo Manso* (Buenos Aires: Espasa Calpe, 1954).

And, as he emerges from the author's inkwell at the beginning of the story proper, he observes: 'El dolor me dijo que yo era un hombre' (11).

I have already tried to describe the story which follows, except for the actual ending, and here Galdós returns to the non-realistic mode of the opening pages. Manso dies, in the gentlest possible manner, and finds himself in a kind of limbo from which he can continue to observe the behaviour of the characters who have accompanied him through the rest of the fiction. The author, he explains, has reversed the spell which originally made him into a fictional character, and he finds a melancholy satisfaction in the speed with which he is forgotten by those who live on.

On the face of it, then, *El amigo Manso* is a realist novel set in a fantastic frame. In practice, however, it is not as easy as it may sound to separate the frame from the rest. Certainly, the main part of the story has all the 'solidity of specification' – the density of social detail – which Henry James required of the novel, and, though James would hardly have approved, one imagines, of the questioning of Manso's status, the degree of bewilderment that Manso exhibits in the course of coming to terms with reality corresponds fairly exactly to James's own prescription for creating what he calls 'intensity of illusion' (1962 edn: 318). Or, as Wayne Booth glosses James's phrase: 'Whatever intensity is achieved must be an intensity of the illusion that genuine life has been presented' (1961: 44). And this is precisely how Manso functions as narrator for the greater part of the novel: the illusion of life is created, not so much by 'lifelike' description (though there is plenty of this), as by Manso's gradual realization that other people are not as he had thought them.

All this is part of the main body of the story. But what is particularly interesting is the trouble Galdós takes to justify Manso's 'non-existence' at a more realistic level. In one sense – and this is the point of the title – Manso doesn't exist because he is the 'friend' everyone else relies on to help them solve their own problems, regardless of any problems he might have himself. And in another, quite different, sense, his 'non-existence' has to do with the fact that he lives in a philosophical ivory tower, and that his moral values continually fail to engage with a life which is based first and foremost on economic relationships. As for his death, it is possible to see this in realistic terms as the result of emotional strain. When he discovers the truth of the relationship between Irene and Manuel, he is filled with 'ideas de muerte' (178); and after he has successfully helped to bring about the marriage of the two lovers, he says to Manuel's mother: 'He dado mi fruto y estoy de más' (222). And when Doña Javiera says that she cannot see any fruit, Manso replies:

> —Es posible. Lo que se ve, señora doña Javiera, es la parte menos importante de lo que existe. Invisible es todo lo grande, toda ley, toda causa, todo elemento activo. Nuestros ojos, ¿qué son más que microscopios? (222)

The microscope image might seem to take us back to Manso's unlimited faith in the power of rational deduction, to his wish to see everything in terms of cause and effect. But, by this stage in the novel, it has more to do with something Manso has painfully acquired in the course of his experience: a sense of wonder in the face of the unknown. By now, his attitude is more like that of the naturalist than of the rational philosopher. When Irene's scheming aunt, Doña Cándida, tries to gloss over the fact that she has allowed Manso's brother to set her up in a new flat so as to have easier access to Irene, Manso's reaction shows how much he has changed:

> La miraba, la observaba con verdadero placer, cosa que parecerá impo-
> sible pero que es verdad. Era yo como el naturalista que de improviso se
> encuentra entre las hojarascas que pisa, con un desconocido tipo o especie
> de reptil, con feísimo coleóptero, con baboso y repugnante molusco. Poco
> afectado por la mala traza del hallazgo, no piensa más que en lo extraño
> del animalejo, se regocija viendo las ondulaciones que hace en el fango,
> o las materias fétidas que suelta, o los agudos rejos con que amenaza
> [...] (169)

All these things are now signs of the inexhaustible variety of nature. Yet at the end of the same conversation, just as he feels that Irene's real situation is about to be revealed, he shrinks back from the truth and is prepared to settle for ignorance: 'Por primera vez en mi vida bendije la ilusión, indigna comedia del alma, que nos hace dichosos [...]' (171). If there are laws of nature, he reflects, then perhaps it is wrong to try to penetrate the mystery which surrounds them. But it is too late, of course, and a few seconds afterwards he meets Manuel by chance and suddenly realizes that he is Irene's unknown lover.

I have tried to show, however, how *El amigo Manso* is also organized in such a way that the non-realistic framework is made to qualify our reading of the rest. The final effect is difficult to pin down. I would argue that the presentation of Manso does not cancel out the realistic treatment of the rest, so much as absorb it into a higher kind of realism, a realism which, as in Proust, includes metaphysical and non-historical values. Thinking back to the two senses of 'illusion' I used at the beginning, we might say that the picture of contemporary society which Galdós presents is truthful in realist terms – that the 'illusion of realism', of a man experiencing reality, is convincing in itself – but that Galdós is not satisfied with accepting what this particular society regards as 'real'. Manso, for all his defects, is the only character in the novel who seriously believes in truth, wisdom and charity; on the other hand, the 'human nature' to which he fails to adapt, and by whose values he stands condemned, is shown to be as relative as any other kind of human construct. And this seems to me the final implication of the novel: Manso learns to take people as they are, but only at the cost of recognizing that the densely registered experience that has brought him to this recognition, is the shadow, not the substance, of 'reality'.

To sum up: the meaning of *El amigo Manso*, it seems to me, is generated, not so much by any steady linear progression, as by the existence of the enigma and by the way this brings about a constant interplay of past, present and future. It is a novel which could well be described in terms of George Eliot's favourite metaphor of the 'web', the idea that things are connected, not by a simple chain of cause and effect, but by an infinite number of differences and similarities which are only revealed by patient comparison. And this, of course, involves the reader in a peculiarly intimate way. A novel like *El amigo Manso*, by forcing us to make our own interpretations as we go, involves us in something like the same process of trial and error which the characters themselves enact. Like them, we are continually tempted to make our own patterns, and perhaps the most sophisticated version of realism consists in showing how often such patterns prove false. So in Galdós, the linear version of history is there, often powerfully so, and if this is what we want to believe in, we may fail to see how deliberately it is subverted. Or to put it another way: in our wish to dominate the text, we may overlook the way in which the text itself evades that process.

At one point in *Middlemarch*, George Eliot talks about 'the stealthy convergence of human lots, [...] a slow preparation of effects from one life on another' (1965 edn: 122), and summing up the whole effect of the novel in the last chapter, she writes:

> Every limit is a beginning as well as an ending. [...] For the fragment of a life, however typical, is not the sample of an even web: promises may not be kept, and an ardent outset may be followed by declension; latent powers may find their long-waited opportunity; a past error may urge a grand retrieval. (890)

Taken out of its context, this may seem no more than a truism: 'life is full of surprises'; yet, coming where it does, at the end of a dense and complex narrative, it suggests two things which I have tried to keep in mind in the course of this chapter. One is that 'realism' is never more truthful than when it questions its own power to tell the truth; and the second, which follows from this, is the suggestion that fiction itself is arbitrary, that there is always a doubt as to why it should end in one way rather than another. Once a writer grasps this, as I think Galdós *does* grasp it, the chances are that she or he will be compelled to move beyond any narrowly defined concept of 'realism', though the experiments which have led her or him to this point would be inconceivable without the various strains which meet in what, for want of a better term, we call the 'realist novel'.

List of Works Cited

Bonet, Laureano (ed.), 1972. Benito Pérez Galdós: *Ensayos de crítica literaria* (Barcelona: Ediciones Península)

Booth, Wayne C., 1961. *The Rhetoric of Fiction* (Chicago and London: University of Chicago Press)

Eliot, George, 1965 edn. *Middlemarch*, ed. W. J. Harvey (Harmondsworth: Penguin Books)

Genette, Gérard, 1969. *Figures II*, Collection 'Tel Quel' (Paris: Éditions du Seuil)

Heath, Stephen, 1972. *The Nouveau Roman: A Study in the Practice of Writing* (London: Elek)

James, Henry, 1962 edn. *The Art of the Novel* (New York and London: Scribner)

Pérez Galdós, Benito, 1954. *El amigo Manso* (Buenos Aires: Espasa Calpe)

Proust, Marcel, 1989. À *la recherche du temps perdu*, ed. Jean-Yves Tadié, 4 vols (Paris: Gallimard)

Rutherford, John, 1975. 'Story, Character, Setting and Narrative Mode in Galdós's *El amigo Manso*', in *Style and Structure in Literature: Essays in the New Stylistics*, ed. Roger Fowler (Oxford: Blackwell)

Stern, J. P., 1973. *On Realism* (London and Boston: Routledge & Kegan Paul)

On Realism, Now and Then:
Martha Stewart Meets Ana Ozores

HARRIET TURNER

This essay focuses on how the techniques of literary realism bridge the gap between our time and the nineteenth century. It proposes a complexly inter-active model of realism, set within a similarly dynamic model of cultural studies. The scope and purposes of cultural studies are framed here in terms of the biosphere, 'an interacting web of plants and rocks, fungi and soils, animals and oceans, microbes and air, that constitute the habit of life on our planet. To understand the biosphere,' writes Freeman Dyson, 'it is essential to see it from both sides, from below as a multitude of details and from above as a single integrated system' (2003: 4). Similarly, through the discipline of cultural studies we focus on highs and lows as these evolve through an interacting web of emotions, conscious and unconscious; we seek to discern, from outside and inside, the nexus of a 'multitude of details' that, all told, sketch out 'el imaginario social' – those collective attitudes, behaviours and social practices that underlie the production of a text and which agitate in lively, often invisible ways, in, among and around words and discourses. Selecting a particular lens or window or a 'crystalline moment', we seek to give, or at least imply, a comprehensive account of the culture in which a text is embedded (Balzar 2001: 5B). At the same time, we strive to highlight those qualities of a writer's art that express a personal view or value, one often affirmed over and against a particular culture or historical moment.

  The attempt to reconcile the social and cultural contexts of a literary work and the power literature achieves through language, voice and formal expres-sion (Dickstein 2003: B8) often exposes, as in the case of the biosphere, gaps in our knowledge, the limitations of our observations and the obfuscations of our theories. Cultural studies emphasize interconnectedness and yet, as Stephen Kern has noted, commenting on 'The Next Big Thing', our findings often appear disconnected from one another. Kern argues for 'some coopera-tion in identifying fundamental [...] universal elements of all cultures (time, space, causality, embodiment, love, vision, death) and then interpreting their distinctive historical and social variants' (quoted in *The Chronicle of Higher Education* 2004: B4). One step toward the articulation of such a thematic, unifying perspective, which allows us to interpret variants, is to adjust the way we view, for example, the dominant literary and artistic movements of an age, examples being Romanticism and Realism in the nineteenth century, and Modernism and Postmodernism in our time. Rather than a set of terms or categories we may envisage these phenomena as repetitive 'waves' and 'troughs', the one eliding with the other – or ebbing from the other – in a reciprocal exchange of moods, techniques, claims and strategies.

Realism in Spain during the nineteenth century encompasses many of the most modern variants and styles, for realism, to recall Lilian Furst's words, is always binary, dualistic and dialogic (1992: 3). Realism as practised by Galdós and Clarín is 'modern' in the root sense of that word – from the old French *moderne*, evolving from the Latin *modernus* and *modus*, meaning something happening 'just now' (Taylor 1999: 26); realism, then, is always with us, in one form or another. It is the great intermediary, the negotiator, the lens that keeps adjusting focus, and thus the concept of realism, when broadly understood, serves to connect various aspects and findings of cultural studies. For once we recognize a world of things that simply exists – 'inanimate, spatially extended, and subject to quantifiable forces' – and once we recognize the powers of the mind – 'the seat of thought, understanding, sensation, and imagination' – then between the extremes of what corresponds to idealism, on the one hand, and to scepticism, on the other, realism continuously becomes the perspective that 'heroically bridges the gap' (Blackburn 2001: 95–6).

Our example of how the literary techniques of realism bridge the gap between now and the nineteenth century is Clarín's 'heroic' first novel, *La Regenta*. In 1884–85, it seemed almost too imitative of life; now, it seems an active agent of modernity: once mediated through film (1994), the novel altered the cityscape of the very social body that had acted, more than one hundred years before, as a catalyst for character, plot and setting. At the same time, contemporary writing and reporting in US magazines and media keep having recourse to the time-honoured 'realist' techniques of writers like Cervantes, Galdós and Clarín, Chekhov and Tolstoy. As James Wood has observed, 'every reader of Cervantes knows that there is abundant 'technique' in *Don Quijote*, and that Cervantes mobilizes all kinds of techniques that are premodern only because they had not yet been identified as techniques' (2003: 25).

The best US news stories take advantage of such realist techniques, identified by Wood as the 'sound of simplicity', the 'direct access to deep emotion; the clarity of phrasings; the willingness to use vernacular and conversational language and repetition rather than obviously literary constructions', as well as their ease in evoking the free indirect style (2003: 25). Journalists today also focus what John Balzar, writing in the *Los Angeles Times*, calls 'crystalline moments': a scene, setting, event, action, or gesture that condenses, in time and space, an essential part of the story (2001: 5B). His term plays upon the trope of the mirror, central to the realist aesthetic of the 1880s. *La Regenta*, among other novels, offers many such moments, such as scenes in Chapters 8 and 16, the one in a precise numerical relation to the other, which capture, almost invisibly, junctures between form and content, surface and idea, the real and the imagined.[1]

Among examples that mark the reciprocity between the literary realism of *La Regenta* and today's press, I have selected Jeffrey Toobin's magisterial account of the trial of Martha Stewart, published in spring 2004 in an issue of *The New Yorker*. For in the moment that Martha Stewart 'meets' Ana Ozores, we see immediately how an interest in the tenets and techniques of realism has become a factor that bridges the gap between writing now and writing then. Each story features a female protagonist, a masculine world of power, comparable social contexts, similar actions of plot, a focus on the telling detail, on 'crystalline moments', which establish patterns and build suspense, and the use of a narrator who reports from the inside while maintaining, from outside, the illusion of objectivity.

Further, as Harry Levin reminds us, '[e]tymologically, realism means "thing-ism". The adjective "real" derives from the Latin *res* [meaning thing] and finds an appropriate context in "real estate" – land, property, things' (1963: 34). Thus realism beckons in Toobin's title, which refers to 'A Bad Thing', while 'thing-ism' itself is a developing theme. It surfaces in objects like the bottles of Evian water and green tea from Japan that stocked the Stewart table at the trial; and there is 'the good thing' – 'not a great one' (Toobin 2004: 72) – that sums up Martha's business, 'Martha Stewart Living Omnimedia'.

This enterprise, in name, echoes the inclusive nature of the nineteenth-century realist novel: 'omnicomprensiva' is Clarín's term (Alas 1972: 137). Yet Martha's business actually only ministers to the 'comforts of middle class life' (Toobin 2004: 66), just as, in *La Regenta*, Clarín maintained his focus on blurred relations between the nobility and the newly rich, leaving the peasant and working classes to linger on the margins, even ignoring university life – a central fact of his own career as a professor of Roman Law. Toobin's account refers at once to Martha's 'homely aesthetic' but also to her odd flair

[1]   See, for example, my chapter on 'The Realist Novel', in *The Cambridge Companion to the Spanish Novel*, ed. H. Turner and A. López de Martínez (Cambridge: Cambridge University Press, 2003), pp. 81–101.

for celebrity (2004: 66). In doing so it points up a contradiction that also afflicts Ana Ozores, who is regarded by everyone as a celebrity – 'la maravilla del pueblo' (Alas 1981: I, 246) – but who, on occasion, aspires only to the 'poetics' of housekeeping – 'la poesía del hogar' (II, 326).[2] Damage done by arrogant social elites, an obsession with things, as well as an overriding passion for money and power and a capacity for lying, all bring home the failed verdict at Martha's trial. Ana's desperate story, in its own way also a 'trial', involves the damaging effects of similar social elites (in her case, a degenerate nobility) and of an obsession with things, a passion for money and power, and the predations of lying minds. Martha, as tabloids have seen, is 'a perfect subject' (Toobin 2004: 64). She is private in her salons and public in her persona, recalling the reclusive Ana, who retreats to her bedroom, anxious to refresh herself by stretching naked upon a tiger skin, but who is careful to present a firmly guarded 'fortress' ('fortaleza inexpugnable'; I, 277) of public virtue, as 'la perfecta casada' (II, 195). This cultural trope is not dissimilar to the kind of 'trustworthiness' and 'good works' that Martha promotes to the general public (Toobin 2004: 64).

Finally, in both stories there is constantly and actively present the classic motif of damaged love triangles: Ana and her aging husband don Víctor rotate among lovers and seducers, male and female; Martha, divorced, wealthy and alone, is caught up in an ambivalent relationship with Sam Waksal, centre of her 'clique' of relationships, at once a close friend of her own age but also a former romantic partner of her daughter Alexis (Toobin 2004: 68). In each story, love triangles keep changing within the exclusivity of inner circles – a 'clique' on the one hand, a *'petit comité'* on the other (II, 298; original italics); these are 'traded' or 'exchanged' relations appropriate to the 'metallic age' ('siglo *metálizado'*; I, 219) of both novels, to their moneyed milieu: a milieu which each narrator analyses from the privileged point of view of an insider who nonetheless promotes the illusion of all-knowing detachment. Having, by his own admission, worked as a summer intern for the same handsome, socially prominent, lawyer who botches Stewart's defence, Toobin now writes for the general public as author of the section 'Annals of the Law' in *The New Yorker* newspaper. Clarín's narrator emerges as an outsider, omniscient and ostensibly removed from the scene, who also writes for the general reading public; in telling his story, however, this narrator inadvertently mirrors certain behaviour traits of his characters; he spies and cracks jokes at their expense and thus, while pretending to be an outsider speaking

---

2   Quotations from *La Regenta* come from the edition by Gonzalo Sobejano (Alas 1981) and, after the first reference, are prefaced only by the volume number. Translations into English come from *La Regenta*, trans. John Rutherford (1984).

through a veneer of objectivity, he characterizes himself as an insider, a voyeur, a *vetustense* (Charnon Deutsch 1989: 101).

Both Ana's story and Martha's trial also make use of constructed 'intertexts': that is, interpolated stories or allusions to other texts. Ana attends the performance of *Don Juan Tenorio* and begins to participate in the play: she sees herself as the virginal novitiate doña Inés, with the town of Vetusta as her cell, and her husband as the rigid Comendador or *convidado de piedra*, a 'guest of stone' concerned only with honour; and, of course, she sees her presumptive lover as the fictional personage of don Juan Tenorio. News items, appearances on television, interviews and other public images may be seen similarly as 'intertexts' that create, in Martha, that imagined *persona* of trustworthiness. This public image is, however, at variance with the 'whole concocted story' that Martha pitches to investigators, as well as with the description of herself – another self-serving 'intertext' – that she presents to her readers in an issue of *Martha Stewart Living* one month before the trial (Toobin 2004: 64–5). A particularly damaging 'intertext' is the message from her stockbroker, which Martha attempts to alter, 'taking the mouse and putting the cursor at the end of the sentence, highlighting it, and typing over it' (Toobin 2004: 63). In Clarín's novel, Vetusta highlights the story of Ana's adultery, typing over it, one might say, to create a scandal in novelistic form – 'aquel gran escándalo que era como una novela, algo que interrumpía la monotonía eterna de la ciudad triste' (II, 584). Vetusta's highlighted 'new novel' coincides in part with the novel that Clarín has created, just as Ana's imaginings had created a series of fictional roles and scenarios that make up the plot of her story and of the novel that contains it.

In *La Regenta*, as in Martha's trial, these competing novels insinuate a metafictive dimension, a literary form of self-reflection that obliquely mirrors those self-regarding aspects of the protagonists. Ana continues to contemplate her own image in her mind, in her dreams, in the eyes of others and in the mirror of her dressing table. Martha's company also reflects her own image: Toobin notes that 'she herself was in many ways its singular product'; as she tells him, her magazine, *Martha Stewart Living*, 'is me, O.K., me, one hundred percent' (2004: 60). Her company, he writes, 'seemed to exist more to serve its founder than the other way around. She was surrounded by people whose jobs were to anticipate and meet her every need' (2004: 60). In such descriptions Toobin makes discreet use of metaphors of monarchy, speaking of 'courtiers' to highlight Martha as 'Queen', just as Ana, from the outset, has been elevated in people's eyes as 'la Regenta'. Self-reflection and image-making are all. In their respective texts, across the centuries, Toobin and Clarín, each in his own way, catch this almost imperceptible shift in representation, from the mimesis of things to a mimesis of perception. It is a shift that correlates, on the one hand, with the rise of mercantilism in nineteenth-century Spain and the replacement of paper bills for coins (Labanyi 2000: 390), and, on the other hand, with the prerogatives of high capitalism in our twenty-first century, when people like Stewart sell and buy at a distance via pixels on a computer screen.

Turning now to the reciprocity of realism between Vetusta, the fictional representation of nineteenth-century Oviedo (capital of Asturias in northern Spain), and present-day Oviedo, we find that the polemic provoked by the publication of *La Regenta* adds an intriguing perspective.[3] In 1884, at the age of thirty-two, Clarín completed the novel's first volume. Previously he had published some short stories and later would write another novel, *Su único hijo* (1891). As a badly paid professor of Law at the University of Oviedo, he also wrote for national newspapers and magazines and, like Jeffrey Toobin, became a sharp critic of legal, political and cultural practices. By April 1885 the second (and final) volume was published in Barcelona. When *La Regenta* appeared in the store fronts of Oviedo, it was viciously attacked as 'an obscene, irreligious monstrosity and as a plagiarism of Flaubert's *Madame Bovary*' (Rutherford 1984: 7). Prominent citizens of the city, as well as ecclesiastical authorities, were shocked to find that the Vetusta of the novel was unmistakably their own Oviedo. They saw *La Regenta* as a 'novela de clave', filled with unflattering, even libellous depictions of themselves, and vicious disputes arose (Alarcos 1982: 227). For Oviedo's citizenry realism, the literary imitation of life, had gone too far.

La Regenta soon slipped from view. Leopoldo Alas died in 1901. While his novel eluded explicit censorship during the Franco years, no major critic promoted it until 1952, the centennial year of the author's birth. In that year, a major conference was held; the proceedings, published in the journal *Archivum*, contained Emilio Alarcos Llorach's brilliant analysis of the structure of the novel.[4] A series of seminal articles, essays and the magisterial edition by Gonzalo Sobejano established *La Regenta* as a canonical text (1976, 1981).[5] The first translation, into English by John Rutherford, was

---

3 This summary of the plot of the novel and of the history of its reception follows John Rutherford's account in the 'Introduction' to his translation of *La Regenta* (1984: 7–17).

4 Emilio Alarcos Llorach, 'Notas a *La Regenta*', *Archivum*, II (1952): 141–60. Reprinted in his book *Ensayos y estudios literarios* (Madrid: Júcar, 1976), pp. 99–118, also in *Clarín y 'La Regenta'*, ed. Sergio Beser (Barcelona: Ariel, 1982), pp. 227–45, and most recently, in the centennial year of the death of Leopoldo Alas, in *Notas a 'La Regenta' y otros textos clarinianos*, ed. José García Martín (Oviedo: Ediciones Nobel, 2001), pp. 141–60. These page numbers, identical to the pagination of the original essay in *Archivum*, refer, in a gesture of honour, to Alarcos Llorach's analysis of the geometrical progressions of the structure of *La Regenta*.

5 See Gonzalo Sobejano, 'La inadaptada', *El comentario de textos*, ed. Andrés Amorós (Madrid: Castalia, 1973), pp. 126–66. This essay offers, to date, the most acutely nuanced inquiry into the formal, structural, and thematic aspects of Chapter 16, showing how, in effect,

published in 1984, followed by a translation into French by a team of five scholars in 1987. During 2001, the centennial year of Alas's death, conferences and commemorations were held in Spain, the US, France, England, Mexico and in several Latin American countries. Unlike those early readers of *La Regenta*, we now can appreciate the novel's daringly modern features – features that link Ana Ozores to Martha Stewart.

Noting the modernity of Clarín's novel, John Rutherford points first to the psychology of characters like Ana, her husband don Víctor, her confessor and would-be lover don Fermín, her seducer don Álvaro, and of their socially elitist milieu. Rutherford finds symptoms of neurosis in general and hysteria in particular, evidenced in the free indirect style, a tumult of self-conscious monologues, and representations of fitful, associative trains of thought. Sex is a principal, although often subconscious, motive for behaviour, manifested in foot-fetishism, sadomasochism, lesbianism, male homosexuality and homosocial relations.

Dreams, either repressed or interpreted, and the fact that childhood trauma forms the crux of the plot, limit action to the inside; in Part I, hardly any event of moment occurs outside the mind of characters. Narration evolves through functions of memory, non-verbal communication, and what Alas called 'el estilo latente', which we may roughly translate as the 'underground speaking of a consciousness'.[6] Melodramatic feeling colours scene and setting, tinged either with nostalgia or with the blackness and bitterness of despairing or vindictive minds. In sum, Clarín's metaphors of mind are as modern as the psychological insights that Toobin delivers in his account of Stewart's trial: the more people tried to help, he observes, 'the more excruciating [her] problems became', while the testimony of friends inadvertently gave 'revealing glimpse[s] into Stewart's emotional life' (Toobin 2004: 70). In each case, the trope of realism's mirror also disguises a subjective narrator who nonetheless claims objectivity by contriving (in Clarín's words) a 'reproduction', an

this chapter sums up the entire novel ('contiene en miniatura toda la novela'). The essay has been reprinted, in part, in *Clarín y 'La Regenta'*, ed. Sergio Beser (Barcelona: Ariel, 1982), pp. 187–224.

Gonzalo Sobejano's subsequent work, particularly his edition of *La Regenta*, with introduction, notes, bibliography, and including Galdós's own 'Prólogo', written in 1901, established Clarín's novel as one of Spain's masterpieces, ranking with the *Quijote* and with Galdós's *Fortunata y Jacinta*. This definitive edition, first published in a single volume (Barcelona: Noguer, 1976), appeared revised in two volumes in paperback (Madrid: Castalia, 1981). The most recent (5th) edition was issued by Castalia in 1990.

6 Clarín refers to the term 'estilo latente' in his review of *La desheredada* (1881), recommending the technique to Galdós. See Leopoldo Alas, *La literatura en 1881*, written in collaboration with Armando Palacio Valdés (Madrid: Alfredo de Carlos Hierro, 1882). Sergio Beser refers to this book in connection with Clarín's essay 'Del estilo en novela', reprinted in *Leopoldo Alas: teoría y crítica de la novela española* (Barcelona: Laia, 1972), pp. 51–86.

'exact reflection of life', of 'life as it really' is (Alas 1972: 141). As Gonzalo Sobejano notes, this image of life as it 'really' is centres on the equation of Oviedo with Vetusta: Vetusta, he declares, is the '[n]ombre ficticio de una ciudad antigua que representa a Oviedo, residencia habitual del autor' (I, 93).

Oviedo–Vetusta

The famous opening paragraphs of the novel offer images of Oviedo as Vetusta. The sentence '[l]a heroica ciudad dormía la siesta' and, in the second paragraph, 'Vetusta, la muy noble y leal ciudad' underline the fact that Clarín's text actually starts in the street. The words reflect, in a mimetic gesture, an inscription graven high on the gate leading into Oviedo: 'MUY NOBLE MUY LEAL BENEMERITA INVICTA HEROICA Y BUENA CIUDAD DE OVIEDO'. At the same time, word-pictures of nobility embla-zoned on high, and of the cathedral tower – a 'poema romántico de piedra', a soaring sign and 'delicado himno' of spiritual grace – keep slipping from high to low as the 'heroic city' digests its soups and stews on a still, warm, October afternoon (I, 93). The south wind, blowing through narrow streets, plays with debris: 'polvo [...] paja y papeles' flitter like butterflies, 'migajas' like 'mariposas', in deserted plazas and twisting alleyways (I, 93). This is Vetusta, its name suggesting, through *vetus*, things worn and rancid with age, underscoring the 'casas viejas y ruinosas' (I, 110). Sandy grit chafes and invades the buildings, biting into stone sills and window casements to lie, Clarín writes, 'incrustados' for a day, perhaps, or for years (I, 110). City streets coil into drains that suck in and expel rubbish, configuring anality but also a spiral that continually reverses high and low, inside and outside; this movement compounds opposites and identities, as lovers and confes-sors, husbands and wives, repeatedly change places. Greyness, blackness, obdurate stone, corrosive mixtures, the staining wetness of mud – each motif conjures the metaphorical equation Oviedo–Vetusta.

Through this basic equation Clarín develops an imagistic discourse that exploits all the senses. To create the impression of density and overlay, he assembles, as we have seen, collages of intertexts and of mixed media: painting, music, architecture and drama. He also projects scenes through sensory expe-rience: fragrance or stench, wetness and dryness, light and darkness. Admix-tures of verbal and visual gestures leech away transparency as words dissolve into glances, glances fade into silences, and silences are encoded in elliptical dots or cinematographic cuts from one chapter to another.

The plot of the novel derives in part from popular literature traditionally sold on the street, such as Spanish imitations and adaptations of the French serial novel. Traces of this mixed and 'translated' origin can be seen, for example, in don Álvaro, whose self-conscious pose as a 'sentimental disimulado' is modelled on the *folletín* (II, 49). The Marquesa reads salon fiction – 'peste nacida en Francia' as Galdós phrased it (1999: 126) – while her son Paco, the dissolute heir, enjoys popular pornographic novels such as the *Historia de la prostitución* by Dufour or Dumas's *La Dama de las Camelias* ... 'y sus derivados' (I: 290).

Everything appears derivative, borrowed, stolen, or appropriated from somewhere else; even the cook, Pedro, spits out half-digested ideas culled from newspapers in an attempt to imitate his fashionable masters. Visitación, in the manner of a magpie, pockets lumps of sugar and borrows language from her past love-affair to enliven the picture of a future seduction, in her 'performance' of Ana in the throes of hysteria. In this realist novel, imitation and copies inform thought and action, as characters ape one another in dress, manner and gesture, and as they style speech and action after cultural artefacts both 'high' and 'low': salon fiction, newspaper articles and classic works of art.

Thus 'popular', street-smart, literary pieces commingle with 'high' or 'classic' cultural icons to shape the vividly dense intertextuality of *La Regenta*. Allusions, copies, parodies, satiric reprises and replays give a particularly 'Spanish' tilt to literary realism, a tilt reminiscent of the translations and interpolated stories that make up the sliding surfaces of the *Quijote* (1605, 1615), or the reiteration of mirror images in Velázquez's *Las Meninas* (1656). Such images and reflections produce the illusion of doubled identities and spaces, inside and outside the novel or the painting.

La Regenta displays its own mixed, mediated, character which is replicated anew in two films (1974, 1994). The more recent of these, a series of 13 episodes made for television, exploits the cinematographic qualities of the original text and returns the novel to the streets.

> Fue feliz [...] la versión de TVE de Méndez-Leite, en capítulos, con la bella, sutil, y sospechosamente perversa Aitana Sánchez-Gijón dando cuerpo a la soñadora y victimada Ana. No faltaron sin embargo voces del canon ovetense que consideraban irreverente el apellido de la actriz, casi una provocación. (Silva Ciénfuegos-Jovellanos 1999: I, 7)

Even now, mediated through film, the production of *La Regenta* continues to provoke comment – reminscent of disputes during the year of publication – while engaging an aesthetic, social and civic reversal. Once again, Clarín's novel has turned a real site, present-day Oviedo, into a textual and pictorial space.

Vetusta–Oviedo

Greyness is gone. The cathedral tower has been restored to a golden glow, and a bookstore commemorates Clarín. Oviedo's new, bright, Hotel Magistral invites us to enter, offering all the cushioned comforts of privacy, as in the house of El Gran Constantino. The Hotel also offers *salones* named Quintanar, Ozores and Mesía, where this adulterous triangle welcomes the 'Asociacion de los Dentistas de Oviedo' for their regular meetings. 'Cafeterías' and estate agencies – 'La Regenta Inmobilario', 'Vetusta Grupo Inmobilario' – reiterate the concept of realism as 'thing-ism', as real estate, while store fronts and shopping malls gesture mimetically towards sites in the novel: 'Óptica Vetusta' recalls both the Magistral's and the narrator's spyglass. Las Salesas – that 'pocilga [...] arrinconad[a] dentro de Vetusta, cerca de los vertederos de la Encimada, casi sepultad[a] en las cloacas' (I: 112–13) – is now a brightly lit 'Centro Comercial'. Traces of the former convent, however, visibly persist through the overlay of this new, refurbished identity; for, as we recall, in *La Regenta* the health of Carraspique's daughter (the tubercular Rosita interned as Sor Teresa in the *convento-cloaca* of Las Salesas) had been 'negotiated' as a commercial object. Sor Teresa's pitiful role was to advertise in Vetusta the ecclesiastical power of don Fermín. In this sense, today's Las Salesas merely exploits an older commercial identity as a specifically underground mall; it retraces the outlines of that ancient, spectral convent 'casi sepultad[o] en las cloacas'.

A mural, which re-envisions the illustrations of Juan Llimoña, inserts the public transformation of a real site into the spectacle of mixed media – painting, novel and film. Clarín as narrator participates visibly in this new, mediated 'text'. Disguised in the novel as an all-knowing outsider, in this mural he almost flaunts his participation in the telling of the story as he presides over the city. The text's mutations have turned Oviedo into a set of civic, artistic and public images that recast the mimetic relation Oviedo–Vetusta as a site of metaphorical exchange. In this exchange, *La Regenta* has become a living event. By generating these copies, the novel also appears to have achieved a kind of knowledge about itself as an urban space, just as Ana and Visitación, through their performative replicas, gained knowledge of themselves and of their past and present lives within the 'framing' environment of Vetusta.

In the opening chapter the narrator adapted his text to the inscription in stone that serves as a gateway to Oviedo, and that today waves as a banner over the Madrid Book Fair. One hundred years later Oviedo has not only replicated the novel's words and signs; it has also reinvented characters and scenes. Walking towards the cathedral on the street named la Rúa we meet Ana Ozores, la Regenta, now a life-size bronze sculpture on her way to that last, devastating, scene. She is seen as more 'real' than Oviedo's own citizens: 'La Regenta, por su parte, es más real que la mayoría de las mujeres (y hombres), en el sentido de no ser una mera pantalla en la que se reflejan los espectros culturales y morales, sino un espectro en estado puro' (Silva Ciénfuegos-Jovellanos 1999: II, 8). Skirts rustle, her gloved hand fingers a rosary, a huge hat slants over her brow, and her eyes – wide and apprehensive – convey a mixture of hope and uncertainty:

> Esos ojos enormes, la carita en forma de corazón, desmintiendo que la perfección vaya en estos tiempos unida al óvalo, la boca grande, la naricilla, el largo cuello, y una presentida melancolía en la mirada, que no llega a derrumbarse en tristeza plena, sino que todavía aguarda una redención, son un acierto, por la ruptura del canón clásico, que casi nunca logra despertar la concupiscencia. Una regenta *resultona*.
>
> (Silva Ciénfuegos-Jovellanos 1999: I, 7)

At night a spotlight picks out her figure, reflecting the action of the spyglass of her priestly lover-confessor. The spotlight also recalls the voyeuristic narrator, who spies on her like the rest of Vetusta, letting his eyes caress her beautiful body as she takes her ease on the tiger skin, half-fearing, but not realizing, that somebody is indeed watching.

Civic Celebrities

In Vetusta–Oviedo *everyone* is watching Ana Ozores. Re-created as an 'escultura', her forms exhibit – quite literally – the 'perfección plástica' that all Vetusta admires and envies (I, 332). Once childless and bereft of friends and family, she stands now as a welcoming civic mother, a celebrity always in the spotlight. And since Martha Stewart was sentenced to five months in a federal jail and five months of 'tasteful house arrest' she, too, in this afterlife, is more in the spotlight than ever (Angell 2004: 21). Every day brings a spate of press comment and cartoons: 'Martha Stewed' pictures Judge Cederbaum placing the lid on Martha's head in a steaming pot; 'Stewart as Muse' informs the winning entry of a bad-writing contest in California; a lead story in the *Wall Street Journal* (reported in *The New York Times*, 18 July 2004) points up the 'Kabuki-like quality to the drama' (4:1).

These representations only enliven the realism of the stories of Ana and of Martha, stories already made melodramatic and *folletinesca* in their mixtures of high and low, truth and lies, fiction and reality. Each is a current piece of cultural production: the bibliography on *La Regenta* grows apace, as shown in the number of volumes catalogued by Noel Valis (in press). The price of stock in 'Martha Stewart Living Omnimedia' went up 37% the day after her sentencing (Angell 2004: 21). Like the temptation of that sequined shawl in Galdós's *La de Bringas* (1884), a temptation as fresh as the day's headlines – '[p]arece que lo han traído los periódicos de anoche' writes the narrator (Pérez Galdós 1967: 58) – nineteenth-century realism holds its own in today's popular press. In July 2004 *Anna Karenina* (1875–77), in a new translation, appeared on the bestseller list of *The New York Times Book Review*.[7]

List of Works Cited

Anon., 2004. *Chronicle of Higher Education*, 10 September: 51–3, B4

Anon., 2004. *The New York Times*, 18 July: 4:1

Alarcos Llorach, Emilio, 1982. 'Notas a La Regenta', in *Clarín y La Regenta*, ed. Sergio Beser (Barcelona: Ariel), pp. 227–45

Alas, Leopoldo (Clarín), 1972. 'Del naturalismo', *La Diana* (April 1882), in Sergio Beser, *Leopoldo Alas: teoría y crítica de la novela española* (Barcelona: Laia), pp. 108–53

——, 1981, *La Regenta*, ed. Gonzalo Sobejano, 2 vols (Madrid: Castalia) [Original edn 1884–85]

Angell, Roger, 2004. 'Comment. Big Doings', *The New Yorker*, 2 August: 21–2

Balzar, John, 2001. 'Latest Bumble Shows Trashy Side of Bush Administration', *Los Angeles Times*, reprinted in the *Lincoln Journal Star*, 31 August: 5B

Blackburn, Simon, 2001. 'Logical Humanism', *The New Republic*, 17 and 24 April: 95–6

Charnon Deutsch, 1989. 'Voyeurism, Pornography and *La Regenta*', *Modern Language Studies*, 4 (Fall): 93–101

Dickstein, Morris, 2003. 'Literary Theory and Historical Understanding', *Chronicle of Higher Education*, 23 May: B7–10

Dyson, Freeman, 2003. 'What a World!', *The New York Review of Books*, 15 May: 4–6

Furst, Lilian R., 1992. *Realism* (New York: Longman)

Kern, Stephen, 2004. 'The Next Big Thing', *Chronicle of Higher Education*: B4

Labanyi, Jo, 2000. *Gender and Modernization in the Spanish Realist Novel* (Oxford: Oxford University Press)

Levin, Harry, 1963. *The Gates of Horn: A Study of Five French Realists* (New York: Oxford University Press)

McLemee, 2004. 'Keeping It Real', *Chronicle of Higher Education*, 30 July: A11

Pérez Galdós, Benito, 1999. 'Observaciones sobre la novela contemporánea',

---

7 Leo Tolstoy, *Anna Karenina*, trans. Richard Pevear and Larissa Volokhonsky (Penguin, 2003), posted number 12 in the list of paperback bestsellers in *The New York Times Book Review*, 25 July 2004: 20.

in *Ensayos de crítica literaria*, ed. Laureano Bonet (Barcelona: Ediciones Península), pp. 123–39

——, 1967. *La de Bringas*, ed. Ricardo Gullón (Englewood Cliffs: Prentice Hall)

Rutherford, John (trans.), 1984. 'Introduction' to *La Regenta* (Athens: University of Georgia Press), pp. 7–17

Sieburth, Stephanie, 1994. *Inventing High and Low. Literature, Mass Culture, and Uneven Modernity in Spain* (Durham: Duke University Press)

Silva Ciénfuegos-Jovellanos, Pedro, 1999 and 2001. 'Prólogo' to Isaac del Rivero, *Leopoldo Alas, La Regenta*, Guión y dibujos, 2 vols (Gijón: Esmena editores)

Taylor, Mark C., 1999. *The Picture in Question. Mark Tansey and the Ends of Representation* (Chicago: University of Chicago Press)

Toobin, Jeffrey, 2004. 'The Bad Thing', *The New Yorker*, 22 March: 60–72

Wood, James, 2003. 'The Unwinding Stair', *The New Republic*, 10 March: 25–30

TRANSLATION STUDIES AND PEDAGOGY

Illustrating the Language: The Cultural Role of Translation in the Spanish Renaissance

JEREMY LAWRANCE

In 1534 Garcilaso de la Vega wrote in his prologue to Juan Boscán's translation of Castiglione's *Il libro del cortegiano*:

> tengo por muy prinçipal el benefiçio que se haze a la lengua castellana en poner en ella cosas que merezcan ser leídas; porque yo no sé qué desventura á sido sienpre la nuestra, que apenas á nadie escrito en nuestra lengua sino lo que se pudiera muy bien escusar, aunque esto sería malo de provar con los que traen entre las manos estos libros que matan hombres.
>
> (1534: fol. 3ᵛ)

In writing off the dead-weight of medieval killer-books as a thing better dispensed with, Garcilaso was proclaiming the advent of the Renaissance on Spanish soil. The prologue was his manifesto for a new prose, just as Boscán's prologue to their collected poetry ten years later was to be a manifesto for a new poetry (Boscán 1543). Boscán advanced the paradoxical claim that the birth of the new depended on imitation of the old – had, in effect, to be a rebirth. Garcilaso likewise asserts that a principal *benefit* one can do one's native language is not by writing original works, but by translating foreign ones.

Behind this claim lay a Renaissance commonplace about 'illustrating' the vulgar languages – that is, making them illustrious, raising them to the lustre of literary speech through imitation of more prestigious languages. But how

A first version of this paper was given at the British Academy's symposium *Translation, Knowledges and Cultures* (4 December 2000) at the invitation of Nick Round, to whom I am grateful for so many marks of long and generous affection, as well as for the gift of his *magnum opus* on Pero Díaz, which set me on the present path. I also thank Lucia Binotti, Pedro Cátedra, Isabel Hernández, Tomàs Martínez Romero, María Morrás, Roxana Recio, Peter Russell, Guillermo Serés and Mirko Tavoni for invaluable gifts of books listed in the bibliography and all kinds of good fellowship; and the editors of this volume for their kindness.

did this differ from the project of the chorus of writers in fifteenth-century Spain who dedicated themselves with earnest passion to the task of translating classical texts? For it appears that Garcilaso's assault on 'libros que matan hombres' was aimed at these very men. It picks up a phrase in Boscán's own prologue to *El cortesano*, where as part of a diatribe against the 'vanidad baxa y de hombres de pocas letras' of those who go about *romançando libros*, Boscán tells the story of a man who found the Roman anecdotalist Valerius Maximus killed dead, as it were, by his Spanish translator:

> hallando a *Valerio Máximo* en romançe y andando rebolviéndole un gran rato de hoja en hoja sin parar en nada, preguntado por otro qué hazía, respondió que buscava a Valerio Máximo. (1534: fols 2r–3r, 'A la muy manífica señora doña Gerónima Palova de Almogávar', at fol. 2r)

The translation in question was the *Valerio Máximo* of Hugo de Urriés, made from the French of Simon de Hesdin and Nicholas de Gonesse in 1477 and printed with a fresh dedication to Ferdinand the Catholic before 1492.[1] That Garcilaso's 'estos libros que matan hombres' is to be taken in relation to these words of Boscán – remembering that the two together prepared *El cortesano* for the press in Barcelona in April–May 1533 – is suggested not only by the demonstrative *estos* but by verbal echoes earlier in the paragraph, where Garcilaso's phrase 'le vía siempre aborrecerse con los que *romançan libros*, aunque él a esto *no lo llama romançar*' (Garcilaso 1534: fol. 3r; my italics) picks up Boscán's passage on those who *romançan libros*,

> acordándome del mal que he dicho muchas veces de estos romançistas, aunque traduçir este libro *no es propriamente romançalle* sino mudalle de una lengua vulgar en otra. (1534: fol. 2r; my italics)[2]

It is no coincidence that in his prolix prologue Urriés boasted that by bringing Valerius Maximus back from his travels in Burgundy he was conferring a

---

[1]   Identified by Russell (1985: 37 n.). The existence of a lost pre-1492 edition of *Valerio Máximo* is deduced from a reference to the progress of the Granada war in Urriés's prologue; the book was reprinted in 1495, 1514, 1529 and 1541.

[2]   Terracini (1964: 84–5 n. 59), 'il cenno di Garcilaso [...] sorge in evidente riferimento (anche nella struttura sintattica della ripresa concessiva) al passo in cui Boscán si sofferma sul termine *romanzar*'. Garcilaso also returns to the target of his attack at the end of his prologue with a remark that 'esta tradución' offers 'vengança de cualquier otra que uviera' (1534: fol. 4r). We may thus discard out of hand the desperate guess that 'libros que matan hombres' refers to romances of chivalry, hazarded in passing by Menéndez Pelayo in 1908 without evidence (1945: 97 n. 1, '¿Aludirá a los de caballería?') and repeated by all commentators (e.g. Garcilaso 1911: 225 n. 54; 1925: 296 n. on 203.17; 1981: 488 n.; doubts only in Terracini 1964: 87 and n. 64). See also n. 12 and n. 18, below.

singular benefit on his homeland (1495: fols 3v–5v). This lent added point to Garcilaso's remarks on the 'benefiçio' done to the Castilian language by Boscán's *Cortesano*.

Fifteenth- and early sixteenth-century Spain produced an extraordinary number of translations like Urriés's, not only of Latin but also of Greek, Hebrew, French and Italian authors; there were perhaps more such translations into Spanish than into any other language in Christendom.[3] This serves to underline how surprising Garcilaso's complaint about the lack of a precedent illustrious tradition in Spanish really is. His prologue goes to the heart of translation's role in illustrating the language by confronting us with the problem of what it was that Garcilaso had in mind that differed from the medieval cult of the antique and the attempts of Juan de Mena and his followers to ennoble Castilian by a wholesale process of Latinization through lexical and syntactical calques.

For these medieval predecessors, as for Garcilaso himself, Latin was a dead language, one that had to be artificially acquired through book-learning; moreover its synthetic grammar differed typologically from the Romance vernacular. Despite such practical disadvantages, they chose Latin as the yardstick of linguistic perfection because of a prestige deriving from its relation to divine scripture and ancient learning. For medieval schoolmen, however, this choice was justified not by cultural factors but by a profound epistemological difference. Since Latin was putatively a language used by God (on a par with the speech inspired in Adam at the ceremonial naming of the world, Genesis 2: 19–20), they posited a difference in kind between this divine language of origin (*grammatica*) and actual human languages (*idiomata*). According to them the spoken idioms were ephemeral, unstable and formless natural sprouts, whereas the written classical grammar was timeless, fixed and artificial (governed by rules or craft, *ars*). Consequently grammar (that is, Latin) could be thought of as prior to and more noble than idioms, as a kind of Platonic idea or archetype of linguistic perfection from

---

3 Alvar (2005) makes statistics from a sample of 90 fifteenth-century translations by 60 hands, from the gross total of 1,782 Iberian translations before 1500 (over 25% of the extant medieval corpus). Since Monfrin (1964, 1972) and Beardsley (1970) first raised the problem of definition posed by the fifteenth-century 'pre-Renaissance' of vernacular humanism there has arisen a sizeable literature on the translators: see the bibliographies, studies and texts in Beardsley (1979), Santoyo (1987, 1996), Santoyo *et al.* (1987–89), Recio (1995a), Hernández González (1998), Martínez Romero and Recio (2001), González Rolán, Saquero Suárez-Somonte and López Fonseca (2002), and Coroleu (2004); Menéndez Pelayo (1950–53, 1952–53) remains indispensable. Surveys are given by Morreale (1959a, 1959b: 15–26), Russell (1985), Lawrance (1986); and see above all the monograph by Round (1993), followed by Morrás (1996), Serés (1997) and Martínez Romero (1998).

which vulgar languages descend – in a metaphysical or dialectic rather than genetic sense – as shadows.

This scholastic notion of the hierarchy of languages and priority of Latin serves to highlight the novelty of what was going forward with the Renaissance project to illustrate the vulgar idioms through imitation. According to the scholastics only the indefectible rationality and compendious abundance of the classical language was capable of representing concepts perfectly; translation was therefore a doomed exercise. Enrique de Villena stated in his *Traslación de la Eneida* of 1427 – with a tortuous diction that encapsulates and enacts the strange drama to be discussed in these pages – that his 'rudiçia e insufiçiençia' did not permit 'tan elevada materia a las usadas humiliar palabras, nin equivalentes fallar vocablos en la romançial texedura para expremir aquellos angélicos conçebimientos virgilianos'.[4]

This traditional attitude, expressed as a formula of modesty in countless fifteenth-century translators' prologues, is given logical form in Dante's *Convivio*, written c. 1305, where the 'sovereignty' of Latin is said to reside in three things: *nobiltà* of uncorruptibility – that is, its existence in a synchronic stasis beyond time and the sublunary realm of linguistic change; *virtù* ('potency') of proximity to original concepts – in medieval terms its realism, its distance from mere nominalism; and *belleza* of harmony, by which Dante seems to mean an aesthetic pleasure in the patterned artificiality of the rules of concord in Latin's inflected grammar (*arte*).[5] However, these statements occur in the context of an apology for *not* writing in Latin (if Latin is sovereign it cannot be subject to the vernacular in a commentary on Italian poetry). In *De vulgari eloquentia*, also dated c. 1305, Dante entirely reverses the argument by stating, this time in Latin, that the spoken *volgare* is 'more noble' than *grammatica*:

---

[4] 'Carta al rey de Navarra', in Villena (1994: 5–13 (p. 5)). In the 'Prohemio', 15–62 (p. 15), Villena repeats, more simply though still not quite in Spanish, that in the 'vulgar lengua [...] por mengua de vocablos non se puede tan propiamente significar los conçebimientos mentales segúnd en la lengua latina se fazer puede'. For the topic of the inferiority of the vernacular in fifteenth-century Spain, see the studies cited in n. 3 above; the most extensive example is El Tostado's commentary on St Jerome's prologue to Eusebius's *Chronici canones*, written for the Marquis of Santillana c. 1450 (Madrigal 1506: fols 5r–25v, Caps. iv–xvii; see Keightley (1977); Recio (1991, 1995b); Wittlin (1998)).

[5] *Convivio* I.v, in Dante (1924: 242): 'Per *nobiltà*, perchè il latino è perpetuo e non corruttibile, e il volgare è non istabile e corruttibile. [...] Per *virtù*: ciascuna cosa è virtuosa in sua natura che fa quello a che ella è ordinata [...]; onde, conciossiacosachè lo latino molte cose manifesta concepute nella mente che il volgare fare non può [...], più è la virtù sua che quella del volgare. [...] Per *belleza*: quella cosa dice l'uomo essere bella, le cui parti debitamente si rispondono, perchè dalla loro armonia resulta piacimento; [...] dunque quello sermone è più bello nel quale più debitamente si rispondono [le voci], e più debitamente si rispondono in latino che in volgare, però che lo volgare seguita uso e lo latino arte.'

vulgarem locutionem appellamus eam qua infantes adsuefiunt ab adsisten-
tibus quum primitus distinguere voces incipiunt; vel, quod brevius dici
potest, [...] quam sine omni regula nutricem imitantes accipimus. Est et
inde alia locutio secundaria nobis, quam Romani *grammaticam* vocaverunt;
[...] ad habitum vero huius pauci perveniunt, quia non nisi per spatium
temporis et studii assiduitatem regulamur et doctrinamur in illa. Harum
quoque duarum nobilior est vulgaris, tum quia prima fuit humano generi
usitata, tum quia totus orbis ipsa perfruitur licet in diversas prolationes et
vocabula sit divisa, tum quia naturalis est nobis, quum illa potius artificialis
existat.[6]

This is designed to combat the medieval argument about linguistic hierarchy
point by point. It asserts that natural speech is prior to and more universal
than written grammar, and more noble precisely because less artificial.
Dante's implied conclusion – that the aptest medium for the expression of
thought is one's native language – set the scene for the ensuing illustration
of vulgar languages. He, indeed, gave currency to the expression 'illustrious
vernacular'.[7]

In cinquecento Italy the details of Dante's argument led to a controversy
known as the *questione della lingua*, but his basic premise, the reversal of the
scholastic linguistic hierarchy, was accepted without demur. 'Io ho per fermo,'
announced the humanist Sperone Speroni in his 'Dialogo delle lingue',

> che le lingue d'ogni paese, cosi l'arabica et l'indiana come la romana et
> l'atheniese, siano d'un medesmo valore, et da mortali ad un fine con un
> giudicio formate. [...] Dunque non nascono le lingue per se medesme a
> guisa di alberi o d'herbe, [...] ma ogni loro vertù nasce al mondo dal voler
> de' mortali. (Speroni 1542: fol. 125)

Speroni's statement sums up in a nutshell the significance of the Renaissance
(if there is one): it replaces a static medieval theocentric induction about the
origins of language with a dynamic, sceptical deduction from historical and

---

6 *De vulgari eloquentia* I.i, in Dante (1924: 379): 'I define *vulgar speech* as that which
infants acquire by practice from those around them when they first begin to distinguish words;
or, to put it more briefly, [...] which we receive without any rules by imitating our nurse.
Besides this we have another, secondary speech which the Romans called *grammar*; [...]
however, few achieve fluency in this because only by long and assiduous study can we teach
ourselves its rules. And of the two, the more noble is the vulgar, both because it was the first
used by the human race, and because everybody uses it despite differences of pronunciation
and vocabulary, and finally because it is natural to us whereas the other is artificial'.

7 *De vulgari eloquentia* I.xi: 'illustrem Italiae [...] loquelam' (Dante 1924: 385); I.xiii:
'Tuscos, qui [...] titulum sibi vulgaris illustris arrogare videntur' (386); I.xiv: 'vulgare illustre'
(387); I.xv: 'aulicum et illustre' (388); I.xvi and xvii–xix, *passim*: 'illustre, cardinale, aulicum,
et curiale vulgare' (388–90).

cultural relativity that puts man's will centre-stage. The significant items are
that Speroni takes it for granted that speech is prior to writing and that no
language can be incomplete or inferior to any other in its ability to express
meanings; from this it is a short step to severing altogether the supposititious
causal relation between God, language and things. With still clearer relevance
to our theme, Joachim Du Bellay wrote in his *Défense et illustration de la
langue française* that the 'diversité et confusion' of human languages after
Babel, since it came into the world 'du vouloir et arbitre des mortelz', admits
no *a priori* reason for thinking that some may be 'plus aptes à porter le faiz
des conceptions humaines':

> on ne doit ainsi louer une langue et blâmer l'autre, veu qu'elles viennent
> toutes d'une mesme source et origine – c'est la fantasie des hommes – et
> ont été formées [...] pour signifier entre nous les conceptions et intel-
> ligences de l'esprit. Il est vrai que, par succession de tens, les unes pour
> avoir été plus curieusement reiglées sont devenues plus riches que les
> autres; mais cela ne se doit attribuer à la félicité desdites langues, ains au
> seul artifice et industrie des hommes.
>
> (1549: fols A4r–A4v, Livre i, Chap. i, 'L'origine des langues')

If all languages are potentially able to express all knowledge, the only reason
why the vernacular should be less good at doing so than Latin must be that
native speakers, unlike the Romans, have been too lazy to foster their own
idiom. Du Bellay therefore attacks the sottish arrogance of those savants
who raise a 'more than Stoic' eyebrow of disdain at everything written in
French, thinking it 'incapable de toutes bonnes lettres et érudition'. The key,
he affirms, lies not in ignoring or despairing of the vernacular, but in cultivating and improving it by imitation of the wealth and excellence of more
prestigious languages.

Such was the theory that lay behind the project of illustration taken up
by writers and thinkers in sixteenth-century Europe. The theory helps us
to understand how the embellishment of the vernacular fitted within the
cultural parameters of the Renaissance, and why it is only an apparent
paradox that an age that takes its name from the revival of Antiquity in fact
witnessed the definitive triumph of the modern languages. Nevertheless,
as Nick Round reminds us, in the field of translation there lie mysterious
and perhaps unbridgeable gaps between theory and practice.[8] As the Italian
concept of *illustre volgare* was exported to other kingdoms it took on specific

---

8   Round ('Translation: Theory and Practice' 1993: 131–47); note especially his distinction
between 'views which are held (or deemed to be held) by a [...] practitioner as their particular
"theory of translation"' and the broader 'context of assumptions' which inform practice but are
not formulated as a theory (131).

configurations according to local conditions; these affected what illustrating the vernacular might mean in practical terms. In Protestant Germany and England religious factors were paramount and it was Luther's and Tyndale's translations of the Bible which set in train the formation of a national *Schriftsprache*. In France the debate depended more closely on Italian models – parts of Du Bellay's *Défense et illustration* are lifted bodily from Speroni – but it ignored the Italian preoccupation with standardization of a supra-regional dialect, substituting instead a chauvinist dispute about the status of the medieval French classics. In Portugal, which preserved little esteem for its indigenous medieval literature, the chief concern of the literature on the dignity of Portuguese was to demonstrate that language's closer proximity to Latin and hence superiority to its rival, Spanish.[9]

The only constant of these national movements of linguistic illustration is their assumption that, in hammering a particular vernacular into a new linguistic canon, the dominant role would be played not by politics or popular culture but by poets and scholars. Spain was something of an exception. Spanish ideologues of the illustrious vernacular showed little interest in the question of adjudicating between regional dialects, less in the competing claims of Aragonese, Galician, Valencian, or Catalan, and none at all in other Iberian languages.[10] Instead they based their assertions of the illustrious pre-eminence of Castilian on the idea of their monarchy's inheritance of Rome's imperial role. A classic example occurs in Antonio de Nebrija's *Gramática de la lengua castellana* (1492), written before the discovery of the New World and long before Charles V's coronation as Holy Roman Emperor. To justify his paradoxical enterprise of writing a grammar of an idiom, Nebrija opens with the following statement:

[9]   See, for example, Dionisotti (1968) and Tavoni (1984) on Italy, Besch (1999) and McGrath (2001) on Germany and England, Norton (1984) on France, and Barros (1959) on Portugal, with further bibliography in Lawrance (2000).

[10]   See the texts in Pastor (1929) and general studies in Terracini (1964), Melczer (1981), Ynduráin (1982), Carrera de la Red (1988) and Binotti (1995). It is true that later enemies of Nebrija sniped at his Andalusianisms (e.g. Asís (1935), Sola-Solé (1974), Asensio and Alcina Rovira (1980); and see especially Valdés (1982: 124): 'aunque Librija era muy docto en la lengua latina, [...] no se puede negar que era andaluz y no castellano, y que scrivió aquel su *Vocabulario* con tan poco cuidado que parece averlo escrito por burla'), but the regional question had long since been decided in favour of standard Castilian; as early as 1493 the Sicilian court humanist Luca de' Marini, after praising Spanish as the least corrupt of the Romance vernaculars and hence the sweetest and most abundant ('Graeca quidem et Latina exceptis, alias sine dubio omnes quae ab his duabas corruptae fuerunt et vocabulorum copia et pronunciationis suavitate longissime prestat; sola namque Hispanorum est lingua quae minus a Latino sermone et loquendi arte discessit'), asserts that of all its dialects – among which he counts Catalan, etc. – Castilian is by far the best, the true Attic of Spanish (Marineus Siculus c. 1495: fol. 33r–33v, Lib. iii, [6] 'De Hispanorum hominum moribus'). See also the quote from Santamaría in the following note.

[Q]uando bien comigo pienso, mui esclarecida reina, i pongo delante
los ojos el antigüedad de todas las cosas que para nuestra recordación et
memoria quedaron escriptas, una cosa hallo et saco por conclusión mui
cierta: que siempre la lengua fue compañera del imperio, et de tal manera
lo siguió que juntamente començaron, crecieron, et florecieron.

(Lebrixa 1492: fol. A2r)[11]

The classical languages of Jews, Greeks and Romans had died with the fall
of their respective empires; now it was the turn of 'nuestra lengua castellana',
which, having lived out its *niñez* in the age of the judges of Castile and flexed
its adolescent muscles under Alfonso X, had spread to Aragón and Navarre
and Italy, 'siguiendo la compañía de los infantes que embiamos a imperar en
aquellos reinos', and was now poised for even greater triumphs (fol. A3v).
This connection between political power and linguistic prestige led Nebrija
to the revolutionary idea that Spanish, as an imperial language, must have a
rational structure of its own which, like Latin, could be reduced to an *arte*
or grammar – an idea which he expounds in a passage that contains both
a precocious variant of the illustration topic and a now familiar claim that
Castilian literature up to that moment consisted of 'things that could be better
dispensed with':

Ésta [*i.e.* la lengua] hasta nuestra edad anduvo suelta et fuera de regla, et a
esta causa á recebido en pocos siglos muchas mudanças [...]. I porque mi
pensamiento et gana siempre fue *engrandecer las cosas de nuestra nación*
et dar a los ombres de mi lengua *obras en que mejor puedan emplear
su ocio*, que agora lo gastan leiendo novelas o istorias embueltas en mil
mentiras et errores, acordé ante todas las otras cosas reduzir en artificio este
nuestro lenguaje castellano, para que lo que agora et de aquí adelante en él
se escriviere pueda quedar en un tenor et estenderse en toda la duración de
los tiempos que están por venir, como vemos que se á hecho en la lengua
griega et latina, las cuales por aver estado debaxo de arte, aunque sobre
ellas an passado muchos siglos, todavía quedan en una uniformidad.

(Lebrixa 1492: fol. A3v; my italics)[12]

---

[11] On the phrase 'compañera del imperio' Asensio (1960: 403–4) points out that language
and empire were coupled even earlier by Gonzalo de Santamaría in his translation of Jerome's
Vitae patrum (Santamaría c. 1486–90: fol. A1, 'deliberé de poner la obra presente en lengua
castellana porque la fabla comúnmente [...] sigue al imperio'); but in this case the point was
to justify Santamaría's abandonment of his native Aragonese for the more prestigious Castilian.
On Nebrija's classical and humanist sources, notably Augustine and Valla, see Braselmann
(1991, 1993), Klein (1995) and Lawrance (forthcoming).

[12] The phrase 'novelas o istorias embueltas en mil mentiras et errores' has been interpreted
as another reference to romances of chivalry (see n. 2 above; the phrase is cited as a parallel
for 'libros que matan hombres' in Garcilaso 1995: 267 n. 9 and 532 n. 267.9°), but a cursory
reading shows that Nebrija meant the works of 'cronistas et estoriadores' referred to a few lines

The startlingly prophetic nature of Nebrija's boast about Castilian's world destiny should not blind us to the way his linguistic concepts sprang from traditional lines of scholastic and humanist debate. The true novelty of his claim was not its political foresight – Nebrija had none, his ensuing statements about imposing the glorious yoke of Spanish on 'pueblos bárbaros' being, at the time of writing, no more than flatulent toadying to his royal patron – but rather in his acute perception of diachronic linguistic change, his ruthless desacralization of the classic languages' prestige, and his conviction that grammar was no distinctive property of the artificial languages but a thing inherent in all language, that needed only to be invented (in the etymological sense) by human ingenuity. The *Gramática* thus sought to demonstrate that Spanish was capable not only of the extraordinary feat of *having* a grammar in the first place, but also of equalling Latin in every department of art and science; it therefore included discussions of prosody and rhetoric as well as orthography, morphology and vocabulary.

Such imperial confidence gave the Spanish humanists' programme for illustrating their language several distinctive features. Not the least striking, given Nebrija's anticipation of Garcilaso's complaint about the lack of an illustrating canon of texts in Spanish, is his declaration in the selfsame prologue to the *Gramática* of almost the opposite view, namely that Castilian had by his day reached its maturity and was 'tanto en la cumbre, que más se puede temer el desçendimiento della que esperar la subida' (Lebrixa 1492: fol. A4r). This curious inflection allowed him to mention with approval – and lickspittle attention to his patron's royal sensibilities – Alfonso X's patronage of the *Siete Partidas*, *General estoria*, and many books 'trasladados [...] de latín et arávigo' (fol. A3r), and to adorn his grammar with examples from Mena and other fifteenth-century writers, so that Persius and Gómez Manrique could be simultaneously adduced to exemplify the substantive use of an infinitive.

Nevertheless, Nebrijas's strictures against 'tales and histories wrapped in a thousand lies and mistakes' show that these gambits, though justified by an impeccable criterion of *uso* as his guiding principle, were a form of denial. Behind them lurked unease at the lack of a canon of Spanish classics on which to base an elegant standard language, an unease compounded, like everything else in Spanish humanism, by envy of Italy.[13] Garcilaso, nearly

later, and that by 'errores' he meant linguistic mistakes, not *erranzas*. This is not to deny the important connection between Nebrija's and Garcilaso's statements (despite the limited circulation of the *Gramática*), but throughout Nebrija's prologue, historiography – or, as he defined it, the glorification of princes – forms the burden of his concern to illustrate and hence eternalize the language.

[13] To Juan Manuel Rozas belongs the merit of having divined the omnipotent role of competition with Italy in early modern Spanish culture (1984: 425–6); the point is developed in relation to Nebrija in Lawrance (forthcoming).

fifty years later, was still preoccupied with the same problem. It was also raised by his Erasmian contemporary Juan de Valdés, like him attached to the Spanish colonial regime in Naples, with his call for the illustration of Spanish at the start of *Diálogo de la lengua*, written *c*. 1535–40. There the authorial character counters a request from the Italians Marcio and Coriolano and his countryman Torres to discourse on his native language – '¡cosa tan baja y plebeya como es punticos y primorcicos de lengua vulgar!' – with the following exchange:

> VALDÉS. —[…] he aprendido la lengua latina por arte y libros, y la castellana por uso; de manera que de la latina podría dar cuenta por el arte y por los libros en que la aprendí, y de la castellana no, sino por el uso común de hablar, por donde tengo razón de juzgar por cosa fuera de propósito que me queráis demandar cuenta de lo que está fuera de toda cuenta. […]
>
> MARCIO. —Me pesa oíros decir eso. ¿Cómo, y os parece a vos que el Bembo perdió su tiempo en el libro que hizo sobre la lengua toscana? [...] Prueba que todos los hombres somos más obligados *a ilustrar y enriquecer la lengua que nos es natural* y que mamamos en las tetas de nuestras madres, que no la que nos es pegadiza y que aprendemos en libros.[14] […] ¿No tenéis por tan elegante y gentil la lengua castellana como la toscana?
>
> VALDÉS. —Sí que la tengo, pero también la tengo por más vulgar, porque veo que la toscana está ilustrada y enriquecida por un Boccaccio y un Petrarca, los cuales […] no solamente se preciaron de escribir buenas cosas, pero procuraron escribirlas con estilo muy propio y muy elegante; y, como sabéis, *la lengua castellana nunca ha tenido quien escriba en ella con tanto cuidado y miramiento cuanto sería menester* para que hombre, queriendo o dar cuenta de lo que escribe diferente de los otros o reformar los abusos que hay hoy en ella, se pudiese aprovechar de su autoridad. (Valdés 1982: 121–3; my italics)

Valdés's concern about the lack of imitable models in Spanish brings us back to the beginning of this paper and Garcilaso's remarks on the role of translation in the illustration of the language. The texts examined so far fail to resolve the initial conundrum of cultural demarcation raised by Garcilaso's attack on the 'libros que matan hombres'; namely, to distinguish in practice between the linguistic work accomplished by Renaissance illustrators of the language and what was done by fifteenth-century translators. The reason for

---

[14] The reference is to Pietro Bembo's dialogue *Prose della volgar lingua* of 1525, whose argument Valdés summarizes, though I do not find a direct parallel for the phrase 'ilustrar y enriquecer la lengua' (but see the discussion, in I.iv, of one's duty to the 'lingua […] propria e naturale e domestica, che è la volgare').

this failure, I submit, is that the Renaissance topic of illustrating the language was flawed by contradictions and ellipses that rendered it problematic both in theory and in practice.

The argument runs like this: fifteenth-century translators of the classics were convinced in theory of the inferiority of the vernacular and resigned to being able to recover only the content of ancient wisdom (as Santillana remarked when asking his son for a translation of the *Iliad* between 1446 and 1452, 'si careçemos de las formas, seamos contentos de las materias', 1988: 456). Yet in practice they strove to adopt new humanist precepts of *traductio*, and manifested a febrile fidelity to form by their cultivation of a contorted and electric style full of violent Latinate hyperbaton and neologisms. Enrique de Villena's outlandish rendering of the *Aeneid* in 1427, already quoted, is the craziest and most delicious of these efforts – not so much illustrating the language, we might say, as reinventing it from first principles; Juan de Mena's and Pedro González de Mendoza's weird stabs at the *Iliad* in c. 1446 and c. 1456 are almost as good, though spoilt by touches of good taste which the adust Villena would surely have disdained.[15]

The despised authors of the 'libros que matan hombres' cannot, then, be denied the merit of having wrestled in their translations with the problem of form versus content, *Stil* versus *Stoff*.[16] This remains the point at stake for Valdés and Garcilaso, who make clear that their strictures on fifteenth-century predecessors concern shortcomings of both matter and manner. To be exact, Valdés gives more weight to style, specifying that what Spain lacked was authors like Boccaccio and Petrarch who not only had 'buenas cosas' to say but also knew how to say them 'con estilo muy propio y muy elegante', whereas Garcilaso seems to foreground content with his remarks about 'cosas que merezcan ser leídas'. But both contradict themselves. Garcilaso slides into admitting that what distinguished Boscán's translation as a national *beneficio* was not in the end its courtly subject matter, but its gentlemanly and unaffected style:

---

15 Translators and lexicographers coined terms such as *interpretar, transferir* and *traduzir* to distinguish this kind of version from the activities embraced by the broad semantic range of medieval *trasladar* (Boscán's *romançar, romançista*, like Italian *volgarizzamento*, did the same in reverse); see Laspéras (1980), Russell (1985) and Nick Round's case study of Pero Díaz de Toledo's Plato (1993). For the humanist background, especially Bruni's influential treatise on *traductio* of c. 1425 (Bruni 1928: 81–90), see Folena (1994), and the inadequate but suggestive note in Sarolli (1962).

16 The merit is nevertheless regularly denied, following Amador de los Ríos (1861–65, VI, 9–54; VII, 194–225) – the first Spaniard to use the Burckhardtian term *Renacimiento* (always in italics), in its historical sense – who, taking his cue from Santillana's dictum, saw the beginnings of the movement under Juan II as the recovery of antique *materias*, and its triumph under Fernando and Isabel as the assimilation of antique *formas*. The present essay sets out to qualify this facile categorization.

> Guardó una cosa en la lengua castellana que muy pocos la an alcançado,
> que fue huir del afetaçión sin dar consigo en ninguna sequedad, et con gran
> limpieza de estilo usó de términos muy cortesanos et muy admitidos de los
> buenos oídos et no nuevos ny al pareçer desusados de la gente. Fue demás
> desto muy fiel tradutor, porque no se ató al rigor de la letra, como hacen
> algunos, sino a la verdad de las sentencias, y por diferentes caminos puso
> en esta lengua toda la fuerça y el ornamento de la otra, y assí lo dexó todo
> tan en su punto como lo halló. (1534: fol. 3ᵛ)

Garcilaso's paradox of the *faithful translator/traitor* (*'fiel tradutor'*) being
one who ignores the literal meaning ('no se ató al rigor de la letra') may
strike us as a novel stroke, but in fact it was a hackneyed allusion to Horace
('nec *verbo verbum* curabis reddere *fidus* | *interpres'*, *Ars poetica*, 133–4; my
italics). Once again, Garcilaso is here picking up on Boscán's own words:

> Yo no terné fin en la tradución de este libro a ser tan estrecho que me
> apriete a sacalle *palabra por palabra*; antes, si alguna cosa en él se ofre-
> ciere que en su lengua parezca bien y en la nuestra mal, no dexaré de
> mudarla o de callarla. (1534: fol. 2v; my italics)

Both men allude to an age-old commonplace, Jerome's celebrated defence
of the translator's licence to attend to the spirit, not the letter ('non *verbo
e verbo* sed *sensum exprimere de sensu'*, Hieronymus 1845: col. 571; my
italics). Jerome in turn adduced the support of Cicero and Horace, and
quoted his own Preface to his version of Eusebius's *Chronici canones*.[17] But
here, too, fifteenth-century translators had got there long before Garcilaso.
Jerome's authoritative prescription formed the backbone of medieval thinking
about translation, and by the fifteenth century had become so clichéd that
even a humble hack like the anonymous translator of Aesop's fables could
curtly allude to *sensum de sensu* as 'the common style of translators':

> non que sean sacadas [sus fábulas] *de verbo ad verbum*, mas cogiendo *el
> seso real según común estillo de intérpretes* por más claro et más evidente
> discussión et clarificación del texto, et aun algunas palabras añadidas et

---

[17] Hieronymus (1845: col. 571, §5), quoting Cicero, *De optimo genere oratorum*, v.14
('nec converti ut interpres, sed ut orator [...]; non verbum pro verbo necesse habui reddere, sed
genus omne verborum vimque servavi') and the Horatian tag; col. 572, quoting Hieronymus
(1846: cols 34–5), this latter being the text glossed by El Tostado (Madrigal 1506, see n. 4
above). Garcilaso probably also had in mind two famous passages in Cicero's *De finibus*, I.4–8,
on illustrating the Latin language by translation from Greek, and III.15 'nec tamen exprimi
verbum e verbo necesse erit, ut interpretes indiserti solent [...]. equidem soleo etiam quod uno
Graeci, si aliter non possum, idem pluribus verbis exponere'.

otras rejectas et exclusas en muchas partes por mayor ornato et eloquencia más honesta y provechosa. (Aesop 1488: fol. 2r; my italics)

More damning than Garcilaso's and Boscán's utter lack of originality in their theoretical postulates, however, was the fact, admitted by Boscán himself, that *El cortesano* was not properly a translation, but an adaptation 'de una lengua vulgar en otra'. Even so, and allowing himself all permissible licence, Boscán bemoaned,

é miedo que, según los términos de estas lenguas italiana y española y las costumbres de entrambas naciones son diferentes, no aya de quedar todavía algo que parezca menos bien en nuestro romançe. (1534: fol. 2v)

But these were crocodile tears. In truth Boscan's job was as easy as translation can ever be. Compared with wresting an equivalence from classical Latin, it has the undeniable look of child's play.

If 'libros que matan hombres' were fifteenth-century versions of the classics, therefore, the complaints levelled at them in Boscán's and Garcilaso's prologues emerge as strangely soft-centred, full of sound and fury but signifying very little. The ideas of the twin champions of the Renaissance on such topics as faithfulness, accuracy and the smoothing away of incompatibilities between source and target were entirely traditional. To find anything novel in their approach we are thrown back on Garcilaso's praise of Boscán for achieving what few had achieved before, 'huir del afetaçion sin dar consigo en ninguna sequedad', and to his concepts of 'limpieza de estilo' and 'términos cortesanos [...] no nuevos ni al pareçer desusados'. What was meant by these terms is glossed in Valdés's *Diálogo*, where *afectación* is any recourse to frigid or unnatural vocabulary.[18] The Valdés character particularly criticizes Juan de Mena's *Laberinto de Fortuna* for this criminal form of diction, revealing that frigidity means barbarisms (*grosería*) or obscure Latinate coinages:

---

18 Valdés (1982: 125): 'quanto al autor de *Amadís de Gaula*, [...] en el estilo peca muchas vezes con no sé qué *frías afetaciones*'; 233: 'el estilo que tengo me es natural, y *sin afetación ninguna escrivo como hablo*; solamente tengo cuidado de usar de vocablos que sinifiquen bien lo que quiero decir, y dígolo quanto más llanamente me es possible, porque a mi parecer en ninguna lengua stá bien el afetación'. It was probably Valdés's critique of *Amadís* that prompted Menéndez Pelayo to identify 'libros que matan hombres' as romances of chivalry (n. 2 above), but when Valdés returns to the subject – in the same passage as his dismissal of translations such as Urriés's (see n. 20) – he grants *Amadís*'s style qualified praise (248), and finally ranks it, alongside *Crónica de Juan II, Palmerín* and *Primaleón*, as the best of the four prose models which may be read 'para lo que pertenece a la lengua' (253). Valdés is hostile to translators, not romances, which gives indirect support to the interpretation of 'libros que matan hombres' advanced in this essay.

quanto al dezir propiamente, ni quanto al usar propios y naturales vocablos, [...] se descuidó mucho [...]; quiriendo mostrarse doto, escrivió tan escuro que no es entendido, y puso ciertos vocablos, unos que por grosseros se devrían desechar y otros que por muy latinos no se dexan entender de todos, [...] lo qual a mi ver es más escrivir mal latín que buen castellano.

(Valdés 1982: 240)

He likewise inveighs against Fernando de Rojas for having used 'vocablos tan latinos que no s'entienden en el castellano' in his *Tragicomedia de Calisto y Melibea*, and calls upon some censor to remedy this fault; only after such a purge will he be willing to admit that 'ningún libro ay escrito en castellano donde la lengua sté más natural, más propia, ni más elegante' (255).[19]

Where does this leave the topic of illustrating the language? To reject syntactic and lexical innovation as 'affectation' is to deny the central thrust of any argument about how translation might enrich a language, or at least to evacuate such an argument of linguistic content. In a seminal document on translation theory Walter Benjamin argued that since the aesthetic essence of literature is agreed to consist in the indefinible, mysterious poetic residue left over after all elements of straightforward communication are discounted, the faithful translator, far from shunning affectation and seeking to smooth the path by rendering the communicable meaning of the original in as natural a form as possible for the target audience – these being 'the credentials of bad translations' – will foreground difference and make the foreignness of the source language as obtrusive as possible; as 'the archetype or ideal' of good translation Benjamin therefore holds up Hölderlin's marvellously opaque and universally execrated calque of Sophocles, or a literal word-by-word inter-linear gloss of the Bible.[20] From this viewpoint – which in effect affirms that

---

[19] Valdés grants merit to only two *librillos* of 'los que an romançado' (244–7), Alberto de Aguayo's *Boecio de consolación* (Seville, 1518), and Alfonso Fernández de Madrid's version of Erasmus's *Enchiridion* (Alcalá de Henares, c. 1527). Urriés's *Valerio Máximo* is named among the *romancistas* dismissed with disdain by the Valdés character (247); we need only read the last sentence of its prologue to gain an idea of the sort of 'unnatural' *language* Valdés had in mind: 'E porque fasta la presente jornada no he fallado scriptor que a mi voluntad trasladar este libro quisiesse, he differido de lo presentar a vuestra excellencia; mas agora que tengo buena oportunidad para lo poner a la emprenta he delibrado, pues en esta guerra santa no puedo personalmente hazer servicio a Vuestra Majestad por el impedimiento de mi senectud, de le servir con este libro' (Urriés 1495: fol. 5v).

[20] Benjamin (1977: 50): 'Was sagt' denn eine Dichtung? Was teilt sie mit? [...] Ihr Wesent-liches ist nicht Mitteilung, nicht Aussage. Dennoch könnte diejenige Übersetzung, welche vermitteln will, nichts vermitteln als die Mitteilung – also Unwesentliches. Das ist denn auch ein Erkennungszeichen der schlechten Übersetzungen. Was aber außer der Mitteilung in einer Dichtung steht – und auch der schlechte Übersetzer gibt zu, daß es das Wesentliche ist – gilt es nicht allgemein als das Unfassbare, Geheimnisvolle, Dichterische'? Das der Übersetzer nur wiedergeben kann, indem er ... auch dichtet? Daher rührt in der Tat ein zweites Merkmal der

the translator's duty is to the original and to his own language, not to the reader – the despised fifteenth-century translations come off looking distinctly good, while Boscán's is definitely bad. Garcilaso's well-worn commonplace to the effect that 'cada vez que me pongo a leer este su libro [...], no me parece que le hay escrito en otra lengua' turns out to have an inconsistent meaning, or no meaning at all, when conjoined with the topic of illustrating the language (1534: fol. 3v). In the early years of the sixteenth century, contrary to what is fondly supposed, no important shift was taking place in redefining the task of the faithful translator, if by that one imagines a watershed between a putatively medieval – read: naïve, clumsy – ransacking of content, and a putatively Renaissance – read: modern, grown-up, hip – concern for equivalent effect and literary form.

But this must be wrong, we cry, because every schoolboy knows that the sixteenth century was the great age of translation. This is true (as witness, for example, Boscán's *Cortesano*), but in the case of Spanish in an unexpected way. W. H. Auden and Norman Holmes Pearson commented on the English case:

> Translation is fruitful in two ways. First, it introduces new kinds of sensibility and rhetoric – for example, the Petrarchan love convention; and fresh literary forms – for example, the pastoral. It does not particularly matter if the translators have understood their originals correctly; often, indeed, misunderstanding is, from the point of view of the native writer, more profitable. Second, and perhaps even more important, the problem of finding an equivalent meaning in a language with a very different structure from the original develops the syntax and vocabulary of the former.[21]

For Garcilaso and Boscán, who were in any case talking about translation from a language with virtually identical structure and vocabulary, the second of these ways remained no more than a pretext. Their debate was solely about the first way, despite the gestures towards the topic of illustrating the language; that is, about aesthetic, and ultimately social, ideals of culture. For all their talk about style, the driving thrust of both men's real concern,

schlechten Übersetzung, welche man demnach als eine ungenaue Übermittlung eines unwesentlichen Inhalts definieren darf'; and 62, on 'das Urbild oder Ideal aller Übersetzung' of Hölderlin and *Interlinearversionen*. A similar argument lay behind Alfonso de Cartagena's celebrated dispute with Leonardo Bruni over the translation of Aristotle, with Cartagena playing the part of Benjamin; see González Rolán, Moreno and Saquero (2000), Morrás (2002).

21 Auden and Pearson (1977: xv–xxxii [p. xv]). They attribute the zenith of translations in this period to the combination of 'the desire of the Protestants for a Bible and a liturgy in the vernacular and the desire of the new aristocracy for secular culture'; it is the second of these reasons that is the heart of the matter for the definition of the Renaissance, as opposed to the Reformation.

as their prologues make abundantly clear, was for the ideological content of Castiglione's work. This ideology was nakedly aristocratic, which made it quintessentially Renascent; it was about the appropriation of a certain kind of power, through a certain kind of culture, by a particular social class; a blueprint for a society in which good table-manners, an elegant accent, civilized relations with the opposite sex, and a strictly amateur familiarity with *belles lettres* would become keys to status and prestige. Garcilaso says all this when he remarks, as a foremost merit of his friend's translation, that

> una de las cosas de que mayor neçesidad ay, doquiera que ay hombres et damas prinçipales, es de hazer [...] todas las cosas que en aquella su manera de bivir acreçientan el punto et el valor de las personas.
>
> (1534: fol. 3r)

In this light his rejection of stylistic affectation can be seen for what it really was: nothing more than a translation into literary terms of Castiglione's key concept of noble *sprezzatura*. The whole linguistic and literary apparatus of his prologue is secretly motivated by this haughty social aspiration. By a last paradox, therefore, our Renaissance gentlemen turn out to have been more concerned with content than with form, even if they conceived of this content as a kind of style – what we should call a life-style. Garcilaso's concept of literary translation as a factor in the illustration of the vernacular touches not so much upon translation theory as upon the larger contexts of ideology and transculturation.

List of Works Cited

Aesop, 1488. *El libro del Esopete ystoriado* (Toulouse: Joan Parix & Estevan Cleblat)

Alvar, Carlos, 2005. 'Acerca de la traducción en Castilla durante el siglo XV', in *Actas del IX Congreso Internacional de la Asociación Hispánica de Literatura Medieval (A Coruña, 18–22 de septiembre de 2001)*, ed. Carmen Parrilla and Mercedes Pampín, Biblioteca Filológica, 13, 3 vols (A Coruña: Universidade), I, 15–41

Amador de los Ríos, José, 1861–65. *Historia crítica de la literatura española*, 7 vols (Madrid: the author) [repr. Madrid: Gredos, 1969]

Asensio, Eugenio, 1960. 'La lengua compañera del imperio: historia de una idea de Nebrija en España y Portugal', *Revista de Filología Española*, 43: 399–413

——, and Juan Alcina Rovira (eds), 1980. *Paraenesis ad litteras: Juan Maldo-*

nado y el humanismo español en tiempos de Carlos V, Humanismo y Renacimiento, 1 (Madrid: Fundación Universitaria Española)

Asís, Eugenio A. de, 1935. 'Nebrija y la crítica contemporánea de su obra', *Boletín de la Biblioteca de Menéndez Pelayo*, 17: 30–45

Auden, W. H. and Norman Holmes Pearson (eds), 1977. *Elizabethan and Jacobean Poets: Marlowe to Marvell*, Viking Portable Poets of the English Language, 2, 2nd edn (London: Penguin) [1st edn New York: Viking, 1950]

Barros, João de, 1959. *'Diálogo em Louvor da Nossa Linguagem': lettura critica dell'edizione del 1540, con una introduzione su la questione della lingua in Portogallo*, ed. Luciana Stegagno-Picchio, Collezione di Testi e Manuali, 45 (Modena: Istituto di Filologia Romanza, Università di Roma)

Beardsley, Jr, Theodore S., 1970. *Hispano-Classical Translations Printed between 1482–1699*, MHRA Monographs, Duquesne Studies Philological Series, 12 (Pittsburgh: Duquesne University Press)

——, 1979. 'La Traduction des auteurs classiques en Espagne de 1488 à 1586 dans le domaine des belles-lettres', in *L'Humanisme dans les lettres espagnoles: XIXe Colloque International d'Études Humanistes (Tours, 5–17 de julio de 1976)*, ed. Augustin Redondo (Paris: Vrin), pp. 51–64

Benjamin, Walter, 1977. 'Die Aufgabe des Übersetzers', in *Illuminationen: Ausgewählte Schriften I*, suhrkamp taschenbuch, 345 (Frankfurt: Suhrkamp), pp. 50–62 [first published as 'Vorwort' to his translation of Charles Baudelaire, *Tableaux parisiens: deutsche Übertragung*, 1923]

Besch, Werner, 1999. *Die Rolle Luthers in der deutschen Sprachgeschichte*, Schriften der Philosophisch-historischen Klasse der Heidelberger Akademie der Wissenschaften, 12 (Heidelberg: Winter) [repr. in *Sprachgeschichte: ein Handbuch zur Geschichte der deutschen Sprache und ihrer Erforschung*, ed. Werner Besch, Oskar Reichmann, and Stefan Sonderegger, Handbücher zur Sprach- und Kommunikationswissenschaft, 2, 2 vols, 2nd edn (Berlin: de Gruyter, 1998–2000), II, 1713–45]

Binotti, Lucia, 1995. *La teoría del castellano primitivo: nacionalismo y reflexión lingüística en el Renacimiento español* (Münster: Nodus)

Boscán, Juan (trans.), 1534. *Los quatro libros del cortesano, compuestos en italiano por el conde Balthasar Castellon y agora nuevamente traduzidos en lengua castellana por Boscan* (Barcelona: Pedro Monpezat) [repr. in Boscán and Garcilaso de la Vega 1995: 637–1019 (prologue, 643–6)]

——, 1543. 'A la duquesa de Soma' [dedication to 'Libro secundo'], in *Las obras de Boscan y algunas de Garcilasso de la Vega, repartidas en quatro libros*, ed. Ana Girón de Rebolledo (Barcelona: Carles Amorós), fols xix^r–xxi^v [repr. in Boscán and Garcilaso de la Vega 1995: 1–498 (pp. 83–7)]

——, and Garcilaso de la Vega, 1995. *Obras completas*, ed. Carlos Clavería Laguarda, Biblioteca Castro (Madrid: Turner)

Braselmann, Petra M. E., 1991. *Humanistische Grammatik und Volkssprache: zur 'Gramática de la lengua castellana' von Antonio de Nebrija*, Studia Humaniora, 21 (Düsseldorf: Droste)

——, 1993. 'Sprache als Instrument der Politik – Sprache als Gegenstand der Politik: zur sprachpolitischen Auffassung Antonio de Nebrijas in der *Gramática de la lengua castellana*', in *Akten des Deutschen Hispanistentages Göttingen 28.2.–3.3.1991*, ed. Christoph Strosetzki, Studia Hispanica, 2 (Frankfurt am Main: Vervuert), pp. 123–35

Bruni Aretino, Leonardo, 1928. *Humanistisch-philosophische Schriften, mit einer Chronologie seiner Werke und Briefe*, ed. Hans Baron (Leipzig: Teubner)

Carrera de la Red, Avelina, 1988. *El 'problema de la lengua' en el humanismo renacentista español*, Lingüística y Filología, 7 (Valladolid: Universidad)

Coroleu, Alejandro, 2004. 'A Preliminary Survey of Greek and Latin Historians in Translation in the Iberian Peninsula (c. 1360–1599)', in *The Iberian Book and its Readers: Essays for Ian Michael*, ed. Nigel Griffin, Clive Griffin, and Eric Southworth (*Bulletin of Spanish Studies*, 81.7–8, November–December), pp. 897–912

Dante Alighieri, 1924. *Le opere*, ed. E. Moore, rev. Paget Toynbee, 4th edn (Oxford: Stamperia dell'Università) [1st edn 1894]

Dionisotti, Carlo, 1968. *Gli umanisti e il volgare fra Quattro e Cinquecento*, Bibliotechina del Saggiatore, 29 (Firenze: Le Monnier)

Du Bellay, Joachim ['I.D.B.A.'], 1549. *La deffence, et illustration de la langue francoyse* (Paris: Arnoul l'Angelier)

Eusebius, *Chronici canones*: see Hieronymus 1846

Folena, Gianfranco, 1994. *Volgarizzare e tradurre* (Torino: Einaudi)

Garcilaso de la Vega, 1534. 'A la muy manífica señora doña Gerónima Palova de Almogávar', in Boscán 1534: fols 3r–4r [repr. in Boscán and Garcilaso 1995: 647–50]

——, 1911. *Obras*, ed. T. Navarro Tomás, Clásicos Castellanos, 3 (Madrid: La Lectura)

——, 1925. *Works: A Critical Text with a Bibliography*, ed. Hayward Keniston, Hispanic Notes and Monographs, Peninsular Series (New York: Hispanic Society of America)

——, 1981. *Obras completas con comentario*, ed. Elias L. Rivers (Madrid: Castalia)

——, 1995. *Obra poética y textos en prosa*, ed. Bienvenido Morros, intro. Rafael Lapesa, Biblioteca Clásica, 27 (Barcelona: Crítica)

González Rolán, Tomás, A. Moreno Hernández, and P. Saquero Suárez-Somonte (eds), 2000. *Humanismo y teoría de la traducción en Espana e Italia en la primera mitad del siglo XV: edición y estudio de la 'Controversia Alphonsiana' (Alfonso de Cartagena vs. L. Bruni y P. Candido Decembrio)*, Bibliotheca Latina (Madrid: Ediciones Clásicas)

——, Pilar Saquero Suárez-Somonte and Antonio López Fonseca, 2002. *La tradición clásica en España, siglos XIII–XV: bases conceptuales y bibliográficas*, Anejos de *Tempus*, 4 (Madrid: Ediciones Clásicas)

Hernández González, María Isabel (ed.), 1998. *En la teoría y en la práctica de la traducción: la experiencia de los traductores castellanos a la luz de sus textos (siglos XIV–XVI)*, Publicaciones del Seminario de Estudios Medievales y Renacentistas, Prospectos y Manuales 1 (Salamanca: SEMYR)

Hieronymus, Eusebius, 1845. *Epistola* LVII *ad Pammachium: De optimo genere interpretandi*, in *Patrologiae cursus completus: series Latina*, ed. J.-P. Migne, 221 vols (Paris: Migne, 1844–65), XXII, cols 569–79

——, 1846. *Interpretatio 'Chronicae' Eusebii Pamphili*, in *Patrologiae cursus completus: series Latina*, ed. J.-P. Migne, 221 vols (Paris: Migne, 1844–65), XXVII, cols 33–675 ('Praefatio', 33–40)

Keightley, Ronald G., 1977. 'Alfonso de Madrigal and the *Chronici canones* of Eusebius', *Journal of Medieval and Renaissance Studies*, 7: 225–48

Klein, Franz-Joseph, 1995. 'Nebrija gab nur das Stichwort: Lesarten des Prinzips der "lengua compañera del imperio" im Siglo de Oro', *Romanische Forschungen*, 107: 285–313

Laspéras, J.-M., 1980. 'La Traduction et ses théories en Espagne aux XVe et XVIe siècles', *Revue des Langues Romanes*, 84: 81–92

Lawrance, Jeremy, 1986. 'On Fifteenth-Century Spanish Vernacular Humanism', in *Medieval and Renaissance Studies in Honour of R. B. Tate*, ed. Ian Michael and Richard A. Cardwell (Oxford: Dolphin), pp. 63–79

——, 2000. 'Medieval Portuguese Literature and the *Questione della lingua*', in *Cultural Links between Portugal and Italy in the Renaissance*, ed. K. J. P. Lowe (Oxford: Oxford University Press), pp. 139–52

——, forthcoming. '*Fabulosa illa aurea secula*: The Idea of the Golden Age at the Court of Isabel'

Lebrixa, Antonio de, 1492. 'A la mui alta et assí esclarecida princesa doña Isabel (Prólogo)', in his *Tratado de gramatica sobre la lengua castellana* (Salamanca: s.n.), fols A2–A4v [repr. in Antonio de Nebrija, *Gramática de la lengua castellana*, ed. Antonio Quilis (Madrid: Editora Nacional, 1980), pp. 97–102]

McGrath, Alister, 2001. *In the Beginning: The Story of the King James Bible and How It Changed a Nation, a Language and a Culture* (London: Hodder & Stoughton)

Madrigal, Alfonso de, el Tostado, 1506. 'Prólogo', in his *El comento o exposiçion de Eusebio 'De las chronicas o tiempos', interpretado en vulgar*, 5 vols (Salamanca: Gysser, 1506–07), I, fols 3r–25v

Marineus Siculus, Lucius, c. 1495. *De Hispaniae laudibus* [*libri VII*] (s.l. [Burgos]: s.n. [Fadrique de Basilea], s.a.)

Martínez Romero, Tomàs, 1998. *Un clàssic entre clàssics: sobre traduccions i recepcions de Sèneca a l'època medieval*, intro. Albert G. Hauf, Biblioteca Sanchis Guarner (València: Institut Interuniversitari de Filologia Valenciana)

——, and Roxana Recio (eds), 2001. *Essays on Medieval Translation in the Iberian Peninsula*, Col·lecció Estudis sobre la Traducció, 9 (Castelló de la Plana: Universitat Jaume I)

Melczer, William, 1981. 'Towards the Dignification of the Vulgar Tongues: Humanistic Translations into Italian and Spanish in the Renaissance', in *Translation in the Renaissance*, ed. Eva Kushner and Paul Chavy (*Canadian Review of Comparative Literature*, 8.2), pp. 256–71

Menéndez Pelayo, Marcelino, 1945. 'Parte 3a.: Boscán', in his *Antología de poetas líricos castellanos: desde la formación del lenguaje hasta nuestros días*, ed. Enrique Sánchez Reyes, Edición Nacional de las Obras Completas de Menéndez Pelayo, 17–26, 10 vols (Santander: CSIC, 1944–45), X, 7–425 [1st edn, Biblioteca Clásica, 14 vols (Madrid: Hernando & Sucesores, 1890–1908), XIII, 1908]

——, 1950–53. *Bibliografía hispano-latina clásica*, ed. Enrique Sánchez Reyes, Edición Nacional de las Obras Completas de Menéndez Pelayo, 44–53, 10 vols (Santander: Aldus & CSIC)

——, 1952–53. *Biblioteca de traductores españoles*, ed. Enrique Sánchez Reyes, Edición Nacional de las Obras Completas de Menéndez Pelayo, 54–7, 4 vols (Santander: Aldus & CSIC)

Monfrin, Jacques, 1964. 'Humanisme et traductions au Moyen Age', in *L'Humanisme médiéval dans les littératures romanes du XIIe au XIVe siècle: colloque organisé par le Centre de philologie et de littératures romanes de l'Université de Strasbourg*, ed. Anthime Fourrier (Paris: Klincksieck), pp. 217–46

——, 1972. 'La Connaissance de l'Antiquité et le problème de l'humanisme en langue vulgaire dans la France du XVe siècle', in *The Late Middle Ages and the Dawn of Humanism Outside Italy: Proceedings of the International Conference, Louvain, May 11–13, 1970*, ed. G. Verbeke and J. IJsewijn, Mediaevalia Lovaniensia, 1.1 (Leuven: University), pp. 131–70

Morrás, María (ed.), 1996. Alonso de Cartagena, *Libros de Tulio: De senetute, De los ofiçios*, Poetria Nova, 2 (Alcalá de Henares: Universidad)

——, 2002. 'El debate entre Leonardo Bruni y Alonso de Cartagena: las razones de una polémica', *Quaderns de Traducció*, 7: 33–56

Morreale, Margherita, 1959a. 'Apuntes para la historia de la traducción en la Edad Media', *Revista de Literatura*, 15: 3–10

——, 1959b. *Castiglione y Boscán: el ideal cortesano en el Renacimiento español (estudio léxico-semántico)*, Anejos del *Boletín de la Real Academia Española*, 1, 2 vols (Madrid: Real Academia Española)

Nebrija: *see* Lebrixa

Norton, Glyn P., 1984. *The Ideology and Language of Translation in Renaissance France and their Humanist Antecedents*, Travaux d'Humanisme et Renaissance, 201 (Genève: Droz)

Pastor, José Francisco (ed.), 1929. *Las apologías de la lengua castellana en el Siglo de Oro*, Nueva Biblioteca de Autores Españoles: Los Clásicos Olvidados, 8 (Madrid: Compañía Ibero-Americana de Publicaciones)

Recio, Roxana, 1991. 'Alonso de Madrigal (El Tostado): la traducción clásica como teoría entre lo medieval y lo renacentista', *La Corónica*, 19(2) (Spring): 112–31

—— (ed.), 1995a. *La traducción en España ss. XIV–XVI*, Anexos de *Livius*, 1 (León: Universidad)

——, 1995b. 'El concepto de la belleza de Alfonso de Madrigal (El Tostado): la problemática de la traducción literal y libre', in Recio 1995a: 59–68

Round, Nicholas G., 1993. *Libro llamado 'Fedrón': Plato's 'Phaedo' Translated by Pero Díaz de Toledo (MS Madrid, Biblioteca Nacional Vitr. 17.4)*, Colección Támesis, B39 (London: Tamesis)

Rozas, Juan Manuel, 1984. 'Siglo de Oro: historia de un concepto, la acuñación del término', in *Estudios sobre el Siglo de Oro: homenaje al profesor Francisco Ynduráin*, ed. Manuel Alvar et al. (Madrid: Editora Nacional), pp. 411–28

Russell, Peter, 1985. *Traducciones y traductores en la Península Ibérica (1400–1550)*, Monografies de *Quaderns de Traducció i Interpretació*, 2 (Bellaterra: Escuela Universitaria de Traductores e Intérpretes, Universidad Autónoma de Barcelona)

Santamaría, Gonzalo García de (trans.), c. 1486–90. *La vida de los sanctos religiosos* (s.l. [Zaragoza]: s.n. [Pablo Hurus], s.a.)

Santillana, Íñigo López de Mendoza, marqués de, 1988. *Obras completas*, ed. Ángel Gómez Moreno and Maximilian P. A. M. Kerkhof, Autores hispánicos, 146 (Barcelona: Planeta)

Santoyo, Julio-César. 1987. *Traducción, traducciones, traductores: ensayo de bibliografía española* (León: Universidad)

——, 1996. *Bibliografía de la traducción en español, catalán, gallego y vasco*, Anexos de *Livius*, 2 (León: Universidad)

—— et al. (eds), 1987–89. *Fidus interpres: actas de las Primeras Jornadas Nacionales de Historia de la Traducción*, 2 vols (León: Universidad)

Sarolli, Gian Roberto. 1962. 'Boscán as Translator: St. Jerome or the Humanists?', *MLN*, 77: 187–91

Serés, Guillermo, 1997. *La traducción en Italia y España durante el siglo XV: la 'Ilíada en romance' y su contexto cultural*, Textos Recuperados, 16 (Salamanca: Universidad)

Sola-Solé, Josep M., 1974. 'Villalón frente a Nebrija', *Romance Philology*, 28.1 (August): 35–43.

Speroni, Sperone, 1542. 'Dialogo [VII] delle lingue', in *I dialogi di Messer Speron Sperone*, ed. Daniele Barbaro (Venice: Figliuoli di Aldo Manuzio), fols 105v–131r

Tavoni, Mirko, 1984. *Latino, grammatica, volgare: storia di una questione umanistica*, Medioevo e Umanesimo, 53 (Padua: Antenore)

Terracini, Lore, 1964. *Tradizione illustre e lingua letteraria nella Spagna del Rinascimento* (Rome: Tipografia P.U.G.)

Urriés, Ugo de (trans.), 1495. *Valerio Maximo* (Zaragoza: Paulo Hurus) [repr. Sevilla: Varela, 1514; Alcalá de Henares: Eguía, 1529; and Toledo: Ayala, 1541]

Valdés, Juan de, 1982. *Diálogo de la lengua*, ed. Cristina Barbolani, Letras Hispánicas, 153 (Madrid: Cátedra)

Villena, Enrique de, 1994. *Obras completas*, II: *Traducción y glosas de la Eneida*, ed. Pedro M. Cátedra, Biblioteca Castro (Madrid: Turner)

Wittlin, Curt, 1998. 'El oficio de traductor según Alfonso Tostado de Madrigal en su comentario al prólogo de San Jerónimo a las *Crónicas* de Eusebio', *Quaderns: Revista de Traducció*, 2: 9–21

Ynduráin, Domingo, 1982. 'La invención de una lengua clásica: literatura vulgar y Renacimiento en España', *Edad de Oro*, 1 (*I Seminario Internacional Literatura Española y Edad de Oro*, Universidad Autónoma de Madrid, 1981): 13–34

The Sense of an Ending:
Leandro Fernández de Moratín's
El viejo y la niña and its Italian Translation

PHILIP DEACON

The ending of a play almost invariably provides a decisive indicator of its overall meaning, and in consequence eighteenth-century European theatrical practice laid stress on the outcome of dramatic works in terms of their agreement with prevailing conceptions of moral justice. Revivals of works from earlier periods, as is notorious in England in the case of Shakespeare's *King Lear*, might have tragic endings re-written to prevent an apparent injustice being visited on a basically good character. Although Spanish theatrical theory from the mid-eighteenth century emphasized the classical division between comedy and tragedy, theoretical orthodoxy was often countered in practice by classicizing comedy assuming some of the moral seriousness and technical features of tragedy in works portraying the mores of the increasingly significant middle orders of society.

El viejo y la niña (1790), the first play by Spain's leading neoclassical comic dramatist, Leandro Fernández de Moratín (1760–1828), was perceived by contemporary audiences and readers to have a particularly sombre ending for a play labelled a 'comedia', in that the nineteen-year-old female protagonist Isabel only manages to escape from her intolerable marriage to the seventy-year-old, thrice widowed Roque by insisting on entering a convent.[1] Fifteen years after the work's publication the Italian translation by Pietro Napoli Signorelli (1731–1815), a dramatist and literary theorist well acquainted with Spanish literature as well as a friend of Moratín, upset the author by modi-

---

[1]   The starting point for recent interpretations of the play has been the chapter on 'La comedia neoclásica' in René Andioc's *Teatro y sociedad en el Madrid del siglo XVIII* (Andioc 1976: 420–42). See too his later summation (Andioc 1995).

fying the ending.[2] Instead of refuge in a convent Isabel agrees to a compromise proposed by her husband's widowed sister Beatriz, whereby Roque has to promise to amend his behaviour in an arrangement to be enforced by Beatriz taking up residence in her brother's house. The present chapter proposes to explore some of the issues surrounding the controversial endings to Moratín's play.

Moratín's attitude to literary culture, as conveyed in statements published in his lifetime and since, portrays a seriousness and sense of purpose indicative of a reverence for his chosen vocation. His five original plays went through multiple versions before and between performance, initial printings and definitive text, a process continued even after the authoritative Paris edition of his *Obras dramáticas y líricas* (1825) was seen into print by their author, then aged sixty-five.[3] *El viejo y la niña* was first published to accompany the play's Madrid première in the Príncipe Theatre on 22 May 1790. Almost immediately the work provoked an anonymous attack in one of the leading intellectual periodicals, the *Correo de Madrid* (Cladera 1790), to which Moratín forcefully replied, in the same journal, directly answering and sometimes ridiculing the claims of his critic, widely accepted to be the Majorcan intellectual Cristóbal Cladera, editor of another important cultural periodical, the *Espíritu de los mejores diarios que se publican en Europa*.[4] Moratín's response made clear his intentions concerning the work and his wish to defend its style, technique and social significance, although its quality is something he preferred to evade, in a rhetorical show of modesty (Fernández de Moratín 1973: 109–21).

It is sometimes forgotten that Moratín's profession in the 1790s was that of official translator for the Government, and it is clear from published and unpublished texts that he had a profound knowledge of French and Italian as well as English. In 1798 he published an annotated prose translation of Shakespeare's *Hamlet*, and in 1812 and 1814 his performing versions of Molière's *Le Médecin malgré lui* and *L'École des maris* appeared in print

2 Napoli Signorelli's links with Moratín have been the subject of studies by Angela Mariutti de Sánchez Rivero (1960) and Franco Quinziano (2002).

3 No monographic study has been made of the changes between manuscripts, first editions and the definitive 1825 texts of Moratín's plays. Belén Tejerina lists and comments on the changes between the 1790 and 1825 texts of *El viejo y la niña*, which result in a cut from 3,146 to 2,684 lines (Fernández de Moratín 1996: 31–43). Fernando Lázaro Carreter, exceptionally, preferred to base his modern edition (Fernández de Moratín 1970) on the 1795 Imprenta Real printing of the play, which incorporates corrections with respect to the *princeps* which Moratín listed in a letter to Melón (Fernández de Moratín 1973: 418).

4 Moratín's only response to criticism of his dramatic works came in his point by point rebuttal of Cladera in the *Correo de Madrid* (Fernández de Moratín 1973: 109–21). It is essential to an understanding of Moratín's explicit intentions in the work. He subsequently refused to respond directly to criticism of his plays.

in Madrid. The version of *Hamlet* is scholarly and faithful to the original, in spite of the odd mistranslation, and Moratín's disagreements with features of Shakespeare's aesthetics are reserved for the prologue and end-notes (Deacon 1996). The Molière texts, on the other hand, are domesticated for a contemporary Spanish audience, in performing editions which give no hint of their French origins. Though the Molière versions came late in his career, Moratín in his practice distinguishes sharply between performing versions and ones which preserve the original features (Andioc 2005: 221–54; García Garrosa and Lafarga 2004: 320–2, 375).

From the 'Advertencia' preceding the authorized text of *El viejo y la niña* in Moratín's *Obras dramáticas y líricas*, we know that *El viejo y la niña* was finished by 1786 and read by the author in that year to one of the Madrid theatrical companies (Fernández de Moratín 1825: I, iii). This version needed severe cuts in order to obtain the approval of the theatrical censors (who would have included a cleric), and we know that Moratín felt the alterations ruined the work: 'toda la obra estropeada y sin orden' (1825: I, iii). Two years later he read the play to the other Madrid-based theatrical company and, in spite of the casting of Isabel not being to his taste because of the actress being too old, performances would have gone ahead had not the ecclesiastical censor refused permission to perform the text as presented. It was at about this moment, in 1788, that Moratín sent a manuscript of his play to Pietro Napoli Signorelli, now back in Naples after having lived in Spain from 1765 to 1783 where he had been a close friend of Moratín's father.

Napoli Signorelli read the manuscript immediately, according to his letter to Moratín of December 1788 (Napoli Signorelli 1867). He is full of praise for the play, especially for its observance of the neoclassical conventions, including the uncomplicated plot, and he singles out for praise scenes which work particularly well. Feeling compelled to add a reservation or two he mentions moments where more compression might be desirable and indirectly expresses a preference for greater comic energy, but he says nothing which directly reveals his attitude towards the ending. A little over a year later Napoli Signorelli would have received the first printed edition of the play (1790), probably very similar to the earlier manuscript, and he subsequently set about producing his Italian translation, which was published in Venice in 1805 (Fernández de Moratín 1996: 91). Moratín's immediate reaction to *Il vecchio e la giovane* is not known, but in 1825, with the translator now dead and his own reputation assured, Napoli Signorelli's translations of all five of Moratín's comedies are vouched for in the 'Advertencia del editor' prefacing the Paris edition of his collected works:

> Esta versión es la mejor de cuantas se han hecho hasta ahora, y á excepcion de uno ú otro defecto muy disculpable, puede asegurarse que el

traductor entendió bien el original, y supo conservar toda su gracia y su energia. (Fernández de Moratín 1825: I, i)

However, in the separate 'Advertencia' preceding *El viejo y la niña*, the author, who is taken to be Moratín, makes clear his specific feelings about Napoli Signorelli's translation of the play:

> en los teatros de Italia [...], fué recibida con aplauso público; pero muchas ilustres damas, acostumbradas tal vez á los desenlaces de la *Misantropía* de Kotzbue, y la *Madre culpable* de Beaumarchais, hallaron el de la comedia de *el Viejo y la Niña* demasiado austero y melancólico, y poco análogo á aquella flexible y cómoda moralidad, que es ya peculiar de ciertas clases en los pueblos mas civilizados de Europa. Cedió el traductor con excesiva docilidad, á la poderosa influencia de aquel sexo que llorando manda y tira- niza: mudó el desenlace (para lo cual hubiera debido alterar toda la fábula) y por consiguiente, faltando á la verisimilitud, incurrió en una contradic- ción de principios tan manifiesta, que no tiene disculpa.'
>
> (Fernández de Moratín 1825: I, iv–v)

Moratín's verdict seems excessively harsh, as a less partisan comparison of the two versions might suggest.

In *El viejo y la niña* the nineteen-year-old orphan Isabel has married, some four to five weeks previously, the ailing, elderly, Cadiz businessman Roque. As the play opens Roque is playing host to Juan, the nephew of a former commercial associate, who unbeknown to Roque, had previously been in love with Isabel, as she had with him. Some five months before the beginning of the action of the play Juan had moved to Madrid with his uncle and main- tained contact with Isabel by letter, but after four months there was silence on her part. A friend in Cadiz then informed Juan that Isabel was to marry someone else. On his return to Cadiz he discovers that he has agreed to stay in the house of the man Isabel has married, which leaves him distraught. Isabel subsequently explains her actions, saying that she had been informed by her then guardian that Juan's marriage to a wealthy woman had been arranged in Madrid. As a consequence of feeling abandoned and betrayed by Juan she had let herself be persuaded into marrying the unsuitable Roque, no doubt conscious of her financial condition as an orphan (Act I, sc. 2). Roque's reaction, once he becomes aware of the previous relationship between Isabel and Juan, is to want Juan to leave his house as soon as possible, but he does not openly broach the matter with him, preferring for the moment to oblige his elderly servant Muñoz to spy on the pair, especially Isabel (Act II, sc. 1). When Isabel and Juan meet they realize the strength of the feelings they still have for one another, but, given Isabel's marriage and their respect for prevailing moral principles, they decide that there is nothing they can do to remedy the situation (Act I, sc. 12). Juan determines to abandon Spain immediately by setting sail from Cadiz for Guatemala, where he has commercial interests. Aware of how she has been cruelly deceived by her guardian, and of the impossibility of a legitimate future with Juan, and repulsed by Roque's behaviour in the short time she has been married to him, Isabel determines to abandon her marriage for life in a convent, an action to which Roque grudgingly accedes (Act III, sc. 4).

Moratín's play closes on this negative note. Though labelled a 'comedia' on the title page, *El viejo y la niña* ends with gloomy prospects for all three main characters. The two virtuous young people end up separated, conscious of having been lied to or deceived, and acquiescing in the hope that time and separation will cure their despair. If the play has, on the one hand, featured their re-encounter and realization of how others have conspired to bring about their misfortune, on the other, the audience has witnessed the behaviour of Roque as a jealous, miserly, unfeeling husband, whose manipulation of Muñoz and general irrationality reach levels which, though intended to make the audience laugh, accentuate the tragic chain of events and the current hopeless situation in which Juan and Isabel find themselves.

It is clear that the author could have made the dénouement less sombre, or at least not emphasized the impossibility of Juan and Isabel finding happiness. Yet we must suppose that Moratín wanted to bring home to the audience the pain which can be produced by a marriage which is inappropriate – the original subtitle is *El casamiento desigual* – and to a large extent outside the control of the woman entering into it. The irremediable fact of the marital contract between Isabel and Roque signifies that the mutual love between Juan and Isabel cannot prosper, except by the adultery of Isabel with Juan,[5] or at a more extreme level by Roque's death. However much Beatriz and Muñoz may criticize Roque's error in marrying a woman more than fifty years his junior the ending exposes the impasse in which Juan and Isabel find themselves and offers no escape route which would provide something approaching a happy ending. Moratín's skill as a creator of dramatic situations is employed in elaborating on the central situation in such a way as to emphasize the injustice of Juan and Isabel's plight, but he offers no morally acceptable alternative solution, and in this sense the ending and much of the plot development revolve around features associated with tragic rather than comic drama.

Moratín had written his play for a Spanish audience, fully aware of the effect that such an ending might provoke. A translator, however, might choose to introduce modifications in accordance with the preferences of the audience

---

[5] The possibility is alluded to by Isabel in the 1790 edition as a 'delito tan horrendo' (Fernández de Moratín 1996: 314).

at whom the translation is aimed. Napoli Signorelli's version of *El viejo y la niña* adopts a hybrid policy as far as fidelity or domestication is concerned (García Garrosa and Lafarga 2004: 6–12, 28–30). Though his translation was intended for performance, he retained most of the Spanish features of the original, setting the work in Cadiz and keeping the majority of its local characteristics.[6] The standard Italian versions of people's names are adopted: Rocco for Roque, Isabella for Isabel, Beatrice for Beatriz, though Juan becomes Carlo, presumably in order not to evoke inappropriate associations by calling him Don Giovanni, and the servants are given names indicative to an Italian audience of their social status (Blasa becomes Giacomina, Ginés is now Fabrizio, and Muñoz is called Alonso). In Act I, scene 5, the Italian text has a footnote to explain 'vale' as 'equivalenti a cambiali', though in Act II, scene 1, the 'reales' in a business deal are left as 'reali'. The Italian follows the Spanish very closely, without becoming unidiomatic, possibly helped by avoiding the assonating *romance* and *redondilla* verses of the original in favour of prose. As the work's recent editor, Belén Tejerina, points out, Napoli Signorelli finds exact equivalences for proverbial expressions, and his overriding aim seems to be to keep close to the original without sounding artificial. Ermanno Caldera had previously demonstrated that the Italian version tones down religious references by finding secular equivalents and reduces the strength of the occasional sexual allusion (Caldera 1980: 156–7).

The most notable feature of *Il vecchio e la giovane*, however, is the change of ending. While Isabella is still pondering on how to escape from her marriage, possibly by entering a convent, Napoli Signorelli provides a different resolution, proposed by Rocco's sister Beatrice, who believes that her brother can be persuaded to reform his behaviour sufficiently for Isabella not to leave him.[7] Moratín claimed in his 'Advertencia' of 1825 that the whole of the rest of the play would have had to prepare the audience for this outcome by being written in a different way; the assertion is debatable at best. Napoli Signorelli may well have explained himself to Moratín by saying that an Italian audience would not accept a play with such a negative ending and that therefore he felt obliged to invent an alternative one. On closer examination it is evident that the modification he carried out could be argued to be close to Moratín's own thinking. It would have been useful to have Napoli's

---

6 Belén Tejerina's erudite edition of Napoli Signorelli's Italian translation, accompanied by Moratín's 1790 text (Fernández de Moratín 1996), is the starting point for all comparative study of the translation and I acknowledge my debt to the editor's scholarship. See my detailed review (Deacon 2001). Quotations from Moratín's 1790 text and Napoli Signorelli's 1805 translation follow this edition.

7 I shall hereafter use the Italian names when referring to the translated version of the play.

written testimony on the matter, but the only evidence is Moratín's words as contained in the 'Advertencia'.

It is not evident from a sympathetic reading of the Italian version that the changed dénouement comes as a surprise or is even written against the grain of the action, as Moratín's criticism seems to imply. An author will naturally feel defensive about their own work, especially a first play, and one that had caused so many problems prior to its first performance. Moratín was no doubt convinced of his original solution and that Napoli Signorelli's changed ending could not be countenanced, but a reading of the primitive version of the Spanish text followed by the alternative ending inserted after line 3029 (Act III, sc. 13) produces a coherent dénouement largely in accord with what Moratín contrived in his later comedies *La mojigata* (1804) and *El sí de las niñas* (1805). What Napoli Signorelli engineers is an ending which provides the opportunity for Isabella to cohabit with Rocco under conditions considerably more acceptable than she enjoyed at the beginning of the stage action, and with the prospect of improvement once Rocco dies, an event which the original Spanish version suggested was not far off.[8] Since there has clearly been no love between Rocco and Isabella, the formal arrangement for a household where the weight of Beatrice's authority would keep Rocco under control and provide Isabella with company and an emotional counterbalance to her husband has much to commend it. Beatrice sympathizes throughout with Isabella, and her future influence might also act as a check on Isabella's conduct, should that concern her husband. Rocco, somewhat isolated through deafness, with a life centred on his business dealings, and whose relationships with his previous wives seemed to revolve around domestic duty rather than companionship and feelings of mutual affection (Act I, sc. 8), might well be prepared to tolerate a shared household, an arrangement which would require him to act more reasonably and exhibit respect for the human rights of his marital partner.

Napoli Signorelli's literary circumstances add support to his case for modifying the ending. In particular, he enjoyed the advantage of knowing the plot structures and dénouements of all of Moratín's plays (with the possible exception of *El sí de las niñas*), when he finalized *Il vecchio e la giovane*.[9] In Moratín's later comedies the endings produce scenes of reconciliation which suggest that effective solutions can be found for seemingly intractable conflictive situations (Lista 1821: 340); it usually requires an overbearing,

---

8   References to Roque's poor health and deafness are frequent in the first edition, though some of these were removed in the definitive text of 1825.

9   It is widely believed that a near definitive text of *El sí de las niñas* had been completed by 1801, but we have no information as to whether Napoli Signorelli might have read a copy before finalizing his translation of *El viejo y la niña*.

elderly, male figure to give way on a matter which suggests irrational behaviour on his part.

Napoli Signorelli's solution for Rocco certainly seems more in line with natural justice than the original ending. Rocco's existence after the curtain falls will require a change in his unacceptable conduct towards Isabella. His self-centredness and despotism will have to be replaced by behaviour which acknowledges his wife's rights. His earlier behaviour had been declared reprehensible by his loyal, long-suffering servant Alonso – a feature criticized by Cladera (1790: 149) – but Napoli now adds to this the almost policing role which the emotionally balanced and rational Beatrice has imposed on Rocco, with his reluctant agreement. If the beginning of the play has presented his behaviour as furthest out of line with rational principles, his acceptance of a need for reform would appear to be a suitable dénouement. He would be recognizing his previous irrationality and, having been subject to persuasion, he would be acknowledging the error of his ways in true enlightenment fashion, as Moratín demonstrated with Diego in *El sí de las niñas* and Martín in *La mojigata*. Napoli might be argued to have understood Moratín's mindset particularly well and merely acted in accordance with the playwright's more recent thinking.

What may also have helped tip the balance for Napoli Signorelli in favour of the change could have been a realistic appraisal of Isabella's situation. As articles in such contemporary Spanish periodicals as *El regañón general* (1803–04) make clear, some women were cynically, or perhaps pragmatically, prepared to put up with an odious elderly husband in the belief that they would soon be widows and able to marry again, should they so wish, and this time to whom they pleased. Moratín's emphasis in the 1790 text – somewhat attenuated in the definitive 1825 version, yet preserved by Napoli Signorelli – on Roque's ill-health ('setentón enfermizo', Act I, sc. 1; 'la quebradura, el flato,/ o la gota se me agrava', Act I, sc. 2; 'que le corrompe el aliento,/ que tiene hinchadas las piernas', Act III, sc. 3) positively invites the belief that a brief period of potential discomfort for Isabella will later give way to liberation from her tyrannical husband.

Moratín's defence of his comedy seems to underline Isabel's moral nature, yet the play had informed us that she let herself be led into marriage with Roque as a 'venganza' (Act I, sc. 12), an irrational attempt to forget the apparent betrayal by Juan. Prolonging a marriage to which she is legally, though not emotionally, committed, seems, as Napoli Signorelli configures it, to be ethically less perverse than her original decision to marry; and her reason for choosing reclusion in a convent seems no more laudable or sensible than continuing to put up with the presence of Roque. What is more, she does not seem impelled to choose the convent option as a result of any religious feelings, and hence her choice appears as an example of bad faith. It is evident that Moratín saw Isabel's assertion of her wish to escape, labelling her husband a tyrant (Act III, sc. 13), as a key moment in the action because he commissioned a drawing of it from Antonio Rodríguez, later converted into an engraving, to accompany the 1825 version of his text (Fernández de Moratín 1973: 418). Moratín appears to argue for treating Isabel's action as indicative of her decisiveness and an assertion of female power against her discredited husband (Di Pinto 1980: 76). He may have chosen the option of the convent because of its frequency among the middle classes (Andioc 1995: 552, 556), but if Isabel's religious feelings reflect his own then the choice seems oppressive of personal liberty, an oppression which would be self-inflicted and arguably less persuasive; if one assumes that her religiosity is uncharacteristically muted during the play, her decision to renounce the world could be perceived as less harsh, but it would nevertheless run counter to the effect Moratín appears to wish to produce.

What is notable about contemporary commentaries on *El viejo y la niña* is that none is by a woman, yet what is significant about Moratín's explanation of the changed ending of the Italian translation is that it is claimed to be the result of pressure from female spectators. Unfortunately we do not know how Spanish female spectators reacted to the original ending. What Moratín's solution achieves is no significant recompense to Isabel for Roque's objectionable behaviour. Judging by his comments, Roque's idea of marriage involves the capacity to be able to treat his wife almost as a slave (Act I, sc. 8), a view no doubt shared by many Spanish male spectators at the time. Yet the late eighteenth century witnessed an increase in the effective, though not necessarily legal, rights of women. If it can be argued that Isabel's decision to enter a convent, which still requires Roque's approval (Andioc 1995: 556), represents a victory for Isabel, it would nevertheless appear that Italian female spectators would not countenance such a dénouement.

One contemporary Spanish critic of Moratín's play, José Luis Munárriz, offered some valuable thoughts on the ending in relation to prevailing concepts of justice (Munárriz 1804: 321–3). Given the situation at the beginning of Act I, he thought that Moratín's capacity to create suspense in the development of the action ('enredo') was severely constrained, which in his view weakened the impact of the dénouement. He expresses disagreement with the author as to the justice of the ending, not appearing to see it as in any sense a victory for Isabel:

> Esta falta de gradación en el enredo, hace que el desenlaze por otra parte melancólico, solo cause la extrañeza de ver víctima de un matrimonio inconsiderado y desigual á la persona inocente. Es verdad que don Roque no puede sufrir la idea de separación; desde que se la sugiere Muñoz en la escena I del acto II. Pero puestos en la necesidad de separarse ¿quién es el

mas desdichado? Isabel, que se condena á una estrecha clausura; donde si
vivirá, será para ver á todas horas la imagen de un amante engañado: de su
amante tan inocente é infeliz como ella, y que á impulsos de su despecho
puede apresurarse su ruina. (Munárriz 1804: 322)

Munárriz's words indicate considerable sympathy for Isabel and disagreement
over the meting out of justice as determined by Moratín. In particular, the
phrase 'se condena á una estrecha clausura' suggests punishment for Isabel
rather than a victory. The situation evokes that of Gutierre in Calderón's
El médico de su honra, whose innocent wife lies dead, while he, as guilty
husband, merely has to suffer her loss while carrying on living.

In Napoli Signorelli's ending Isabella suppresses the consequences of her
feelings for Carlo to the extent of persuading him to abandon her and all
hope of a future relationship. Her decision to accede to Beatrice's solution to
remain married, but as if in name only, still constitutes a sacrifice, but one
that will only cause distress in the short term at having to share a house with
Rocco. Ironically Rocco's future demise is likely to evoke the same lack of
grief which, in his perverse way, he attributed to Beatrice when the death of
her husband left her a rich widow (Act I, sc. 2). Rocco's final situation in *Il
vecchio e la giovane* is more in line with the punishment deserved by someone
as inhuman as he has proven himself to be, an individual whose objectionable
qualities are so effectively portrayed in Moratín's characterization. Taken in
conjunction with his imperious treatment of his wife (underlined in the word
'tirano' used to describe him, Act I, sc. 2), his obsessive miserliness, absurd
jealousy and lack of sympathetic, humanizing characteristics would seem to
merit more than the privation of Isabella which Moratín's ending provides.
Andioc sees Napoli Signorelli's ending as a 'reconciliación' (Andioc 1976:
432); in some respects the ending would seem more like a truce, with an
external agent (Beatrice) called on to enforce the peace. Sceptical contemporary spectators, especially female ones, might have imagined that Beatrice
would need all her persuasive powers to keep Rocco to his word.

The modified ending forces Rocco to a rethink, to accept something
approximating the separation to which he had earlier voiced objections (Act
II, sc. 1), but it is an arrangement which will be worked out in practice under
the one roof. The pressure on him occasioned by Beatrice's solution, which
finds the support of Isabella, produces the acceptance of a modification in
his behaviour and constitutes a victory for reason, subtly avoiding the trans-
gression of the social convention which requires respect for the institution
of marriage. Rocco's situation, as overseen by Beatrice, parallels the ending
of *La mojigata,* in which the re-education of Martín, after his moral failure
over his daughter's upbringing, is enforced by his brother Luis. Moratín had
portrayed Beatriz as balanced, reasonable and sympathetic; Napoli Signorel-

li's ingenious alternative ending seems inspired by Moratín's characterization. The mature Napoli Signorelli was able to understand women's feelings and aspirations and give them imaginative expression. His alternative ending was a provocative act, but one whose principles, I would argue, faithfully reflected Moratín's thinking in 1805 when he revisited the same social and moral ground in the more overtly comic *El sí de las niñas*.

List of Works Cited

Aguilar Piñal, Francisco, 1984. *Bibliografía de autores españoles del siglo XVIII* (Madrid: Consejo Superior de Investigaciones Científicas), III, pp. 341–402

Andioc, René, [1976] 1987. *Teatro y sociedad en el Madrid del siglo XVIII* (Madrid: Castalia)

——, 1995. 'El viejo y la niña', in *Historia de la literatura española. Siglo XVIII*, ed. Guillermo Carnero (Madrid: Espasa Calpe), pp. 550–9

——, 2005. *Del siglo XVIII al XIX. Estudios histórico-literarios* (Zaragoza: Prensas Universitarias de Zaragoza)

Caldera, Ermanno, 1980. 'Pietro Napoli Signorelli traduttore di Moratín', in *Studi di letteratura italiana in onore di Fausto Montanari* (Genoa: Il Melangolo), pp. 149–60

[Cladera, Cristóbal] Fulgencio del Soto, 1790. 'Artículo V', *Correo de Madrid*, 371 (19 June): 147–51

Deacon, Philip, 1996. 'La traducción de *Hamlet* de Leandro Fernández de Moratín', in *Teatro clásico en traducción: texto, representación, recepción*, ed. Ángel Luis Pujante and Keith Gregor (Murcia: Universidad de Murcia), pp. 299–308

——, 2001. Review of Leandro Fernández de Moratín, *Il vecchio e la giovane. Traduzione di Pietro Napoli Signorelli*, ed. Belén Tejerina, *Dieciocho*, 24: 178–81

——, 2004. '"Efectos de la crianza": *La Mojigata* de Leandro Fernández de Moratín', *Dieciocho*, 27: 87–100

Di Pinto, Mario, 1980. 'La tesis feminista de Moratín. Una hipótesis de lectura de "El viejo y la niña"', in *Coloquio internacional sobre Leandro Fernández de Moratín, Bolonia, 27–29 de octubre 1978* (Abano Terme: Piovan), pp. 75–91

Fernández de Moratín, Leandro, 1825. *Obras dramáticas y líricas* (Paris: Imprenta de Augusto Bobée), I

——, 1867. 'Prólogo', *Obras póstumas* (Madrid: Imprenta y Estereotipia de M. Rivadeneyra), I, pp. 154–60

——, 1970. *Teatro completo, I. El viejo y la niña. El sí de las niñas*, ed. Fernando Lázaro Carreter (Barcelona: Labor)

——, 1973. *Epistolario de Leandro Fernández de Moratín*, ed. René Andioc (Madrid: Castalia)

——, 1996. *Il vecchio e la giovane. Traduzione di Pietro Napoli Signorelli*, ed. Belén Tejerina (Naples: Liguori)

García Garrosa, María Jesús and Francisco Lafarga, 2004. *El discurso sobre la traducción en la España del siglo XVIII. Estudio y antología* (Kassel: Edition Reichenberger)

Hufton, Olwen, 1995. *The Prospect Before Her. A History of Women in Western Europe*. I: *1500–1800* (London: HarperCollins)

[Lista, Alberto], 1821. 'Teatros. *El sí de las niñas*: comedia en tres actos en prosa. Su autor Inarco Celenio P.A.', *El Censor*, 11: 336–42

Mariutti de Sánchez Rivero, Angela, 1960. 'Un ejemplo de intercambio cultural hispano-italiano en el siglo XVIII: Leandro Fernández de Moratín y Pietro Napoli Signorelli, *Revista de la Universidad de Madrid*, 9: 763–808

Munárriz, José Luis, 1804. *Lecciones sobre la retórica y las bellas letras, por Hugo Blair* (Madrid: Imprenta Real), IV, pp. 321–3

Napoli Signorelli, Pedro, 1867. 'Carta a Moratín', in Leandro Fernández de Moratín, *Obras póstumas* (Madrid: Imprenta y Estereotipia de M. Rivadeneyra), II, pp. 119–23

Quinziano, Franco, 2002. 'Pedro Napoli Signorelli y Leandro Fernández de Moratín: amistad, afinidades e influjos literarios', *eHumanista*, 2: 188–236

A Poem For All Seasons: Gil Vicente in Translation

PATRICIA ODBER DE BAUBETA

Twenty-first-century readers may be surprised at the ease with which the poems of Gil Vicente (1465?–1536?) continue to travel across temporal, spatial and linguistic borders, thus becoming new – or renewed – lyrics for the enjoyment of successive generations. One Vicentine poem in particular illustrates this phenomenon, 'En la huerta nasce la rosa', included in the *Auto de los cuatro tiempos*, written and performed for the court of D. Manuel I and first translated into English just over three centuries ago.

> En la huerta nasce la rosa
> quiérome ir allá
> por mirar al ruiseñor
> cómo cantaba.
>
> Por las riberas del río
> limones coge la virgo
> quiérome ir allá
> por mirar al ruiseñor
> cómo cantaba.
>
> Limones cogía la virgo
> para dar al su amigo
> quiérome ir allá
> para ver al ruiseñor
> cómo cantaba.

This chapter brings together a love of Gil Vicente, an abiding interest in translation, and a perverse enthusiasm for the arcane, all of which I can honestly attribute to Nick Round. Much of the 'detective work' was already done by the North American scholar Constantine Stathatos, who has produced and published a series of bibliographies to facilitate the task of the Vicentine scholar. Much of the data retrieval was facilitated by my generous collaborators, Dr Manuela Carvalho, Dr John Hobbs, Dr Amélia Hutchinson, Dr Helen Kelsh, Dr Ann MacLaren, Dr Sonia Pérez Villanueva, Dr Maria Helena da Fonseca de Oliveira Rodrigues, Dr Jane Whetnall, Dr Claire Williams.

The author holds the University of Birmingham's *Cátedra Gil Vicente*.

Para dar al su amigo
en un sombrero de sirgo
quiérome ir allá
para ver al ruiseñor
cómo cantaba.[1]

In fact, this poem has been rendered in English, in whole or in part, by ten different translators, and their translations have appeared in print and on the Internet at least 23 times. This may not seem especially significant, until we consider that the 1824 translation was reproduced as recently as 2003, thus prevailing, in a Darwinian sort of way, over its successors and rivals.

The first English translator was Sir John Bowring (1792–1870), remembered as a diplomat, political commentator, linguist, minor poet and the compiler of *Ancient Poetry and Romances of Spain* (1824), in which he included seven Vicentine lyrics:

'Muy graciosa es la doncella' (*Auto de la sibila Casandra*)
'En la huerta nasce la rosa' (*Auto de los cuatro tiempos*)
'Del rosal vengo, mi madre' (*Triunfo do Inverno*)
'Si dormís, doncella' (*Quem tem farelos?*)
'Mal haya quien los envuelve' (*Auto de los cuatro tiempos*)
'Sañosa está la niña' (*Auto de la sibila Casandra*)
'¿Cúal es la niña/ que coge las flores?' (*O Velho da Horta*)

The acknowledged source text is the *Copilaçam de todas as Obras*, Lisbon, 1562 (1824: 315), but his selection and ordering of the poems are identical to those made by Johann Nikolaus Böhl von Faber (1821), an important participant in what Osório Mateus has described as 'a revolução bibliográfica nas cidades da Alemanha' (2002b: 258). Indeed, on more than one occasion Mateus refers to 'o Gil Vicente que a literatura romântica privilegiou', though he did not have Gil Vicente's English translators specifically in mind (2002a: 153).

Bowring was extremely interested in the ballad tradition of Europe, and, I would argue, was very much the product or follower of the Romantic tendencies that prevailed at the end of the eighteenth and beginning of the nineteenth centuries, namely the 'conscious revivalism' identified by Gillian Beer (1970), and explained more fully by Breen and Noble (2002: 20). This

---

[1] This version is taken from *As Obras de Gil Vicente*, vol. I (Camões 2002: 95–6). It should be borne in mind that within the play, the song is interspersed with speech. Those who read it in translation are therefore reading not only a mediated version of the poem, but one that has been taken completely out of its context. On the other hand, as Arthur Terry has noted, some Vicentine lyrics are 'self-contained' and can stand alone (1965: xvii).

'conscious revivalism' describes cultural trends such as antiquarianism as well as retrospectively defined movements such as Orientalism. In poetry, this antiquarianism and exoticism was variously characterized by collections of old ballads and oral poetry, such as Percy's *Reliques* (1765), by works of pseudo-antiquity such as MacPherson's Ossian poems (1760–63), and by works that drew on the popular ballad such as Wordsworth's *Lyrical Ballads* (1798) (Breen and Noble 2002: 20).

Bowring deliberately integrates himself into the antiquarian movement and adopts the poetic diction of the English Romantic poets. As Entwistle points out:

> They [the ballads] came back to favour with the Romantic movement of the early nineteenth century [...] the Romantics, furthermore, were digesting all their past national traditions simultaneously. (1939: 187)

It is surely no coincidence that Keats's 'Ode to a Nightingale', with its references to summer and warmth,[2] was published in July 1819, barely five years before Bowring's own compilation, which combines both the antiquarian (medieval and late medieval) with the exotic (Peninsular and Moorish). Fascinated by various national traditions simultaneously, his work bridges the divide between late medieval or Renaissance Portugal, and nineteenth-century England, but always, I believe, with Shakespeare in the background.[3] All three are concerned with the natural world, the seasons, the passing of time.

Bowring felt it necessary to give his translations English titles, adopting the domesticating approach. In her study *Tradition and the Individual Poem. An Inquiry into Anthologies*, Anne Ferry draws our attention to:

> the ways anthologies are arranged, and of how arrangements of entries and other devices for presenting them – for instance, titling them and revising their language and form – can exercise authority over poems and readers. (2001: 2)

Thus for Bowring, 'En la huerta nasce la rosa' becomes 'The Nightingale', simultaneously harking back to the medieval lyric (Provençal and Peninsular), as well as paying homage to Keats:

> The rose looks out in the valley,
> And thither will I go,

---

2   See also the 'Ode on a Grecian Urn', 'To Autumn'.
3   Both the *Auto de los cuatro tiempos* and the *Triunfo do Inverno* bring to mind certain Shakespearian songs, for instance 'Under the Greenwood Tree' from *As You Like It*.

To the rosy vale, where the nightingale
Sings his song of woe.

The virgin is on the river side
Culling the lemons pale;
Thither – yes! thither will I go,
To the rosy vale, where the nightingale
Sings his song of woe.

The fairest fruit her hand hath cull'd,
'Tis for her lover all:
Thither – yes! thither will I go,
To the rosy vale, where the nightingale
Sings his song of woe.

In her hat of straw, for her gentle swain,
She has placed the lemons pale.
Thither – yes! thither will I go,
To the rosy vale, where the nightingale
Sings his song of woe.

Our interpretation of this poem may vary according to whether the translator gives prominence to the rose, symbol of burgeoning female sexuality, as Alan Deyermond has explained (1990: 130; 2001: 27), or the nightingale, traditionally associated with Spring, the messenger of love, representative of the lover himself and eventually symbol of sorrow and pain (Shippey 1970: 46–60; Pfeffer 1995; Devoto 1990: 259–307; Pampín Barral 2001: 63–71). Certainly, Bowring introduces a note of sadness into his translation, with the 'song of woe'. He also translates 'sirgo' as 'straw' instead of 'silk', which in conjunction with 'swain', renders it rather more rustic than the original poem, which was, after all, included in a play destined for a court (and courtly) audience. He also unwittingly removes an allusion to an earlier poetic tradition, the Galician Portuguese women's-voice songs, as represented by Estevan Coelho's *cantiga de amigo* (a spinning song), 'Sedia la fremosa seu sirgo torcendo' (Brea 1996: I, 245).

Bowring's book is one of the earliest English anthologies of poems composed by Spanish and Portuguese poets, and it seems highly likely that his choice of texts for translation established the pattern for those who came after.[4] If Bowring followed Böhl von Faber, Bowring's successors were equally influenced by his preferences in making their own selections for subsequent

---

[4] An earlier anthology (Herbert 1806) also includes a Portuguese poem, Camões's 'Vão as serenas águas', which also appears in volume XV of Longfellow's *Poems of Places* (1876–79).

compilations, which demonstrates the fundamental role played by anthologists and translators in creating a canon:

> Those who are in positions to edit anthologies and prepare reading lists are obviously those who occupy positions of cultural power; and their acts of evaluation – represented in what they exclude as well as in what they include – constitute not merely recommendations of value but [...] also determinants of value. (Smith 1984: 29–30)

Numerous readers and scholars have had recourse to Bowring's work, and his translations have continued to be selected for inclusion in a series of anthologies, the first of which was Henry Wadsworth Longfellow's monumental work *The Poets and Poetry of Europe* (1845). This contains 'How fair the maiden' and 'The rose looks out in the valley'. (Longfellow's compilation was published in London in 1855.)

In the 1870s Bowring's translation of 'En la huerta' was included in another major North American anthology, William Cullen Bryant's *Library of World Poetry, being the Choice Selections from the Best Poets* (1870). Again we see an anthologist exercising his authority, which, in Bryant's case, was not inconsiderable:

> Because their own status was so great, the judgments about the 'best' that Bryant, Emerson, and Whittier made in their anthologies had great influence, And those anthologies kept the canon stable, self-perpetuating. (Golding 1983: 291–2)

Golding also makes the point that the New England poets, while responsible for the 'conservation of European literary tradition', also 'used their anthologies to preserve or enhance their own reputations' (1983: 292).

Translation theorists Helga Essmann and Armin Paul Frank make a distinction between external and internal translation history research, suggesting that, for the former, a series of 'institutional' questions should be asked:

> Which texts by which authors do we find in an anthology? Who were the translators? When and under what circumstances was the anthology made? [...] (What texts are placed in sequence? What other relations are recognizable between the selected works – between the works of various authors or, if applicable, between works of several literatures?) (1991: 73)

If we apply these questions to Bryant, we note that he includes the poem, with minor differences of punctuation, in the section 'Poems of Nature' (1999: 295–373), and that, within this section, Bowring's nightingale perches alongside poems dedicated to the lark, cuckoo, belfry pigeon, thrush, robin, swallow, owl, pelican and stormy petrel, among others. From this we may speculate that the Vicentine nightingale found its way into the anthology as much on the strength of Bowring's title as on the actual content of the poem. Had Bowring chosen to give precedence to the rose or the maiden, perhaps his translation might have passed unnoticed. Instead, because Bryant's compilation has been reissued repeatedly, and almost continuously available since its first appearance, the most recent edition dating from 1999, Gil Vicente's nightingale continues to sing.[5]

Throughout the twentieth century, Bowring's Vicentine translations continued to satisfy anthologists' needs. Thus, in 1920, Thomas Walsh (1875–1928) included 'En la huerta' in *Hispanic Anthology* (reprinted in 1969). Walsh included the same translation in *The Catholic Anthology* (1927; revised edition 1932, with subsequent reprints). And as recently as 2003, Bowring's translation was published on the Poetry Archive on the Internet, taken from Walsh's *Hispanic Anthology* of 1920.[6] So we may very reasonably argue that Bowring's translation has withstood the test of time.

The second translation of 'En la huerta nasce la rosa' appeared in a review of the Hamburg edition of the *Obras de Gil Vicente* (1834), published in the *Quarterly Review* in 1846.[7] While the translator is not named, I believe it could have been John Adamson, the noted English Lusophile.[8] In a letter to Almeida Garrett, dated 17 February 1845, Adamson writes:

> I waited sometime expecting you w^d have procured me the works of Gil Vicente, but as they did not arrive I sent to Hamburgh for them, and am busy translating the prefatory matter etc. with a view to making them known here. (Estorninho 1954: 720)[9]

Adamson had already mentioned Gil Vicente almost twenty years previously, in his letter of 28 January 1826:

---

[5] As for the reasons for this latest re-editing, my personal view is that it was a response to the publication of *World Poetry* (Washburn et al.) in 1998. The Bryant volume might not have been intended to compete directly with this new anthology, but it could certainly benefit from renewed attention to this kind of publication.

[6] At http://poetry-archive.com/v/the_nightingale.html, accessed 23 July 2003.

[7] This article is mentioned by Georgiana Goddard King in her monograph (1921: 47, n. 5).

[8] The article has traditionally been attributed to Edward Quillinan, and Miguel Alarcão e Silva certainly presents convincing arguments for Quillinan's authorship (1986, 1995). However, I believe that the case for Adamson is equally convincing.

[9] This and Adamson's other letters came to my attention in Silva's monograph (1990: 106–7).

I hope your friend will persevere in his intention of republishing the too long neglected work of Gil Vicente. In consequence of the sad state of affairs in Spain the finest libraries of that country have been sent to England and I have been earnestly looking forward to a copy of this author arriving in England for which I would give almost any money but none has yet made its appearance. (Estorninho 1954: 712–13)

We know that Adamson was not able to bring this translation project to fruition, not only because of the difficulty of the language, which he also mentions in his 1845 letter, but also because his library was destroyed by fire in 1849. However, given (a) the timing of this article, 1846; (b) the length and detailed knowledge it contains; (c) the fact that it contains translations of excerpts from plays and entire poems; (d) the coincidence that it is followed by a review of Almeida Garrett's *Um Auto de Gil Vicente*; and (e) that other nineteenth-century Lusophiles tended to focus on Camões, it is possible that it was Adamson, turning his work on Gil Vicente to good account, who wrote this article. The translation comes after a brief synopsis of the play:

Spring glides in singing a charming song. To translate it closely would be to cage the nightingale; but the following imitation of a portion of it is a faint echo of its sweetness:–

I'll away to the garden,
For winter is over;
The Rose is awake
To the song of her lover!
I will go and discover
The passionate Nightingale singing above her.

From the boughs green and golden
That slope to the river,
A Nymph gathers lemons
To give to her lover:
I will go and discover
The shy little Nightingale singing above her.

Near the vineyard, where often
I have spied out a rover,
Sits a damsel who sings
To be heard by her lover:
I will go and discover
The bold little Nightingale singing above her.

This translation dispenses with the repetitions and *leixa pren* of the original, and introduces a gradation of feeling or behaviour: the nightingale – or lover – grows more daring with each verse: 'The nightingale can also be a highly charged sexual image' (Pfeffer 1985: 4). The translator also makes the seasonal context explicit: 'for winter is over'. There is some degree of translator's licence in this version, given that there is no reference in the original to vineyards. One could criticize this modification on the grounds that it deletes the allusion to the traditional *locus amoenus* of medieval verse, with all its connotations and metonymic value. On the other hand, a vineyard is no less a symbol of fertility. This translation is reprinted in another North American multi-volume anthology, Charles Dudley Warner's compilation, *Library of the World's Best Literature*. Bowring's translation appears in Volume 28, with the addition of a title 'The Song of Spring' (1896–97: 16498).

The next translation to appear was that of Aubrey Bell, published in his *Lyrics of Gil Vicente*.[10]

> In the garden the roses blow:
> Thither, thither would I go
> To hear the nightingale in song
> All the night long.
>
> By the bank of the stream
> She is gathering lemons:
> And thither would I go
> To hear the nightingale in song
> All the night long.
>
> She was gathering lemons
> To give to her love:
> And thither would I go
> To hear the nightingale in song
> All the night long
>
> In a silken hat
> To give to her love:
> And thither would I go
> To hear the nightingale in song
> All the night long. (1914: 51; 1921: 55; 1925: 55)

Bell makes an explicit reference to the nightingale singing at night, which is in keeping with folkloric, literary and natural traditions. He retains the original tense scheme and tries as far as possible to incorporate rhyme into his version. This is not unexpected in the light of his comments about the

---

10 It should be noted that the editions are not identical, either in the selection of poems, or in the critical comments adduced. There are a number of differences between the first and second editions. The third is a reproduction of the second.

'modern' editions of Gil Vicente, in which 'the utmost indifference has been shown in the matter of rhyme, to which he himself was very attentive' (1929: 408).

In 1951 Gerald Brenan offered a partial translation to exemplify 'a villancico which develops from a little popular ditty':

> In the garden the rose is born.
> I want to go there
> to see how the nightingale is singing. (1976: 140)

In 1953, C. M. Bowra discusses the poem in his article, 'The Songs of Gil Vicente', but includes a translation of just two lines:

> To listen to the nightingale,
> How it sings its song.

Eleanor L. Turnbull, on the other hand, offers a complete and more dynamic translation in her anthology *Ten Centuries of Spanish Poetry: An Anthology in English Verse with Original Texts: From the XIth Century to the Generation of 1898*:

> In the garden blossoms the rose:
> Would that I could be there
> To see how the nightingale sings
> In that garden so fair!
>
> On the banks where the river flows
> Picking lemons the maiden goes:
> Would that I could be there
> To see how the nightingale sings
> In that garden so fair!
>
> Picking lemons the maiden goes
> To give to the loved one she knows:
> Would that I could be there
> To see how the nightingale sings
> In that garden so fair!
>
> To give to the loved one she knows
> In her silken hat the fruit she stows:
> Would that I could be there
> To see how the nightingale sings
> In that garden so fair! (1955: 129–31)

J. M. Cohen opted for a literal prose translation, in *The Penguin Book of Spanish Verse*:

> In the garden is born the rose, I want to go there to see the nightingale, how he sings.
> On the banks of the river, the maiden gathers lemons. I want to go there, to see the nightingale, how he sings.
> The maiden was gathering lemons to give to her love. I want to go there to see the nightingale, how he sings.
> To give them to her love in a hat of silken stuff. I want to go there to see the nightingale, how he sings. (1956: 122)

Cohen is extremely honest about his own limitations: 'The prose translations at the foot of each page aim at no literary merit; they are intended purely as aids to the reading of the Spanish' (1956: xxxviii), a disclaimer that is repeated in the third edition (1988). No changes are made to his Vicente translations.

Not unexpectedly, Cohen's rendering stands in contrast to the translation made by American poet Willis Barnstone, as a version that preserves the simplicity of the original, which is the key to its poetic quality:

> In the garden the rose is born:
> I want to go there
> to see how the nightingale
> is singing.
>
> Along the riverbanks
> the girl is picking lemons:
> I want to go there
> to see how the nightingale
> is singing.
>
> The girl was picking lemons
> to give her friend.
> I want to go there
> to see how the nightingale
> is singing.
>
> She had lemons in a silk hat
> to give her friend:
> I want to go there
> to see how the nightingale
> is singing. (1964: 90)

Barnstone has written on translation theory and anthologized/translated a number of Galician Portuguese and Portuguese poems, for which he continues to feel great affection.[11]

The most unusual translation, however, is that by Grover I. Jacoby:

> There's a rose's new life in the garden.
> How greatly I find to my liking
> The sight of the nightingale
> And its readiness to sing.
>
> And now, down banks of the river,
> The girl plucks the lemons there.
> How greatly I find to my liking
> The sight of the nightingale
> And its readiness to sing.
>
> The girl plucks the lemons there
> To give to a friend of hers.
> How greatly I find to my liking
> A sight of the nightingale
> And its readiness to sing.
>
> To give to a friend of hers
> The fruit in her silken hat goes.
> How greatly I find to my liking
> A sight of the nightingale
> And its readiness to sing. (1969: 212)

This translation stands out from the others because the translator introduces an unusual rhythm to the English version. Thus the first line can actually be sung to the tune of 'Oh what a beautiful morning', from the musical *Oklahoma*:

> There's a rose's new life in the garden
>
> ...
>
> There's a bright golden haze on the meadow,
> There's a bright golden haze on the meadow,
> The corn is as high as an elephant's eye,
> An' it looks like it's climbin' clear up to the sky.[12]

---

[11] 'I love medieval Portuguese poetry', in an email dated 5 May 2003, in response to my email of 26 April 2003. Most notable is the poet's generous offer: 'If I haven't translated the 'En la huerta nasce la rosa', I'll do so for you.' Had he not already translated this poem, it would have been a welcome addition to this chapter.

[12] A full transcription of the lyrics can be found at numerous Internet sites, some with musical accompaniment. See, for example, http://www.niehs.nih.gov/kids/lyrics/ohwhata.htm.

The reader – or listener – is tempted to imagine that this tune was running through Jacoby's head at the time he was engaged in translating the lyric. While any such speculation may seem far-fetched, there is some common ground: both poems do aim at a 'pseudo-rusticity' and it is not difficult to imagine that, like the lyrics from a popular American show, Gil Vicente's songs remained with their listeners long after the performance was over, and were sung or hummed for some time afterwards, acting as a reminder of a good night's entertainment.

Finally, we come to the translation made by Stephen Reckert:

> In the garden the rose is born:
> I will go there
> to see the nightingale,
> how he was singing.
>
> Along the riverbank
> the maiden is picking lemons:
> I will go there
> to see the nightingale,
> how he was singing.
>
> The maiden was picking lemons
> to give them to her friend:
> I will go there
> and see the nightingale,
> how he was singing.
>
> To give them to her friend
> in a hat of silk:
> I will go there
> and see the nightingale,
> how he was singing. (1993: 97)

This translation comes from both the head and the heart: a knowledge of poetry down the ages and across three continents, an understanding of the conventions which did *not* constrain their makers, and an unashamed love of poetry. Thus Reckert's translation, like the source poem, deliberately recalls the *cantigas de amigo* in its repetitions of words and structures and guilelessness, but still has a powerfully erotic subtext, due to the presence of those key symbols, the rose, nightingale, river, lemons and silken hat. Not an element is missing, nor has anything superfluous been added.

From the perspective of external translation history, viewed as a corpus the English translations of Gil Vicente's poems offer an excellent example of the politics of the anthology, the consequences of which may be seen as positive or negative. We may opt for pragmatic acceptance of certain publishing realities, such as the undeniable fact that '[t]he poetry of minorities is also dependent on anthologies for reaching a wider audience, and again anthologies have played an important role in making that poetry known' (Korte 2000: 11). Moreover, according to this critic, 'only poets and poems that have been anthologized have a good chance of becoming items of cultural memory or even inter-cultural memory' (2000: 12). Or we may experience a certain unease at the appropriation of Gil Vicente's lyrics in the interests of representativeness, and the projection of the Portuguese and Spanish as 'exotic others', recalling at the same time Eric Hobsbawm's trenchant observations in *Nations and Nationalism since 1780* on the position of 'small' peoples and languages in nineteenth-century Europe:

> The small people, language and culture fitted in with progress only insofar as it accepted subordinate status to some larger unit or retired from battle to become a repository of nostalgia and other sentiments – in short, accepted the status of old family furniture. (1991: 41)

Anne Ferry, for her part, points out how the anthologist 'supplants the author of the poem in choosing how it should be presented, with interpretative consequences',[13] and warns that 'the unique role and presence of the anthologist can give a different direction to the experience of reading a poem than if it were read elsewhere' (Ferry 2001: 2). This is undeniably the case when songs are taken out of plays in which they fulfil a specific artistic or structural function. And when the poems undergo the process of translation, yet another layer of mediation is imposed. On the other hand, not all of Gil Vicente's translators have been anthologists: some are theatre producers, composers or singers, whose performance-driven agenda produces a different kind of retextualization.

As far as internal translation history is concerned, the poems transcribed above present an illuminating microcosm of the range of options and challenges that face translators of Gil Vicente, his Galician Portuguese predecessors, and indeed, translators of poetry in general. A reading of the translated poems reveals the choices and decisions made over the course of time by translators who are quite naturally the product of their own time, formal education and wider reading. For example, how do they deal with the vexed question of rhyme? We have seen Aubrey Bell's opinion on this subject. On the question of whether to translate into prose or verse, the prizewinning translator Willard Ropes Trask (1900–1980) had unequivocal views on how

---

[13] In fact, this process was well established in respect of Gil Vicente's work. The *Copilaçam* of 1562 was compiled after his death by his son, who exercised his own judgement about the genres and ordering of the plays.

to deal with this 'problem'. Writing about his own translations of medieval Galician Portuguese lyrics he stated: 'Those in which structure predominates over content, I have put into verse; those in which the thought predominates over the structure, into prose (Trask 1978–79: 11).[14]

Translators also have to choose how to deal with repetition, deciding whether it truly exists and what purpose it fulfils. If they perceive it as integral to the meaning of the poem, they may retain it; if not, it is deleted. And they may not always be aware of subtle shifts within poems (Wardropper 1974–75; Reckert 1998). Certain lexical items, such as *amigo* and *amado*, may also present difficulties.

Versions of Gil Vicente's plays or individual poems have been published and performed on both sides of the Atlantic for almost two centuries. They still have much to say to an audience, in any language, because of Vicente's treatment of universal themes, love and the passing of time. For instance, in 'En la huerta nasce la rose', the mental picture conveyed by each stanza could be visualized as a medieval manuscript illumination, of the kind we find in Books of Hours or Calendars. This would certainly illustrate the seasonality of Gil Vicente's poetry. The first stanza might be the textualization of the painting of a walled garden with a rose bush in bud and a nightingale, both emblematic of Spring, renewal, and offering the promise of fertility. A second picture would show a solitary maiden on a riverbank picking lemons from a tree in summer or early autumn. A third miniature would depict the maiden, perhaps with a young man in the background making his way towards her. And finally, a representation of the girl offering her beloved the highly symbolic gift of fruit in a silk hat. This may be fanciful, but the static quality of the scene described in the poem has as much in common with the visual arts as with the lively performance of a song. There are obvious precedents for the diachronic representation of the maiden on the riverbank in those Galician Portuguese *cantigas de amigo* by Airas Nunes, 'Bailemos nós ja todas três, ay amigas' (Brea 1996: I, 122), and Joan Zorro, 'Bailemos agora, por Deus, ai velidas' (Brea 1996: II, 571). Commenting on the symbolic character of the landscape in the light of Kenneth Clark's seminal study *Landscape into Art* (1991: 1–31), Deyermond offers a convincing explanation for the compression of a whole natural (reproductive) cycle into one short poem:

> It is true that, as Sir Kenneth Clark emphasizes, medieval artists and writers offer us a landscape of symbols, not a landscape realistically observed for

---

[14] While he is not commenting directly on the Vicentine lyrics, it should be pointed out that Trask did translate at least one poem by Gil Vicente, 'Muy graciosa es la doncella', for inclusion in his *Medieval Lyrics of Europe* (1969: 142).

its own sake, but they knew the natural world around them, and they knew that trees do not simultaneously bear flowers and hazelnuts. (1990: 138)

This goes some way towards explaining how Gil Vicente can have roses coming into bud and lemons ripe for the picking within the same poem. Both are symbolic of the maiden about to surrender her virginity, like the young women of the *cantigas de amigo*:

Stanza 1 is set in spring, the season of fertility; stanza 2 in autumn, the season of fruition. The girls who were dancing in their courtship rituals, passing from virginity into sexual experience, as the hazel-trees flowered, are now, months later, dancing again, but big with child as the trees are heavy with nuts. (1990: 138)

Gil Vicente's poem also takes us from spring to autumn, and yet, paradoxically, it is curiously timeless – for Stephen Reckert 'the sun stands for ever at noon' (1993: 97). It is these qualities which ensure that Gil Vicente's 'En la huerta nasce la rosa' is, indeed, a poem for all seasons.

List of Works Cited

Anon., 1846–47. 'Ancient Portuguese Drama. Gil Vicente', *Quarterly Review*, LXXIX, 157 (December 1846-March 1847): 168–202

Alarcão e Silva, Miguel, 1986. *Edward Quillinan e Portugal* [texto policopiado] Lisboa. Dissertação de Mestrado em Estudos Anglo-Portugueses, apresentada à F.C.S.H. da UNL Faculdade de Ciências Sociais e Humanas da Universidade Nova de Lisboa

——, 1995. 'Home is Where the Heart is: A Obra Lusófila de Edward Quillinan (1791–1851)', *Revista de Estudos Anglo-Portugueses*, 4: 87–132

Barnstone, Willis, 1964. 'Poetry of the Spanish Renaissance', *Antioch Review*, 24: 88–93

Beer, Gillian, 1970. *The Romance*, The Critical Idiom, 10 (London: Methuen)

Bell, Aubrey F. G., 1914. *Lyrics of Gil Vicente*, 1st edn (Oxford: Blackwell) [2nd edn 1921, different in some respects from the previous edition; 3rd edn 1925, reprint of the second]

——, 1929. 'Notes for an Edition of Gil Vicente', *Revue Hispanique*, 77: 382–408

Böhl von Faber, Johann Nikolaus, 1821. *Primera parte de la Floresta de Rimas Antiguas Castellanas*, ordenadas por Don Juan Nicolás Böhl de Faber (Hamburgo: en la librería de Perthes y Besser), pp. 301–3

Bowra, C. M., 1953. 'The Songs of Gil Vicente', *Atlante*, 1: 3–21 [repr. 1955 with minor alterations, in *Inspiration and Poetry* (London: Macmillan), pp. 90–111]

Bowring, John, 1824. *The Ancient Poetry and Romances of Spain* (London: Taylor & Hessey)

Brea, Mercedes (coord.), 1996. *Lírica Profana Galego-Portuguesa*, 2 vols (Santiago de Compostela: Xunta de Galicia/Centro de Investigacións Lingüísticas e Literarias Ramón Piñeiro)

Breen, Jennifer and Mary Noble, 2002. *Romantic Literature* (London: Arnold, Contexts)

Brenan, Gerald, 1976. *The Literature of the Spanish People: From Roman Times to the Present Day*, 1st paperback edn (Cambridge: Cambridge University Press) [first publ. 1951]

Bryant, William Cullen, 1870. *Library of World Poetry, being the Choice Selections from the Best Poets*, intro. William Cullen Bryant (New York: Avenel Books) [reissued many times, including 1970 (New York: Avenel Books), 1995 and 1999 under a slightly different title, *The Illustrated Library of World Poetry* (New York: Grammercy)]

Camões, José (dir.), 2002. *As Obras de Gil Vicente*, vol. I (Lisboa: Centro de Estudos de Teatro, Imprensa Nacional-Casa da Moeda)

Clark, Kenneth, 1991. 'The Landscape of Symbols', in *Landscape into Art* (London: John Murray), pp. 1–31 [first publ. 1949; new edn 1976, repr. 1991]

Cohen, J. M., 1956. *The Penguin Book of Spanish Verse* [revised in 1960, repr. In 1970; 3rd edn 1988, with the slightly modified title: *The Penguin Book of Spanish Verse: New Parallel Text Edition*]

Devoto, Daniel, 1990. 'Calandrias y ruiseñores', *Bulletin Hispanique*, 91: 259–307

Deyermond, Alan, 1990. 'Sexual Initiation in the Woman's Voice Court Lyric', in *Courtly Literature: Culture and Context* (Selected Papers from the 5th Triennial Congress of the International Courtly Literature Society, Dalfsen, The Netherlands, 9–16 August 1986), ed. Keith Busby and Erik Kooper (Amsterdam and Philadelphia: John Benjamins), pp. 125–58

——, 2001. 'Las imágenes populares en cancioneros musicales', in *Lyra Mínima Oral. Los géneros breves de la literatura tradicional* (Actas del Congreso Internacional celebrado en la Universidad de Alcalá, 28–30 octubre 1998), ed. Carlos Alvar, Cristina Castillo, Mariana Masera and José Manuel Pedrosa (Alcalá de Henares: Universidad de Alcalá), pp. 17–29

Entwistle, William J., 1939. *European Balladry* (Oxford: Clarendon Press)

Essmann, Helga and Armin Paul Frank, 1991. 'Translation Anthologies: An Invitation to the Curious and a Case Study', *Target*, 3.1: 65–90

Estorninho, Carlos, 1954. 'Letters from British Correspondents to Almeida Garrett', *Annual Report and Review of the Historical Association, Portugal Branch, Twelfth Annual Report and Review* (Lisbon), 711–22

Ferry, Anne, 2001. *Tradition and the Individual Poem: An Inquiry into Anthologies* (Stanford, Ca: Stanford University Press)

Golding, Alan, 1983. 'A History of American Poetry Anthologies', in *Canons*, ed. Robert von Hallberg (Chicago and London: University of Chicago Press), pp. 279–307 [see also 1995. *From Outlaw to Classic: Canons in American*

Poetry, The Wisconsin Project on American Writers (Madison: University of Wisconsin Press)]

Herbert, W., 1806. *Translations from the Italian, Spanish, Portuguese, German and Danish etc.: To Which Was Added Miscellaneous Poetry* (London: Longman, Hurst, Rees & Orme)

Hobsbawm, E. J., 1991. *Nations and Nationalism since 1780: Programme, Myth, Reality* (Cambridge: Cambridge University Press, Canto) [first publ. 1990]

Jacoby, Grover I., 1969. *Translations: Comment in Motion* (Versions of poems by Petrarch, Michelangelo, Hölderlin, Heine, Christine de Pisan, Charles d'Orléans, Gil Vicente, Garcilaso de la Vega, Lope de Vega, Calderón, Bécquer, Rosalía Castro), no. VII (Los Angeles, Cal: The Variegation Publishing Company)

King, Georgiana Goddard, 1921. *The Play of the Sibyl Cassandra* (Pennsylvania: Bryn Mawr College and New York, Bombay, Calcutta and Madras: Longmans, Green)

Korte, Barbara, 2000. 'Flowers for the Picking. Anthologies in (British) Literary and Cultural Studies', in *Anthologies of British Poetry. Critical Perspectives from Literary and Cultural Studies*, ed. Barbara Korte, Ralf Schneider and Stefanie Lethbridge (Amsterdam and Atlanta GA: Rodopi), pp. 1–32

Longfellow, Henry Wadsworth (ed.), 1845. *The Poets and Poetry of Europe*, 1st edn (Philadelphia: Carey & Hart) [I refer to the 1855 edn publ. in London by Sampson Low]

—— (ed. and trans.), 1876–79. *Poems of Places* (Boston: R. Osgood)

Mateus, Osório, 2002a. 'Vicente, Santarém, 1531', in *De teatro e outras escritas*, ed. José Camões (Lisboa: Quimera in collaboration with the Centro de Estudos de Teatro), pp. 153–61

——, 2002b. 'Vicente na Edição Romântica', in *De teatro e outras escritas*, ed. José Camões (Lisboa: Quimera in collaboration with the Centro de Estudos de Teatro), pp. 258–62

Pampín Barral, Mercedes, 2001. 'Cantan ruyseñores cantares más de ciento': la evaluación del canto del ruiseñor en la poesía cancioneril', in *Lyra Mínima Oral. Los géneros breves de la literatura tradicional* (Actas del Congreso Internacional celebrado en la Universidad de Alcalá, 28–30 octubre 1998), ed. Carlos Alvar, Cristina Castillo, Mariana Masera and José Manuel Pedrosa (Alcalá de Henares: Universidad de Alcalá), pp. 63–71

Pfeffer, Wendy, 1985. *The Change of Philomel. The Nightingale in Medieval Literature*, American University Studies Series III. Comparative Literature, vol. XIV (New York: Peter Lang)

Reckert, Stephen, 1993. *Beyond Chrysanthemums: Perspectives on Poetry East and West* (Oxford: Clarendon Press)

——, 1998. *Play it again, Sam* ('The Question of Repetition and Is There Any Such Thing?'), The Kate Elder Lecture (London: University of London, Queen Mary and Westfield College, Department of Hispanic Studies)

Shippey, Thomas, 1970. 'Listening to the Nightingale', *Comparative Literature*, 22: 46–60

Silva, João Paulo Ascenso Pereira da, 1990. *Memórias de Portugal. A Obra Lusófila de John Adamson* (Ponta Delgada: Eurosigno Publicações)
Smith, Barbara Herrnstein, 1984. 'Contingencies of Value', in *Canons*, ed. Robert von Hallberg (Chicago and London: University of Chicago Press), pp. 5–39 [revised version (1988), included in *Contingencies of Value: Alternative Perspectives for Critical Theory* (Cambridge, MA and London: Harvard University Press)]
Stathatos, Constantine C., 1975. 'A Bibliography of Translations of Gil Vicente's Work since 1940', *Vórtice*, Stanford University, I: 3, 83–8
——, 1977. 'Anglo-American Contributions to the Study of Gil Vicente: A Bibliography (1940–1975)', *Sillages*, 5: 127–56
——, 1980. *A Gil Vicente Bibliography (1940–1975)* (London: Grant & Cutler)
——, 1997. *A Gil Vicente Bibliography (1975–1995), with a Supplement for 1940–1975* (Bethlehem, PA: Lehigh University Press, and London, Cranbury, NJ: Associated University Presses)
——, 2001. *A Gil Vicente Bibliography (1995–2000)*. Teatro del Siglo de Oro, Bibliografías y Catálogos, 36 (Kassel: Edition Reichenerger)
Terry, Arthur (ed.), 1965. *An Anthology of Spanish Poetry 1500–1700, Part I: 1500–80* (Oxford: Pergamon Press)
Trask, Willard Ropes (ed.), 1969. *Medieval Lyrics of Europe* (New York and Cleveland: World Publishing Company)
——, 1978–79. 'Songs from the Galician Portuguese', *Translation*, 6 (Winter): 8–22
Turnbull, Eleanor L. (ed.), 1955. *Ten Centuries of Spanish Poetry. An Anthology in English Verse with Original Texts: From the XIth Century to the Generation of 1898* (Baltimore: Johns Hopkins Press)
Walsh, Thomas (ed.), 1920. *Hispanic Anthology: Poems Translated from the Spanish by English and North American Poets*, Hispanic Notes and Monographs (New York and London: G. P. Putnam's Sons) [reprinted 1969 (New York: Klaus Reprint Co.)]
—— (ed.), 1927. *The Catholic Anthology: The World's Greatest Catholic Poetry* (New York: Macmillan) [revised edns 1932 and 1947 (New York: Macmillan)]
Wardropper, Bruce, 1974–75. 'On the Supposed Repetitiousness of the *Cantigas de Amigo*', *Revista Hispánica Moderna*, 38: 1–6.
Warner, Charles Dudley (ed.), 1896–97. *Library of the World's Best Literature*, 30 vols (New York: Peale & Hill)
Washburn, Katherine, John S. Major and Clifton Fadiman (eds), 1998. *World Poetry: An Anthology of Verse from Antiquity to Our Time* (New York: Quality Paperback Book Club)

Knocked Down with a (Vulture's) Feather: Some Issues of Everyday Argumentation, Humour and Translation

ROBIN WARNER

The possibility that the practical interests of those engaged in second-language-related activities may afford a distinctive insight into language theory has fairly recently been endorsed by Stephen Levinson, who, in his influential *Presumptive Meanings*, specifically commends the concern of students of translation and second language learning with 'a great body of language lore beyond knowledge of grammar and semantics' (2000: 23). Appropriately encouraged, I embark here on discussion of some applications of a particular area of discourse pragmatics – that of argumentation – to a field to which the dedicatee of this volume has made important contributions: the interface of humour studies and translation (Round 1995, 1996, 1998, 2005). On the assumption that linguistic theory can make useful contributions to practical activity by providing guidelines for reflexive monitoring of intuitive or *ad hoc* procedures, it is proposed here that greater familiarity with argumentational structures and strategies can both help identify certain ways in which verbal humour is produced and offer guidance in the search for equivalent effects. If, as someone once observed, one of the problems with jokes is that they are not taken seriously, another is certainly the fact that individual responses to humorous presentations are notoriously diverse. What amuses and provokes laughter in one person can leave another unmoved and even irritated. In terms of intentionality or function, however, it is feasible to categorize certain text-genres – such as cartoons appearing in newspapers – as expressly oriented towards the creation of humour, and it is from material of this type that virtually all the examples analysed here are drawn.

One of the obstacles often faced by translators is that verbal humour does not, on the whole, travel well. When the humour is derived from linguistic forms themselves the difficulties are immediately obvious. Puns and double-meanings, for example, often oblige the translator to opt for a 'second best'

solution by finding a lexical item in the co-text more amenable to translation as a polysemous term or a homonym. So called 'garden path' sentences
(such as 'we saw her duck', or 'es gato y araña') are even more intractable,
as this sort of ambivalence cannot be transferred when the different syntactical categories concerned are clearly differentiated in the morphology of the
target language. We should also bear in mind, however, that verbal humour is
not limited to the specific semantic/phonological properties of given lexical
items or expressions, but is deeply embedded in a particular linguistic culture,
a circumstance that raises for translators problems that are often difficult to
pin down let alone solve. Indeed, in one pessimistic view, the interlocking of
formal linguistic features and socio-cultural elements in some types of joke is
often 'so specific to a single language community that, beyond its frontiers,
the joke is unlikely to succeed' (Chiaro 1992: 78).

On the other hand, there is one frequently encountered type of verbal
humour that seems able to cross the language-gap without much difficulty. Of
the two examples below, the Spanish joke, taken from an anthology featuring
the popular Latin American cartoon character Condorito de Oro (depicted
here with his fiancée on a park bench), was published some fifty years later
than its English counterpart; yet, give or take one or two details, each piece
of dialogue could virtually stand as a translation of the other:

> Bert and Florrie were at the point of discussing where and how the honey-
> moon should be spent. 'Let's go to Margate by boat,' suggested Bert. 'No
> dear, that won't do, I'm always seasick,' replied the girl. 'Rubbish. Love is
> a good remedy for that.' 'Yes,' said the young lady thoughtfully, 'but what
> about the return journey?' (Aye 1933: 246)

> CONDORITO: Yayita, ¿qué te parece un viaje de novios por el mar?
> YAYITA: Ya sabes el miedo que le tengo al mar.
> CONDORITO: No te preocupes. El amor es el mejor remedio para el mareo.
> YAYITA: Sí, pero ... ¿y a la vuelta?[1]

The Spanish cartoon, as do all those in the *Condorito de oro* series,
concludes with the legend '¡PLOP!' as a character (in this case the little
vulture himself) falls over backwards, stupefied by a retort that constitutes the
punch line. Before investigating further the particular feature of language use
exploited in this type of verbal humour, it is worth mentioning briefly some
existing contributions of linguistic theory to the study of this topic.

It has become virtually axiomatic that humour involves a perception of
incongruity, of the yoking together of elements that are substantially incompatible; in verbal humour the form taken by this effect can range from the

[1] *Condorito de oro: selección de los mejores chistes*, 1987, without page numbers.

conjoining of two different meanings of an utterance to the co-presence of two mutually incompatible definitions or interpretations of a given situation.[2] The investigation of this sort of incongruity in joke-telling has been facilitated by the emergence, in recent decades, of a number of approaches to language use that share a focus of attention on communicative function rather than linguistic form and on the way the interactive and social contextualization of an utterance makes at least as important a contribution to its meaning as what is linguistically encoded. Areas of linguistic pragmatics such as Speech Act Theory, Politeness Phenomena and Gricean or Relevance-Theory approaches to inferencing provide effective tools for analysing humour, especially when an element of miscommunication – real or apparent – is involved. By and large, it would be fair to say that speakers described and reported in jokes provoke amusement because they opt for highly unsuitable politeness strategies, signally fail to satisfy the felicity conditions for their speech acts, produce utterances of minimal relevance and overlook conversational implicatures or unwittingly create inappropriate ones.[3]

The contention here is that everyday argumentation (EA) should be added to the list of discursive competences in which mistakes and failures are often linked with humour. EA is characterized for present purposes as an integral feature of all language use – including everyday uses of language, rather than as a specialized mode or genre (as it is often presented in manuals of composition). Indeed, it is viewed as something that plays an important role in discourse coherence. What is proposed is a broad definition along the following lines:

> Speakers giving reasons for or against their own or others' utterances with a view to getting hearers to think or do something.[4]

At a local level of coherence (that of the connectedness of consecutive utterances and the avoidance of non-sequiturs), EA has to do with the

---

[2]   The question of whether successful jokes involve some sort of *resolution* of such contradictions, along the lines envisaged in, for instance, Oring's notion of 'appropriate incongruity', is more contentious, though the approach adopted here, postulating higher-order sense-making of superficially incoherent elements in a piece of discourse, is necessarily sympathetic to his view. See Oring (1992: 1–15).

[3]   See, for instance, as an example of Neo-Gricean analysis, Attardo (1993).

[4]   Considerations of space rule out any thorough unpacking of the intentionally simple-seeming definition that I give here. My approach draws eclectically on a number of models (all of which share a refusal to downgrade argumentation to the status of a specialized discourse genre), such as the speech-act-based model of Eemeren and Grootendorst, the utterance schematics and natural logic of French or Swiss theorists such as Anscombre and Ducrot, and a number of individual British and American approaches that focus on functional sequences of utterances or conversational moves.

functional linking of utterances. It is important to bear in mind, however, that argumentational coherence is not simply or even basically a matter of morphosyntactically-realized connections between contiguous clauses, but rather an important resource in the functional–interactional organization of discourse. In other words, the persuasive orientation of EA (and even when what addressees are intended to do or think is fairly trivial) inevitably raises the issue of higher-level coherence, 'what makes words and sentences into a unified discourse that has cultural significance for those who create or comprehend it' (Tannen 1984: xiv). The perlocutionary success of speakers, that is, depends on making sense to their audiences in terms of culturally-shared definitions and evaluative standards, consensual norms of the sort that make genuinely rational debate possible in Jürgen Habermas's theory of communicative action.[5] These include, on the level of everyday conversation, our expectation that a competent member of the linguistic community will know what sort of speech act requires reasons to be given for performing it, and know, moreover, which reasons count as valid ones. Whether reasons count as valid, of course, depends on all sorts of shared beliefs and assumptions about the world and linguistic representations of it. Where the production of humorous effects is concerned, it is precisely the perception of deviation from such shared standards of evaluation that creates the core element of incongruity. We are invited to regard the presenter of reasons that fail to convince as comically eccentric, slow-witted, naïve or in other ways cognitively challenged. Humour is also often generated when arguments are viewed in the light of what could be called critical coherence, that is, identified as a conspicuously unsuccessful attempt at manipulation. The amusement that accompanies the realization that a piece of argumentation is transparently self-serving was famously demonstrated by the laughter generated in court by the rejoinder 'he would say that, wouldn't he'.[6]

It is precisely this kind of reaction that is counted on by the Spanish cartoonist who, toward the end of the Felipe González administration, depicted the opposition leader José-María Aznar encouraging a meeting of Partido Popular supporters with the exhortation:

---

[5] Habermas (1989 edn). While all language use is, for Habermas, by its nature predicated on the possibility of open and rational persuasive interaction, he does recognize the possibility of using language *strategically*, that is, with an intent to deceive and/or manipulate.

[6] This now standardized expression was originally made by a witness in the 'Profumo' case who, in effect, was being pressurized by the counsel for a defendant to admit that a call girl's account of events (her own) should not be believed in preference to that of a doctor (the defendant).

La sequía se agrava cada día. El agujero en la capa de ozono sigue aumentando. ¡Dimita Sr González![7]

In terms of the definition of argumentation proposed above, we could say here that a contentious speech act – the call for resignation – is prefaced by two utterances that function as justifications for performing it. The reasons given are, of course, patently inappropriate, since the weather is widely regarded as a canonical example of a state-of-affairs for which heads of government cannot be held accountable.[8]

Such humorous depiction of crass opportunism is not, however, the most frequent source of argumentationally derived humour. Attention is more frequently focused on speakers who fail to convince because they produce reasons that are clearly based on substantial misjudgement of situation or motive. The following example features Condorito's fiancée Yayita (in this instance representing the comic stereotype of the stunningly attractive young woman who seems ingenuously oblivious to her effect on males), coming out of a bank and producing the '¡PLOP!' effect on a friend:

Este banco es formidable; abrí una cuenta con el depósito mínimo y el gerente me invitó a cenar.

Yayita's remarks are neither discursively complex nor do they raise any particular problem for the translator, but it is worth remaining with them briefly because they offer a useful illustration of some important features of EA. First, we should note that hearers/readers are often expected to recognize the relationship of one utterance to another without the benefit of an explicit linking expression such as 'porque', or when the neutral 'y' is used rather than, say, 'pero' or 'sin embargo'. In fact, Yayita's strategy is to enhance the effectiveness of her argument by using a popular variant of the assertion–justification model in which the justifying element is itself contrastively enhanced:

---

[7]   Juan Ballesta, *Cambio 16*, 30 October 1997. The intention, of course, was to suggest that all Aznar's accusations against González – such as having authorized anti-terrorist death squads – were similarly lacking in foundation.

[8]   It is worth noting, though, that the importance of the consensual validity of reasons is well illustrated here. The absence of political responsibility for unwelcome meteorological phenomena that Spanish readers are expected to acknowledge might well be less consensual among North American readers in the aftermath of government repudiation of the Kyoto accords. A translator might even consider whether to make the specifically Spanish remit explicit ('the drought in Spain', for example).

1. I declare this bank is wonderful
   (because)
2. (a) I deposited only the minimum amount
       (but nevertheless)
   (b) The manager asked me out on a dinner date

While counter-expected with respect to reason (a), reason (b) is presented as, in fact, compatible with it, and is thereby lent considerable argumentational force.[9] We might further note (and this is probably a basic ingredient of amusingly unsuccessful argumentation of this sort) that the contextual assumptions on which Yayita's reasoning depends are consensual up to a point. Banks do indeed offer incentives to open new accounts and the value of such incentives normally matches the value of the new business; her friend and the readers, however, will more readily access background knowledge of the socio-sexual significance of dinner dates, information which enables them to recognize that Yayita's assumption that the manager is acting in a purely professional capacity is comically mistaken.

Contrastive/adversative relations also occur at the level of interaction between participants and the organization of their exchanges rather than that of the compatibility of informational content in adjacent clauses. Both 'pero' in Spanish and 'but' in English are often employed as discourse markers, signalling not so much provision of counter-expected information as non-compliance with expected norms of response – 'arguing', as it were, in the sense of 'disagreeing'. Again, when such disagreement is not explicitly marked it is sometimes advisable, as a translator, to make it clear that a dispreferred response is being produced. In 'Imitar', a cartoon involving Yuyito, Yayita's naughty little niece, a classic theme of humour involving children appears: inadvertent exposure of adult guilty secrets. The little girl is overheard talking to her doll and mimicking the speech-style of her young nanny:

> YAYITA: ¡Yuyito, deja la muñeca y no le hablas imitando a la niñera! ¡No quiero que la imites más! Y ahora ve a darle un beso a tu tío Condorito, que acaba de llegar.
> YUYITO: ¿En qué quedamos, tía? ¿No dices que no debo imitar a la niñera?

Yuyito's argumentation here is condensed but not without a certain complexity of structure. '¿En qué quedamos, tía?' has the force of a refusal to

---

[9] According to Rhetorical Structure Theory, the effect is to increase what is termed the addressee's 'positive regard' for the counter-expected utterance. See W. C. Mann and S. A. Thompson (1992: 39–78).

comply with a directive, on the implied grounds that to perform the requested action would infringe a previously established rule; it is thus appropriately followed by an explicit mention of the prohibition in question. An English version, of course, would similarly need to make the implied protest clear, for example by including 'but' as a 'dissentive' discourse marker ('but Aunty, didn't you say I mustn't …?') rather than routinely (and unnecessarily) reproducing the allusion to an agreed rule of behaviour. What is also worth noting, perhaps, is that the comic inappropriateness of the child's reasoning does not stem simply from faulty disambiguation of a given expression (as is the case with many 'stupid person' jokes); the important infringement here is the exposure of transgressive behaviour of a sort that is, as a rule, tactfully overlooked.

We have already seen that an appropriate conjunction is not required for an utterance to be seen to function as a reason, and that, similarly, when an utterance has the force of a speech act of the sort for which reasons are normally expected to be given, this function is not necessarily explicitly encoded (as with Yayita's '¿En qué quedamos …?'). Often the further step is taken of combining the two functions in the same conversational move, a feature of EA that, again, can have important consequences for translators. A functional conflation of this sort, together with the familiar mixture of consensual and idiosyncratic standards of evaluation, is found in the following example, a piece of theatre dialogue:

LA SACRISTANA: ¿Quieres tú echar un trago, Ginera?
LA BIGARDONA: Luego los mozos me sienten el aliento.[10]

In this exchange (between a mother and her teenage daughter in rural Galicia) much of the humour depends on the fact that the girl simultaneously declines the offer of a swig of local hooch, and, in line with norms for dispreferred responses to offers, provides a justification for doing so. It would be important in translation into English (a linguistic culture more prone to include explicit markers of politeness) to ensure the girl's words have the force of turning down the offer, or to add a stage direction with a gesture of refusal, in order to highlight the comical irony of her simultaneous provision of a 'polite' justification. Her excuse, that is, reveals that she is motivated not by maidenly abstemiousness and the concern for respectability valued by polite society, but rather by concern not to lessen her attractiveness to the village lads she plans to get to grips with later in the evening.

Indeed, one of the principal sources of humour in EA is exploitation of consensual norms of politeness in verbal interaction, precisely because, with

---

10 Valle-Inclán, *Cara de plata*, ed. A. Risco (1992: 187).

requests and other impositions, providing the requestee with reasons is a standard redressive move. In the following example Condorito, in the guise of an official guide, addresses a group of tourists animatedly chatting on an observation platform at the side of a huge waterfall:[11]

> ¡Por favor! ¡Si las señoras tuvieran la bondad de callar un momento, oiríamos el potente rumor de las cataratas!

Although on the level of syntax (and again we are dealing with a standard device for mitigating an imposition) the guide's remarks have a protasis/ apodosis form, interactively the functional structure is recognizably one of a directive followed by a justification for uttering it. 'Por favor', far from signalling deferential politeness in Spanish, is often used as an expression of protest at others' behaviour and as a demand for it to stop. A translation, of course, should make it clear that the illocutionary force of 'por favor' is one of calling the group to order, thus clarifying the argumentational link with the utterance that follows ('Ladies! Please! If you would be so kind as to ...'), in order to convey fully the sarcasm of the guide's flagrant disregard of consensual standards of evaluation and, indeed, of norms of politeness. Since there is obviously a huge incongruity of scale between the decibel level of the massive falls and that of a few human voices, the justification he provides is manifestly implausible and the over-elaborate politeness formula he uses is clearly a form of mockery.

In the next cartoon example, not only does the controversial nature of the first utterance ensure that some attempt at justification will be expected, but an explicit connector is also provided. However, in order to appreciate fully the extent to which the argument put forward is seriously at odds with consensual scales of values, the reader needs to make a series of inferences. The drawing shows two fashionably-attired women sitting at an outside table of a café.[12] The face of one registers utter astonishment as the other remarks:

> ¡Ojalá se muriera, así sería sólo mío!

The main inferencing task is that of deducing the topic of a conversation encountered *in medias res* as it were, but even a decision so normally routine as the assignment of reference is an important part of this problem, since the reader – as opposed to the speaker's woman-friend in the cartoon – has missed the earlier part of the conversation, in which the antecedent of the anaphoric referring term 'se' has been established. (This, presumably, is the

---

[11] See *Condorito de oro* 'Condoricosas'.
[12] Juan Ballesta in *Cambio 16*, 12 October 1986.

same as the subject of the verbs 'muriera' and 'sería', which, as is customary in Spanish when the antecedent is readily recoverable by the hearer, is elided in both cases.) The perennial translation issue of explicitation of underdetermined meaning is raised here in a particularly pointed manner, since English is not one of the somewhat inelegantly termed 'pro-drop' languages, and thus the number and/or gender of verb subjects cannot be left unspecified.[13] In the last resort, some sort of guess needs to be made as to whose death the speaker is expressing a desire for, but familiarity with the norms and structures of EA as well as contextual knowledge in general (such as the sorts of topic two leisured women-friends are likely to chat about) can help make the guess a relatively well-informed one. Not only is openly expressing a hope for someone to die normally taboo, but the justification given here, instead of serving as mitigation, actually reveals that the wish itself is crazily self-defeating. A deceased person, that is, would obviously be unsatisfactory as a partner in a sentimental liaison. The humour here seems to stem rather from perceiving a startling lapse from standards of reasoning and sense-making on the part of a sufferer from strong feelings of jealousy.[14]

Although the point has not been explicitly made, parts of the foregoing analysis have touched on the interfaces between EA and other pragmatic approaches to discourse coherence. In fact, one of the strengths of argumentation theory as an analytical tool lies in the useful ways it can be combined with and supplement other approaches to discourse coherence. In the final example to be considered, it is instructive to note that it is effectively through interlinking a series of EA units, each with its own comic effect, that the larger-scale coherence of the piece as a humorous short narrative is achieved. The example is taken from a cartoon series whose protagonist is a pre-adolescent boy. The strip begins with Gutanda, the housekeeper, answering the door to Eulalia, an adult neighbour:[15]

> EULALIA: ¡Gutanda, menos mal que estás en casa! ¿Puedo ver tu televisión?
> ¡La mía se ha estropeado!
> GUTANDA: Por supuesto Eulalia, pasa, pasa.

[13] This is a clear instance of required explicitation attributable to a difference between two linguistic systems and not of the generalized translational tendency to explicitation first postulated by Shoshana Blum-Kulka. See Blum-Kulka (1986: 19).

[14] The referential underdeterminacy is combined here with a variant protasis/apodosis structure (if a, then b) to suggest a traditionally bleak (or 'black') view of the existential paradoxes involved in matters of life, love and death. It is possibly of interest to note that a group of students of Spanish as a second language, in a recent tutorial, unanimously found this cartoon 'not funny'.

[15] Mique Beltrán, 'Marco Antonio', in *Pequeño país*, 8 February 1997.

EULALIA: ¡Es que hoy es el último capítulo de 'Semilla Rosa'! ¡Y por fin se sabrá si Ana Luisa María se casa con Edelmiro José, pese a la oposición de sus padres, los vecinos, el vaticano, la ONU y su cuñada Kelly Ramírez!

GUTANDA: Se casarán, ya verás.

Eulalia here not only gives an explanation (the broken TV) to justify her intrusive request, but goes on to provide a further set of justifying reasons, stressing the urgency of her need, with a description of the crucial stage reached in the story-line of a serialized soap opera she wants to watch. Even discounting the cartoonist's satirical hyperbole, these reasons might well strike many readers as comically unconvincing (although Gutanda certainly seems to find them plausible), because they are manifestly grounded on an uncritically enthusiastic evaluation of the crude strategies for creating empathy and suspense that are typical of soaps. The narrative continues to develop via argument and counter-argument, as Gutanda, with an exclamation that signals an unwelcome realization, implies she will have to rescind her offer. The cartoon concludes with a large frame of Marco Antonio and his cronies in front of the television set, festooned with soccer fans' accessories, yelling and gesturing with bug-eyed fervour as they watch the big match, while in the doorway we see Eulalia blithely countering Gutanda's argument and backing up her own prediction that the boys will not mind changing channels.

GUTANDA: [...] ¡Jesús Eulalia! Me había olvidado que los chicos están viendo la tele. Creo que hoy daban un partido de fútbol.

EULALIA: Oh, bueno ... pero son unos críos muy simpáticos, ya verás como son tan amables de cambiar de canal.

This punch-line is basically a 'fundamental misappraisal of situation' type of argumentational joke, but it is worth noting that the humour of the cartoon as a whole – the 'point' of the story – has to do with the way the obsessive passions of fans in general override consensual standards of polite interaction.

To conclude, the varied uses of EA in the examples analysed seem to support the hypothesis that humorous effects are created when reasons given are conspicuously problematic in some respect. Where related translation issues are concerned, when humour is argumentationally generated the source text can provide the translator with helpful structural guidelines as to the shape of characteristic types of functional relations between utterances. A number of such functional structures have been identified in the examples studied here. There is also some support for the intuition – one that, if sound, must give some encouragement to translators daunted by the culture-specific nature of many jokes – that many of the basic principles underlying the humorous use of EA transcend differences between linguistic cultures. At the same time, however, given that hearers and readers invariably test reasons against the consensual evaluative standards and expectations of their linguistic community, the successful transfer of argumentationally-based humour to the context of a different culture will depend on there being at least some degree of correspondence between the evaluative norms of the two cultures concerned.

Where more specific aspects of translational methodology are concerned there are also helpful insights to be derived from central notions of EA. An instructive example is the question of the use or omission of connectors, bearing as it does in important ways on the pervasive problem of explicitation. Indeed, the discursive principles governing the status of conjunctions as sufficient but not necessary ingredients of pieces of argumentation can be applied to many other types of underdetermined meaning. By and large, speakers and hearers use explicit connectors, whether needed or not, when they wish their utterances to be acknowledged as cogent. This function may be generic (as in religious or political sermons, opinion articles, formal and informal debates, etcetera), or the explicit connection may be used to reinforce reasons too idiosyncratic to be readily recognizable as reasons.[16] The concept of presumptive meaning has an important application here: given that underdetermination is a central feature of ordinary language use, to specify what is normally left unspecified amounts to substituting a marked form of expression for an unmarked one, inevitably giving rise to inferences of one sort or another.[17] Such inferences, when created through a translator's intervention, are unlikely to be appropriate. In particular, if an argumentational connector that was originally left implicit is explicitized, there is a distinct risk of, at best, attributing to the source writer a strong concern to be up front and on record as to her persuasive intentions and, at worst, of giving the impression that reasons firmly grounded on consensual values are deviant or unsound in some way.

It is true that there will always be occasions when the grammar of the target language makes explicitation unavoidable (the already-mentioned

[16] Advertisements might possibly warrant inclusion in this list, but many advertising texts make a show of open argumentation (beginning sentences with 'Porque ...' is a typical ploy in Spanish ones), quite possibly as a smokescreen for some more manipulative strategies. See Warner (2000: 64–75).

[17] For Levinson what is minimally specified is stereotypically exemplified, whereas marked forms give rise to marked meanings: 'If the utterance is constructed using simple, brief, unmarked forms, this signals business as usual, that the described situation has all the expected, stereotypical properties. If, in contrast, the utterance is constructed using marked, prolix, or unusual forms, this signals that the described situation is itself unusual or unexpected or has special properties' (Levinson 2000: 6).

verb–subject ellipsis, normal in Spanish but not in English, is a case in point) and others when a modicum of textual tweaking on the part of the translator may be advisable in order to clarify the argumentational slant of a segment of source text. Nevertheless, alternative means of marking this type of coherence should probably be preferred to the seemingly more obvious solution of inserting conjunctions the original writer did not deem necessary. Particularly when dealing with argumentation (and with humour for that matter), whenever enhancement of precision is a tempting option rather than an absolute necessity, translators should probably pay heed to the dictum that warns against presuming to fix what isn't broken.

List of Works Cited

Anon., 1987. *Condorito de oro: selección de los mejores chistes* (Panama: Editorial América)

Attardo, Salvatore, 1993. 'Violation of Conversational Maxims and Cooperation: The Case of Jokes', *Journal of Pragmatics*, 19: 537–58

Aye, John, 1933. *Humour in Our Streets* (London: Universal Publications)

Ballesta, Juan, 1986. *Cambio 16*, 12 October

——, 1997. *Cambio 16*, 30 October

Beltrán, Mique, 1997. 'Marco Antonio', in *Pequeño país*, 8 February

Blum-Kulka, S., 1986. 'Shifts of Cohesion and Coherence in Translation', in *Interlingual and Intercultural Communication*, ed. J. House and S. Blum-Kulka (Tübingen: Narr)

Chiaro, Delia, 1992. *The Language of Jokes* (London: Routledge)

Habermas, Jürgen, 1984. *The Theory of Communicative Action*, trans. Thomas McCarthy, vol. I (London: Heinemann); vol. II (Cambridge: Polity, 1989)

Levinson, Stephen C., 2000. *Presumptive Meanings. The Theory of Generalized Conversational Implicature* (Cambridge, MA: MIT Press)

Mann, W. C. and S. A. Thompson (eds), 1992. *Discourse Description: Diverse Linguistic Analyses of a Fund-Raising Text* (Amsterdam: Benjamins)

Oring, Elliot, 1992. *Jokes and Their Relations* (Kentucky: University Press of Kentucky)

Round, Nicholas G., 1995. 'Translation, Cultural Influence and Semantics: Notes towards a Theoretical Convergence', in *Translation and Meaning, Part 3 (Proceedings of the 2nd Maastricht/Lodz Duo Colloquium)*, ed. M. Thelen and B. Lewandowska-Tomaszcyk (Maastricht: Hogeschool Maastricht, School of Translation and Interpreting), pp. 175–84

——, 1996. 'Interlocking the Voids: The Knowledges of the Translator', in *The Knowledges of the Translator*, ed. M. Coulthard and P. Odber de Baubeta (Lewiston/Lampeter: Mellen), pp. 1–30

——, 1998. *Translation Studies in Hispanic Contexts*, edited with introduction, *Bulletin of Hispanic Studies*, 75, no. 1 (January)

——, 2005. 'Translation and its Metaphors: The (N+1) Wise Men and the Elephant', *SKASE Journal of Translation and Interpretation*, 1: 1, 47–69

Tannen, Deborah, 1984. *Coherence in Spoken and Written Discourse* (Norwood, NJ: Ablex)

Valle-Inclán, Ramón del, 1992 edn. *Cara de plata*, ed. Antonio Risco (Madrid: Espasa Calpe)

Warner, R., 2000. 'This Is Your Lifestyle: Self-identity and Coherence in Some English and Spanish Advertisements', in *Advertising and Identity in Europe*, ed. J. Cannon, R. Warner and P. Odber de Baubeta (Bristol: Intellect), pp. 64–75

Assessing Assessment

ANTHONY TRIPPETT

First, do no harm.[1]

When Nick Round remarked at an examiners' meeting that 'marks are a metaphor' he demonstrated that, for him, the discourse and lexicon of assessment are inseparable from those of teaching and learning; the untidiness and subjectivity of assessment are ill-matched to numbers and mathematical operations.[2] When – after another examiners' meeting – Nick celebrated the anecdote of the man who looked for his lost keys underneath a lamp-post because that's where the light was, rather than further down the road in the darkness at the place where he first discovered they were missing, he was again recognising the problematic character of assessment.[3]

---

[1] This familiar dictum, widely but wrongly assumed to come from the Hippocratic Oath, expresses the minimum that can be expected of those engaged in teaching and associated assessment practices.

[2] In his *What Good are the Arts?* (2005), John Carey reflects that subjectivity when he defends the proposition that criticism is camouflaged autobiography.

[3] Such have been typical concerns of a man whose astonishingly prolific and diverse research output has accompanied a lifetime's dedication to teaching and learning in higher education. I have particular grounds for being grateful to Nick Round for his wonderful contributions to two *pedagogical* projects at Sheffield University with which I have been involved. In the first we staged the opera *La púrpura de la rosa*, in the second the early religious work *Oratorio sacro al nacimiento de Christo Señor Nuestro*. (See www.shef.ac.uk /hispanic/purpura/ and www.shef.ac.uk/hispanic/armonya/ for details.) For the first of these Nick provided a full English translation and English surtitles.

Preamble: The Case for Pedagogy[4]

With the pressing concerns of the Research Assessment Exercise (RAE) evaluations in the UK, research has tended to become pre-eminent in most universities, while teaching and learning are relegated to a secondary role (Brown 2006: 3). In some cases teaching competence is accorded little or no weight when promotion is considered. This focus is unsurprising, given that universities' research income has almost invariably to be earned or won in open competition whereas teaching income is more or less stable and difficult to lose. Yet the fact that even in very successful UK research-led universities teaching and learning brings in around 60% of income should give pause for thought.[5] We might also note that in the new climate created by the introduction of 'top-up' fees (the new system of charging UK undergraduates for tuition, introduced in 2006–07), students are likely to become much more demanding in respect of how they are taught, and to compare one institution or department with another on that basis. The suggestion that they should fend for themselves while the academic staff get on with their research – the institutional advice given to me during my first week as a university student in the early 1960s – is not likely to cut much ice.

My more substantive point, however, is that in almost every case a university lecturer's impact on society and the world is likely to be greater as a teacher of the hundreds if not thousands of students with whom she or he will come into contact over a career than through research articles and books produced. This is in no sense to deny the value of research, nor underestimate the links between teaching and research, nor yet the ways the one may be much enhanced by the other. It is not at all an either/or choice, though opinions are often unhelpfully polarized. I would like simply to argue for the importance of pedagogy in its own right, particularly insofar as it can help us as teachers. This conviction has been strengthened by the M.Ed. course for university teachers that I recently completed at the University of Sheffield, and I would like to highlight four points that emerged from that experience.

First of all, the M.Ed. encouraged reflection on the nature and design

4   Not all pedagogy, I hasten to add; pedagogy comes in many shapes and sizes and may be used as much to control as to liberate or empower, and there is much disagreement as to both theory and practice. Certain colleagues in my own institution, for example, contend that criterion referencing, beloved of many educationalists, is educationally damaging; and figures as different as the Poet Laureate, Andrew Motion, and the president of the UK's Confederation of British Industry (CBI), Sir Digby Jones, have been critical of the stifling effects on creativity of the current school curriculum and exam system. (See *The Independent, Educational Supplement,* 29 June 2005: 3; 'The Today Programme', BBC Radio 4, 28 June 2005.)

5   The statistic was supplied by Paul White, Sheffield University's Pro-Vice-Chancellor in charge of teaching and learning, at a Teaching and Learning Forum held at the University on 9 June 2006.

of the curriculum, something I had never been invited to do as an undergraduate, excellent though I had found my degree course in other respects.
If one is not careful, the content of the curriculum implicitly becomes a
given that the student accepts. While there is nothing wrong with trust, it is
important within an academic context for all to recognize when value-laden
assumptions are being made. Secondly, pedagogy also encourages reflection
on the relationship between teacher and student, and the kind of authority
that the one exercises over the other. Authority needs to be won by persuasion and argument, rather than being simply the prerogative of position. I
believe that the desirable model is one of collaboration and dialogue, and it
is only when these occur that the student is able to develop the power to think
for him or herself.[6] Thirdly, of course everything depends on what model
of learning you have in mind: and we all *do* have models in mind, usually
without consciously reflecting on them. D. Fox clearly and wittily indicates
some of the models:

1. the discipline-centred, information-based approach which sees students
   as empty vessels into which their tutors pour knowledge;
2. the student-focused approach which sees students as clay to be modelled
   by their tutors;
3. another student-focused approach, this time indifferent to the particular
   discipline involved, which sees the student as a plant, the (independent
   and unpredictable) growth of which is fostered by the tutor;
4. the approach which sees the tutor as a traveller engaged on a journey of
   discovery in the company of students who have rather less experience
   than s/he.

Such reflections on the model of learning helped me formulate my contribution to a conference on the Crisis of Golden Age Studies in International
Hispanism, held at the University of Nottingham in March 2003. Whereas
the delegates focused on disciplinary content, I felt much could be gained
by looking at the model of learning and the quality of the learning experience. It seemed to me that performance – musical or theatrical – could
encourage a degree of engagement that other approaches did not.[7] Fourthly
and finally, reflecting on the student experience of learning makes us aware of
how painful and difficult some learning situations can be. This awareness can
make us more sensitive teachers, while also helping us to be a little kinder

---

6   Stephen Brookfield, a strong advocate of dialogue, points out that if we take the trouble
to find out what students think, instead of assuming that we already know, we may get some
pleasant surprises (Brookfield 1995: 127–8).

7   In this I was drawing on my experience of organizing a departmental choir to sing
Spanish songs and of the *Púrpura de la rosa* Spanish opera project (see n. 3 above).

to ourselves as researchers. I would now like to apply these considerations to the area of assessment – one that is particularly apt to provoke anxiety in the student.

Assessment

Assessment is at the sharp end of education. It occupies a huge amount of our time and permeates all aspects of our activities: tutors assess students, Higher Education Funding Councils assess tutors and university departments, students assess tutors through questionnaires, universities conduct internal audits of teaching and assessment and so forth, and in the UK each of these processes has generated its own acronym: TQA, IET, RAE, QAA …

The history of education provides many examples of discredited testing and assessment systems driven by racism, gender bias, or other forms of prejudice. This prejudice is often masked by claims to scientific rigour and objectivity; nineteenth-century cranial anthropometrists such as Paul Broca, for example, measured skull sizes and maintained that: 'The relationship between intelligence of subjects and the volume of their head is very real and has been confirmed by all methodological investigators without exception' (quoted in Gould 1996: 77). In the twentieth century, IQ tests were designed with the object of identifying 'the feeble-minded' for their subsequent sterilization; a practice which continued in the American state of Virginia until 1972 (Gould 1996: 365). Underlying such practices is the assumption that ability, even if not biologically determined, is fixed and immutable, or that there is only one valid form of ability or intelligence.

Such views, while they can still be found, have now been largely discredited.[8] Yet controversy about assessments continues to fill the press and the lives of politicians and educationalists: the institutional games-playing associated with the RAE assessments and the heated debates around their assessment criteria are recent examples. The British Academy has argued that the authors of Humanities books may suffer as the consequence of the decision of some RAE panels not to distinguish between books and articles,[9] and Simon Blackburn, Professor of Philosophy at Cambridge, observes that Plato, Leibnitz, Hume, Kant and Wittgenstein would not have fared well with the RAE Philosophy subpanel (Blackburn 2006: 14). Similarly the UK 1995–96

---

[8]   Oliver James, for example, argues very strongly in *They f*** you up* (2002), particularly in Appendix 3, that the environment is considerably more significant than genetic factors in determining intelligence, mental abilities and psychological health, and states that this can be demonstrated with regard to studies of twins.

[9]   www.britac.ac.uk/reports/rae/rae-2005/rae2005.html

Teaching Quality Assessment (TQA) Teams and their procedures have been criticised.[10] There has been disagreement, too, concerning the value of school students' A-level results as an indication of higher education potential.[11] And there have been disputes between the government and the independent Office for Standards in Education in England (Ofsted) with regard to failing schools, with the first keen to close schools which the second had assessed as performing well in difficult circumstances (Judd 2000: 1 and 12).

These cases underline the point that assessment is a problematic area in which different interest groups, assumptions and prejudices do battle, and where claims for objectivity and absolute values need to be treated with considerable caution. In this context, the high levels of assessment experienced by school children in the UK when compared with their peers in other countries may be something that we should view with concern (Asthana 2006: 4).

The Dangers of Assessment

Necessary though it often is, assessment can be profoundly counter-productive. Confidence and self-esteem can be undermined; those assessed can be marginalized and, in extreme cases (as I suggest below with reference to dyslexia), even criminalized. Part of the problem lies in the authority invested in the assessor. In any liberal, democratic society the authority one person or group is allowed to exercise over another needs to be justified carefully. It is easy to assume that our students think and understand exactly as we do; but because we cannot easily check those assumptions, we often get it wrong. Not so very long ago, much of modern languages teaching was centred on written work and grammar-based study, and scant recognition was given to the fact

10 Three different teams assessed Sheffield University's modern language departments and came to different conclusions as to the *shared* learning resources: the Iberian Studies team criticised and penalised the Department of Hispanic Studies for the inadequacy of the provision of IT facilities; the French Studies team made no comment on that but criticised and penalised the Department of French for the lifts and paternoster; the Russian and Eastern European Languages and Studies Team awarded Russian and Slavonic Studies full marks, see *Quality Assessment Reports* (HEFCE, Bristol, February 2006). So much for consistency!

11 When admissions tutors at Bristol University, under pressure from Higher Education Funding Council England (HEFCE), sought to counteract the disproportionately high number of successful independent school student applicants by taking into consideration the A-level success rate of the applicants' schools – consistently higher in most independent schools – some independent school heads reacted in outrage at what they saw as prejudice against them and boycotted the University (see Hodges 2000: 10). Obliged to recognize the problems associated with admission into Higher Education, the Government set up the investigation which culminated in the Schwartz Report (see: www.admissions-review.org.uk/).

that some students underperformed in those areas yet possessed a sensitive ear and a good auditory memory. The result was that these different and valuable learning skills were neither encouraged nor appropriately assessed. Students who were not deemed successful in terms of the limited parameters of learning and assessment then current were taken to be of limited ability or worse. Music, languages and mathematics abound with such cases, but it can happen with any subject or activity, and those affected often internalize this negative evaluation: '*I* am no good at this or that'.

A Particular Example: Dyslexia[12]

Dyslexia is particularly illuminating with regard to these negative assessments. Until very recently, dyslexics were often judged to be idle, disorganized, inattentive or unintelligent. Unless they had strong parental support they were likely to have difficulty with assessments at school and often failed to progress educationally. Many would be unhappy, disruptive and marginalized. Today it is recognized that, with the right support, dyslexics can overcome the very specific handicaps under which they labour and which prevent the display of their true abilities. Educational institutions in the UK are now legally required to ensure that there is no discrimination against dyslexics.

This is no insignificant matter. The British Dyslexic Association estimates that 10% of the population is dyslexic, and 4% severely so (Hartley-Brewer 2001: 13).[13] Furthermore, the same source indicates that 70–80% of the prison population is dyslexic, which raises the possibility that the marginalization suffered by many dyslexics over the years as a result of inappropriate assessments may have contributed in some way to the behaviour that led to their incarceration.

While dyslexia may be an extreme example, it does illustrate the central difficulty for assessors of understanding the mental processes of their students, and the risks that assessment poses as a consequence. Without more effective communication and understanding, summary judgements may be inaccurate and potentially damaging. Even at university level the unscrambling of confused thinking or expression in the work of students, and the devising of appropriate feedback, may be time-consuming and demanding, but it remains crucially important (Black and Wiliam 1998). Underlying this is the more

---

12 Dyslexia is given by way of an example. There has been a good deal of attention given recently to SLI (Specific Language Impairment), which presents in a very similar way to dyslexia and is thought to be genetic in origin.

13 The British Dyslexia Association further maintains that dyslexia is a reading disorder that affects a much larger proportion of the population than is usually seen as dyslexic.

fundamental question of the very different ways in which each of us learn. It ill behoves us to make judgements on the student who has produced a particular piece of work if we do not understand their learning style, and have not adapted our teaching to accommodate it.

Comparative Assessment

Of the different kinds of assessment in wide use, comparative assessment can be the most counter-productive. Students learn at different paces and in different ways; the learning process may be complicated by other maturation processes and, taken together, these can compromise the effectiveness of any assessment, and especially comparative assessment. Nor is the speed with which people learn always significant. Penelope Leach notes indignantly that parents sometimes engage in similar comparisons with regard to infant behaviour:

> Child development is a process, not a race. In the first years each infant recapitulates the evolutionary stages that produced humanity, so major landmarks like walking and talking are important and exciting. But that does not mean that it is necessarily better to reach them faster and pass them sooner. (Quoted in James 1998: 113)

It is a sad fact that negative comparisons of their own abilities with others' lead some students to stop making an effort in their work. Readers will call to mind their own examples, as did members of the audience when I delivered the first draft of this chapter as a seminar paper. It is my contention that comparative assessment is not compatible with actively encouraging students to develop their individual potential.[14] This is chiefly because it can lead many students to feel that they are a failure; and when this experience is repeated at every educational stage from around the age of seven this can have a very negative effect on learners' self-esteem and emotional well-being. Yet our education system relies increasingly on assessment. Oliver James suggests that this is one of the reasons why the incidence of depression among 25-year-olds is now five times what it was in the 1950s (James 1998: 42–127).

---

[14] Nick Round has shown himself to be very wary about judging or prejudging student potential on the basis of comparative assessment. When he was introducing a new module of sequential interpreting at Sheffield University he was most insistent that no student should be excluded on the grounds of how they had fared in previous language tests. He wanted all to have the opportunity of stretching themselves and discovering their potential in the new and different performative demands of the new module.

Assessment Training

I noted earlier that some assessments require the use of imagination in that we need to be able to empathize with our students. Assessments also require a high degree of professionalism; our personal dislikes, frustrations and hopes have no place there. Assessing students is a demanding process yet most of us became involved in it, like teaching itself, without any training at all. A recent and relevant example concerns the retiring headmaster of Westminster School (a well-known private secondary school in the UK) who offered his services as a teacher of Mathematics to the state system, only for his offer to be rejected on the grounds that he had no formal training. While the conservative press had a field-day criticizing the local authority concerned for excessive political correctness, few acknowledged that it is desirable for those engaged in education to receive relevant training – a need that is now recognized in the UK's Higher Education institutions. After all, we would not employ an unqualified lawyer, accountant or doctor.

Qualified or not, we are required to assess – by employers, society at large, and not least by our own students. Students ask us what strategies they need to employ in order to score a particular mark. We become caught up in the intricacies of institutional systems and procedures which cannot easily reflect the fact that a given student is evidently troubled and his larger educational needs would be best served by some kind of counselling rather than penalties for not handing in work on time. If we are not careful we find ourselves losing sight of the larger picture.[15]

Who Needs Assessment?

Assessment is clearly necessary: in many situations we need to assess the competence of aspirants to specific roles: doctors, for example, engineers, or linguists. But there are many situations where assessment is decidedly problematic, whoever is undertaking it. Most problematic are those Kafkaesque situations in which assessees are judged by people they don't know, by criteria they don't understand, and at times and in circumstances not of their choosing.

I have argued that some types of assessment undermine our ability to encourage students to think independently and challenge authority. Limits on academic freedom in Franco's Spain, for example, or in Castro's Cuba

[15] The excellent 'Guide to Good Practice: Principles of Assessment' by Caroline Clapham on the Higher Education Academy website – www.llas.ac.uk/resources/goodpractice. aspx?resourceid=1398, whilst immensely helpful on the practicalities, does not look at the larger principles discussed here.

remind us that education systems and their assessment processes can be used to inhibit thought as well as to free it. It has long been recognized that the tendency to conform, to accept received opinion or authority without question, can be compelling. This was underlined in the work of social psychologist Dr Stanley Milgram who, working at Yale University in the early 1960s, asked volunteers to administer painful electric shocks in an experiment which, they had been led to believe, was designed to investigate the effects of punishment on learning.[16] In fact it was their own behaviour and performance which was under scrutiny, rather than those of the subject to whom they believed they were administering the shocks in response to her or his failures in learning. The experiment demonstrated the alarming willingness of many to obey a source of authority even when this involved doing something with which they disagreed. In this case the volunteers were prepared to cause distress to the subject at the behest of a researcher wearing a white coat. Milgram's experiment serves here to underline the importance of our role, as educators, in encouraging students to think independently and critically, and to question authority. If our assessment processes are in any way opaque we ourselves become mysterious authority figures whose thought processes are incomprehensible to our students, with the inevitable consequence that they will find it difficult to challenge us. Indeed, certain assessment processes may be anti-educational in the sense that they actively undermine student autonomy and the ability to respond critically to authority.

Assessment: Some Recommendations

So how can assessment processes be made more useful? Wherever possible, assessment should be subordinated to the learning process. Learning is our main concern, and we need to ensure that assessment facilitates it.[17] If it impedes learning in any way we will need to be able to justify this. Like learning itself, assessment also needs to be, as far as possible, anxiety-free. Whilst limited nervousness may be a spur to extra effort, anxiety can stimulate the psychological defence mechanisms, effectively closing down the higher centres of the brain to allow instinctive responses to occur: in such situations, students may find their ability to think significantly impaired.

Assessment should lead to feedback, so that lessons can be learnt from

---

[16] The experiment was originally described in Milgram (1963: 371–9). A later summary was reproduced in Cooper (1968: 31–2).

[17] As the former principal of Leeds Metropolitan University, Christopher Price remarked: 'Measuring students does not make them cleverer any more than weighing pigs makes them fatter' (Price 2005: 3).

the effort expended (Black and Wiliam 1998). It may also be appropriate to discuss it prior to its taking place so that the assessment becomes part of a dialogue between teacher and learner, a collaborative reflection on the learning process. In language learning, for example, one might lay bare the rationale of assessment, saying to a student: if you make mistakes in the person of the verb, there may well be a communication breakdown; if you don't pay attention to the structure of the sentence its meaning will be obscured and the thread of your argument lost. The assessment itself could become a focus of attention in the learning process, because through it we are saying what is important in the discipline. Everything should be done to try to ensure that the student is actively involved in the assessment process; for example, students and teachers could devise and discuss essay questions and assessment exercises together. Peer assessment can be productive too, although it is important to ensure that it is not perceived as threatening by those taking part.[18] Above all, assessment should be *active*; some traditional systems encourage passivity, resignation and unreflecting deference to authority.

In accordance with the most basic educational aims, we want to encourage our students to become active, confident and reflective individuals. We do this best by example, and by making ourselves and our procedures transparent and open to scrutiny. I contend that we need to divest ourselves of authority arising from our position or role, and regain it by our practice or by force of argument in open debate. And if we have assessed our own assessments with due rigour we should be able to have confidence in our students' assessments of us, united in a single collaborative pedagogical endeavour.[19] In these circumstances, it is to be hoped that any marks we might be called upon to generate for students' work would be rich metaphors of which Nick Round could approve.

---

[18] As part of an exercise to encourage the very productive practice of peer *observation* amongst university staff, a protocol was established by which the person observed set the agenda and decided by whom, when and how s/he would be observed. This arose from a HEFCE-funded research initiative centred at Leeds Metropolitan University (see *Develop News*, no. 2 (November 1998)).

[19] Our efforts in this regard can be helped by the work of pressure-groups such as www.assessment-reform-group.org.uk. Another source of inspiration is the Brazilian educationalist Paulo Freire, who writes: 'Education must begin with the solution of the teacher–student contradiction by reconciling the poles of the contradiction so that both are simultaneously teachers *and* students (Freire 1972: 46).

List of Works Cited

Anon., 1998. *Develop News*, no. 2 (November 1998)

——, 2003. www.shef.ac.uk/hispanic/purpura, website accessed 15 July 2007

——, 2005. www.shef.ac.uk/armonya, website accessed 15 July 2007

——, 2005. 'The Today Programme', BBC Radio 4, 28 June

——, 2005. *The Independent, Educational Supplement*, 29 June: 3

——, 2006. www.assessment-reform-group.org.uk, Assessment Reform Group website, accessed 19 July 2006

——, 2007. www.britac.ac.uk/reports/rae/, website accessed 15 July 2007

——, 2007. www.admissions-review.org.uk, website accessed 15 July 2007

Asthana, Anushka, 2006. 'Exam Strain on Schools "Too Great"', *Observer*, 26 March: 4

Black, Paul and Dylan Wiliam, 1998. 'Inside the Black Box', *Phi Delta Kappan*, 80(2) (October): 139–48

Blackburn, Simon, 2006. 'Give That Philosophical Master a Big, Brown Star', in *The Times Higher Education Supplement*, 30 June: 14

Brookfield, Stephen, 1995. *Becoming a Critically Reflective Teacher* (San Francisco: Jossey-Bass)

Brown, R., 2006. 'Brown must stop playing with higher education', *The Independent, Education Supplement*, 11 May: 3

Carey, John, 2005. *What Good are the Arts?* (London: Faber & Faber)

Clapham, Caroline, 2003. 'Guide to Good Practice: Principles of Assessment', Higher Education Academy website: www.llas.ac.uk/resources/goodpractice. aspx? resourceid=1398, accessed 19 July 2006

Cooper, David (ed.), 1968. *The Dialectics of Liberation* (Harmondsworth: Penguin)

Fox, D., 1983. 'Personal Theories of Teaching', in *Studies in Higher Education*, 8.2: 151–63

Freire, Paulo, 1972. *Pedagogy of the Oppressed* (London: Penguin)

Gould, S., 1996. *The Mismeasure of Man* (New York: W. W. Norton)

Hartley-Brewer, E., 2001. 'How Space Science could Beat Dyslexia', *The Independent, Education Supplement*, 11 January: 13

Hodges, L., 2000. 'Elitist, exclusive, too posh ... but we're changing says Bristol', *The Independent, Education Supplement*, 12 October: 10

James, Oliver, 1998. *Britain on the Couch* (London: Arrow)

——, 2002. *They f*** you up* (London: Bloomsbury)

Judd, J., 2000. '"Humiliation" of 101 schools facing closure', *The Independent* and *Special Supplement*, 16 November: 1, 12

Leach, Penelope, 1994. *Children First* (London: Michael Joseph)

Milgram, Stanley, 1963. 'Behavioural Study of Obedience', *Journal of Abnormal and Social Psychology*, 67: 371–9

Price, Christopher, 2005. 'The Government is obsessed with elitism', *The Independent, Education Supplement*, 24 November: 3

Civilization and Barbarism: The Perpetual Question

PAUL JORDAN

> Much mediaeval writing can still connect with us and with our experience; often it does so in ways more pertinent and alive than are achieved by most authors closer to our own age.
>
> (Round 1980: 156)[1]

Nick Round wrote these words a quarter-century ago, commenting on the 1980 Modern Languages Association Presidential Address, by Professor Philip Thody, of Leeds University. Essentially, Thody considered university modern languages education, as then constituted, to be inadequate for the modern world (because of the stranglehold of mediaevalists and historical philologists). Echoing the fears expressed by Matthew Arnold in the nineteenth century about the overthrow of civilized culture, Thody feared that the perceived cultural deficiency of graduates was likely to hasten the future emergence of a centralized bureaucratic state. His proposed remedy was modern language studies based on three elements: increased language teaching; history and social structure; a range of literature (this last to generate understanding, not of the foreign culture, but through it, of the home culture).

While accepting a good deal of Thody's analysis, Round denies the existence of a mediaeval hegemony: 'The unicorn', said the lady in the Thurber story, 'is a mythical beast.' The 'dominant position of mediaeval studies in most modern language courses' is another; 'there is no such animal' (1980: 155).[2] He concedes that sometimes mediaeval texts were used 'not as imaginative witnesses but as specimens in a linguistic museum' (1980: 157), but asserts that 'the *Celestina* [...] can speak as directly and as valuably to my

---

[1]   In this essay, the spelling *mediaeval* (rather than *medieval*) is preferred, for reasons which will in due course become apparent.

[2]   Thody's analysis is also challenged by my sister, J. E. Bradley, who read languages at Leeds (where Thody was professor of French) from 1970 to 1975. Modern literature and society were major constituents of the curriculum.

students as, let us say, the latest Latin-American novel' (1980: 157).[3] He regards language acquisition as an inexact science, denounces quantitative arguments as naïve, and argues that teachers should facilitate students' engagement, which in turn will bring about their internal transformation.

As to how engagement might be achieved, Round observes that, since students spend a great deal of time outside formal literature classes on private study, the same should be true for their language studies. He then asks what might stimulate motivation to learn the language. The year abroad is considered essential, because then students see real results from language skills.[4] How, Round wonders, can similar engagement be encouraged at university, where (except for students with a vocational orientation) the relationship between skill and result is purely formal? He proposes that students need a sense of validity and coherence in their courses – and that literature, if it works '*as a culture*', provides these (1980: 161). The rationale is that a literature has a wealth of internal relationships (it is a multi-dimensional cultural entity) and that, through its expressiveness, literature generates external relationships (readers engage with it), just as residence in a foreign country does. Unlike Thody, Round regards engagement with a foreign culture not as instrumental, but as thoroughgoing and unconditional. He considers that literature in education should not be a paradigm for imitation or a body of information to be possessed, but a medium which draws the student into engagement with the foreign culture, the field to be inhabited.

How, he wonders, and through which texts, can cultural engagement be achieved? As to method, 'target language' teaching (unless by native speakers) is rejected on two grounds. First, it is seen as a threadbare simulacrum of the year-abroad environment; secondly, Round adduces a relative poverty of communication, which results from an imperfect grasp of the language. In relation to choice of texts, rejecting both canonical and eclectic approaches, he suggests, quite simply, that the literature used (which should be texts with which the teachers themselves genuinely engage) should reinforce language learning, and provide a way in to literary and cultural history, as a means of understanding both a specific culture, and culture in a broader sense.

> No course [...] restricted to its own time [...] could function properly as a cultural experience. It could not do justice to the themes which ought to concern it most, because it could not begin to illustrate their actual histor-

---

[3] It is tempting to associate the remark with an article written in 1980 (although published in 1991), in which Round takes Cortázar to task for misunderstanding Galdós, and misrepresenting him in *Rayuela*.

[4] In some institutions such as Cambridge, the year abroad was until relatively recently not obligatory, although it was encouraged. And in the early 1990s – at least in Scotland, where language degrees take five years – politicians questioned the necessity of a year abroad.

ical diversity. It could only reinforce the habit of abstraction – especially abstraction from time – which is the particular bane of so much study in the humanities. If we are to promote a right understanding of real languages, real societies, real cultures, that habit needs to be broken. [...] The way to do this is to recognize [...] the extent to which all linguistic or social or cultural states are the products of time and change. If literary studies are to help this recognition to happen, they must [...] show the literary culture in some measure of its historical variety. [...] It does demand enough of a historical range to display the double process which is always at work: the one-way, irreversible line of historic development, and the ever-renewed and renewing interplay between present and past. If students can grasp these patterns within literary culture, they stand a better chance of recognizing them in language and in society. For in literature as elsewhere, our relationship with the past is compounded at once of kinship and of differentiation. (1980: 163)

Round concludes by asserting that university language department staff must continue to be competent literary critics, linguists and language teachers. Further, expertise needs to extend to new fields of historical and social inquiry, either through linguists moving into them, or by inter-departmental teaching: modern language departments should occupy the interdisciplinary centre of the Arts curriculum.

The Thody–Round exchange of 1980 is not untypical of debates within modern languages: as we shall see, generally speaking, however different their approaches and underlying philosophies may be, most commentators tend to share a concern with the active maintenance of non-materialistic values in education, within social contexts where these cannot be taken for granted. In the course of this chapter, I shall discuss key issues in the development of Hispanic Studies, in the political and intellectual contexts of the last twenty-five years: it has been a period of major change for higher education, and it seems that the process of change will continue for the foreseeable future. Nick Round has witnessed and reflected on these developments and, as we shall see, has made a telling contribution to the debate.

Ten years after the Thody–Round exchange, in 1990 – no Golden Age this, but a time when many of today's trends started to emerge clearly – the debate was renewed, when Barry Jordan published *British Hispanism and the Challenge of Literary Theory*. Many important issues, including those relating to the selection and reading of texts, are raised; to these we shall return. For the present, however, I am interested in the re-emergence of the question of the hegemony of the mediaevalists, within whose enemy ranks Jordan places Round. Round, of course, argued that the hegemony was, like the unicorn, mythical, belonging in the realm of fiction – and it is to that plane that the next part of the discussion draws us.

Nowadays (as Jordan observes), we customarily remove the distinction between 'literary' and 'critical' writing, in order to discover similar types of rhetorical structure. This procedure might be taken further: if critical discourse is about a fictitious object, then it cannot be 'read' as a representation of the world, but must be deconstructed through fiction-theory.

A suitable fiction-theory for the case of the mediaeval hegemony is provided by an Argentine critic, J. L. Borges, who, in the essay 'Tlön, Uqbar, Orbis Tertius', speculates that objects could exist before discovery, and/or endure after being forgotten. In the (Tlön) world, of course, objects' existence depends on sustaining consciousness (not necessarily a human or divine one). An instance is cited of the power of animals' consciousness. 'A veces unos pájaros, un caballo, han salvado las ruinas de un anfiteatro' (1981: 30). Presumably, if a horse – perhaps a mere carthorse, not a thoroughbred – can sustain a physical structure, then the imaginary (and imaginative) unicorn could maintain in existence a subtler entity, such as a mediaeval-philological hegemony: if unicorns existed, so too could a hegemony (in theory).[5]

A second property of (Tlön) objects is that they may be rediscovered independently by more than one person, thus acquiring multiple simultaneous existences. However, the different instances of rediscovered objects (*hrönir*) are not identical. As Borges observes:

> Dos personas buscan un lápiz; la primera lo encuentra y no dice nada; la segunda encuentra un segundo lápiz no menos real, pero más ajustado a su expectativa. Esos objetos secundarios [...] son, aunque de forma desairada, *un poco más largos*. (1981: 28; my italics)

The mediaevalist hegemony fits this pattern. Clearly, 'J' (Jordan's) is the same object as 'T' (Thody's) hegemony, although like Borges's second pencil, it is longer than the original: it is the '*longstanding* hegemony of Renaissance and especially Medieval Studies' (Jordan 1990: 76; my italics). However, there is in what we call 'Jordan's text' an excess, which the theory as it stands cannot process: 'T' is also present, as 'the dominant position of medieval studies in most modern language courses' (1990: 77).[6] This empirical textual discovery (that one person can find both the original object, and a *hrön*) requires the following theoretical refinement. A person, 'J', finds the object ('lo encuentra'), says nothing to others ('y no [les] dice nada') – simultaneously enunciating a *hrön* nothing to him/herself ('y no [se] dice

---

[5] Similarly, if a flock of sparrows could preserve an amphitheatre, then an articulate bird such as a parrot might sustain a hegemony.

[6] Thody (1980: 7). Actually, the text is not, strictly speaking, 'T', but another text which closely, though imperfectly, resembles it.

nada'), enabling his/her subsequent rediscovery of the same object ('[']lo encuentra[']').

If the mediaeval hegemony is a *hrön* (a subjective object), then we should investigate the nature of the texts where it is discovered. Again, Borges has a useful hypothesis. In the essay 'La biblioteca de Babel', he postulates a library constructed of hexagonal chambers containing books, each of 410 pages. Throughout history, various hypotheses about the ideological structure of the library have been proposed. Empirical observation, however, has thus far only produced the conjecture that no two books are identical, and that 'sus [the library's] anaqueles registran todas las posibles combinaciones de los veintitantos símbolos ortográficos (número, aunque vastísimo, no infinito)' (1981: 94).

If Borges's idea is applied to further dimensions of reality, such as that constructed of volumes with 202/228 pages (rather than 410) – then the conceptual framework is in place to approach the 1980 volume of *Modern Languages*, which contains Thody's and Round's articles.

There is evidence that dimensions of the library are indeed structured on Borgesian principles, as a fragment of Jordan (1990) reveals:

> Much medieval writing can still connect with us and with our experience; often it does so in ways more pertinent and alive than are achieved by most authors closer to our own age. (1990: 78)

This text resembles – indeed, it purports to be a direct citation of – Nick Round's statement, which was given at the beginning of this essay; but it is in fact a quite different text: *medieval* has replaced *mediaeval*. The implications are far-reaching indeed: potentially, the number of texts in the library is greater, by orders of magnitude, than has previously been suspected – just as Borges predicted. Clearly, no canon – mediaeval or otherwise – can exist, since notions of textual boundary, and author, become extremely problematic.

While of course acknowledging the limitations of our ability to 'read' such texts as these, nevertheless, we may still consider that their study could be of relevance to the concerns of our contemporary culture. Let us therefore consider symbol sequences from the arbitrary text, which for convenience we designate 'Jordan (1990)': (a) 'Could *Don Quixote*, Cervantes's "great" novel, possibly be construed as being about football? Who knows? In the future, it might well be, for [...] if we do not allow for this possibility, we are attempting to pre-empt history' (1990: 27); and (b) [Terry Eagleton] 'afirma que *Macbeth* trata de Manchester United' (1990: 44).

It seems that these sequences may be examples of the work of the 'far-reading' school of the ludic period, whose devotees are thought to have projected their cultural preoccupations onto a limited number of so-called canonical literary texts.[7] Modern scholarship, of course, has identified and described thousands of ballgame-related texts, two well-known examples relevant to the present case being Shakespeare's drama about corner kicks: *King Leap*; and Martorell's treatise on the penalty shoot-out: *Tirant al blanc*.

Returning to the main argument, and to Round's 1980 article, Jordan criticizes it on three grounds. First, he assumes that Round's creed is 'of common sense, those values and beliefs embodied in literature's timeless wisdom and whose unquestioned presence seems to confirm everything we take for granted' (1990: 78). (We have already seen that this is not Round's ideology.) Secondly, he thinks that a text cannot belong within a national canon, while simultaneously having more universal resonance. (If this were true, then literature would have lost its expressive power – and we could not read, say, the *Quijote*.) Finally, he calls literary canons 'cultural mandarinism' (1990: 79). (Again, as we have seen, Round, too, is sceptical of the validity of a canon.)

Why, though, should not writings from long ago connect with the contemporary reader? I for one enjoyed *La Celestina* in the 1980s.[8] I studied it as a first-year student with Tony Watson, and it certainly connected to my thinking 'as directly and valuably as any Latin-American novel', to paraphrase Nick Round's words. (In fact, if anything, it connected rather more directly.) And I do not dismiss as irrelevant the *Siete partidas*, the work of an author who, in heart and mind, engaged with all three of the major religious traditions which emerged from the Semitic world. For Jordan, though, the modern reader cannot connect to literature from a previous age, and a curriculum which advocates such a connection is a universalizing, complacent project. True learning, he maintains, comes through awareness of difference.

It is not just the choice of literary texts which Jordan attacks, but a pervasive 'nostalgic elitism' (1990: 100), in which mediaeval professors, who were reluctant to teach language, did so through archaic methods (i.e. through literary texts) – a procedure long abandoned by teachers of English as a foreign language.

Language learning is a problematic issue, although the assumption in universities was – and is – that students are experienced second-language learners. One question over which I take issue with Jordan is that of literature in language learning. This was not (as Jordan claims) a mechanical routine of prose and translation – at least in the University of London, whose 1981

---

[7] It must be acknowledged, however, that many doubt that the school ever existed.

[8] Presumably twenty-first-century Spaniards do too, since the *Celestina* was the first of a series of literary classics given away with Sunday editions of *El País*, in 2005, the much-celebrated quatercentenary of the *Quijote*.

regulations emphasized a critical attitude to language use. There, a group of Spanish lecturers produced a language-learning volume, based on diverse literary texts. They reasoned that in a non-vocational modern language degree, 'it makes sense to make the literary part of the course serve as the end to which language study is the means' (Fishburn and Ife 1981: unnumbered). Jordan was oblivious to, or had no time for, such developments, preferring to attack the wicked mediaevalists. And yet, he was certainly aware of, and apparently concerned about, what was happening in the wider world.

[T]he left's relatively successful attack on literature looks like being over-taken, if not hijacked, by a far more powerful radicalising force from the right, that of Thatcherite Education Policy. Indeed, it is the now pervasive official discourse of rationalisation, relevance, vocationalism and market realism that is setting the agenda and unsettling the very material and ideo-logical foundations on which literary studies, among many other things, actually take place. (1990: 96)

In this context, it is puzzling that Jordan (whose allegiance in the struggle between civilization and barbarism seems clear enough) should be so fasci-nated with the basically utilitarian discipline of teaching English as a foreign language: even as he praises it, its limitations are evident. It is a discipline which has 'done remarkably well without literature. [...] literature has been virtually purged from course programmes and materials production, on the grounds that it makes no useful contribution to the purpose of learning a language for practical use' (1990: 100).

Later in this discussion we shall explore why foreign languages and cultures should be studied. For the present, however, I shall make some brief reflections on teaching languages, based on my own practical experi-ences: 1974–79 in teaching English as a foreign language (TEFL); since 1989 in Hispanic Studies, in British universities. Leaving aside questions of resourcing and motivation, I shall consider one central issue, which has exercised many of us, including Nick Round: how may learners progress from dependency (performing a limited Spanish which has been acquired through structured dialogues and the like, and/or explanations of grammar and syntax) to autonomy, in which consciousness and identity within the language develop? The first stages of the TEFL methodologies which I was expected to use were based primarily on the spoken language: a teacher, working with a small group, 'dominated' the students' minds through inten-sive dialogues. By contrast, advanced teaching consisted of seminars, usually on business-related texts; or work with grammar and syntax, as preparation for Cambridge certificate examinations. As to how one made the transition between these two very different states, this was achieved either through residence in an anglophone country, or, less successfully, through immersion courses which attempted to simulate it. Both options are expensive. It was, in other words, clearly recognized within TEFL that it did not have the answers: an identity in the foreign language can only be created within the culture.

Of course, the study of literature has long provided access to cultures. At the same time, a central pedagogic practice for basic mother-tongue literacy, and the advanced skills which are developed from it, is the reading (and production) of narrative, which is to say, literature. One reason for this is that narrative is central to our being.[9] We have a deep affinity with literature, a willingness to enter its worlds – as a reader-character – and, in so doing, learn. Learning may be at a basic linguistic level, or it may relate to cultural information, or systems of ideas – or it may, by analogy, foment (for example emotional) self-understanding. Literature, in other words, is an environment in which a linguistic consciousness may develop – or, in Round's terms, a propitious location for the transformation of the learner.

If mother-tongue literature provides important linguistic and cultural knowledges, which go far beyond the immediately 'useful', might not foreign-language literature do likewise? Of course it does. In an important sense, therefore, the decision whether to use literature is a political act. In this context, while there is still – perhaps – time for debate about how the balance can be struck in higher education, events elsewhere might give pause for thought. In the 1980s the Inner London Education Authority (ILEA), perceiving that residence in a foreign culture (i.e. Britain) was not, on its own, necessarily sufficient to advance acquisition of English, promoted the use of literature in second-language learning in schools, through the Language Division of the Centre for Urban Educational Studies. The unit was abolished in 1989, when ILEA fell victim to Thatcherism.[10]

Jordan, who advocated abandoning a literature-based undergraduate curriculum, nevertheless made two proposals for safeguarding the study of cultural artefacts, such as literature. He proposed that students, before reading literature, should study theory, so as to 'look *at*, not *through* the tools by which they perceive literature. This sort of work could help students [...] ask on what grounds some texts are seen as better, more important than others' (1990: 92). Where students spend a great deal of time studying literature, such an approach might be appropriate. However, undergraduates

9   There are numerous writings on fiction and the young consciousness. Richard Gregory even asserts that fiction liberates us from 'the tyranny of reflexes triggered by events'; it 'gives – in forms to be shared – the essential need of all intelligent organisms: alternative views and courses of possible action' (1977: 394). It is the basis of higher consciousness, in other words.

10   See *Multi-ethnic Education Review*, and *Issues in Race and Education*. I am grateful to my partner, P. J. Kidner, who worked in the unit from 1984 to 1987, for this information.

nowadays rarely study a single language, and many study little literature as part of their course. How, precisely, would compulsory theory modules, which would further erode the time available for literature, enhance engagement with literature, and thereby consolidate its position in the curriculum?

Jordan's second proposal is to adopt a 'cultural studies' approach. If these are cultural studies as understood by Raymond Williams and Richard Hoggart, which use 'serious' cultural products such as art-house cinema, the novel and the like, (and they probably are, since Jordan is a cinema specialist), this would surely find support. Really, the main difficulty with Jordan's proposal is that, while he mentions issues which have arisen in the cultural studies debate, he simply does not pursue the argument in the Hispanic context.

What, then, are the issues? Raymond Williams's words (and it was largely thanks to Nick Round that I became interested in Williams) are a useful starting point:

> It is only in our own century that the regular reading even of newspapers has reached a majority of our people, and only in our own generation that the regular reading of books has reached a bare majority. (1965: 177)

Basic mass literacy, and books as a mass cultural resource, are recent phenomena: the new mass media. Far from being an entrenched traditional institution, we should ask whether books are yet established – or whether they ever will be. It is all very well for García Márquez (in written narrative) to seek to privilege the oral, the popular over the written, and allegedly authoritative:[11] perhaps it is too early in history for this – or perhaps it is already too late. As a character in Ariel Dorfman's *Reader* observes: 'Oh you know I don't read. Not me. Not us, Pops. We're into screens' (1995: 5). What real evidence is there that 'serious' literature is an elite form which underpins the status quo, and diverts attention from more useful matters? Is not literature in reality the multi-voiced entity at the heart of freedom of expression, a stimulant to the imagination, the key cultural phenomenon which ensures that literacy leads to freedom, not tyranny?

This is the view expressed by one very well known literary figure (who promoted progressive society-wide education, and who subsequently fell victim to tyranny) on the occasion of the opening of a public library:

> The poet spoke on the subject of books – their origin and development and the vital role they play in forming free men and women. It was a passionate speech, very much in tune with the Republican fervour wafting at these moments through the land. Lorca expressed agreement with the

---

11 Notably, in 'Los funerales de la Mamá Grande' (1962).

> great philologist Ramón Menéndez Pidal, who had said that the Republic
> should mean, above all, Culture, and explained, [...] taking Voltaire as his
> authority, that the civilized world has been governed by a handful of great
> books: the Bible, the Koran, the works of Confucius and Zoroaster. He
> argued that true wisdom lies in the contrasting of ideas [...]. There should
> be room for both the mystics and the revolutionaries: for St. John of the
> Cross and Tolstoy; side by side [...] Augustine, Nietzsche and Marx.
>
> (Gibson 1989: 318)

Richard Hoggart, in *The Uses of Literacy* (1957), argues that economic
progress could bring intellectual enslavement: social solidarity declines,
as people become increasingly isolated, and attached to material objects.
He identifies as part of this process the capture of popular culture, and its
standardization into a mass culture which masquerades as popular, and which
– unlike serious art – breaks no new ground, does not challenge, but is used
to manipulate the reader/consumer.

Some cultural critics correlate these stereotyped 'popular' products with
the portrayal of political events in the real world; Richard Johnson (1986),
for example, who notes cultural studies' literary roots, finds popular literary
stereotypes in the media coverage of the Falklands war. Others focus on
the struggle between hegemonic and popular currents within mass-culture
phenomena, such as sports and certain types of music.

Such analyses, while insightful, prompt the questions: Why separate
culture into a theoretical discourse of evaluation, and stereotypical cultural
products? Why not study overtly mediated cultural products such as 'serious'
novels and films, which problematize both sides of the equation? Fred Inglis
makes this point: stressing cultural studies' roots in 'high' art, he acknowledges a debt to F. R. Leavis, and identifies art as 'the *essential* category [of
intellectual inquiry] for serious thought about and interpretation of the world'
(1995: 202).

By contrast, Antony Easthope (1991) identifies literature as elite art, and
cinema as popular culture. Gradually, however, he abandons this dichotomy,
conceding that literature and cinema overlap. (While Easthope sees this as a
product of postmodernism, I would argue that cinema and written narrative,
of different types – for example: experimental, politically engaged, consum-
erist – have overlapped and connected throughout the century.)

One sceptic of literary studies in the 1980s was Terry Eagleton. He characterized what he calls the literary humanist discourse thus:

> Its role was to be marginal: to figure as that 'excess', that supplement
> to social reality which in Derridean style both revealed and concealed a
> lack, at once appending itself to an apparently replete social order and
> unmasking an absence at its heart where the stirrings of repressed desire

could be faintly detected. This, surely, is the true locus of 'high culture' in late monopoly capitalism: neither decorative irrelevance nor indispensable ideology, neither structural nor superfluous, but a properly marginal presence, marking the border where that society both encounters and exiles its own disabling absences. (1984: 92)

Doubtless this exemplifies that successful leftist assault on the old establishment, which Jordan identifies. However, times change: in an early twenty-first-century world which (however briefly) seems to offer only one vision of modernity, Eagleton has become literature's advocate. He observes of Joyce's *A Portrait of the Artist as a Young Man*: 'because there are so many styles in the book [...] we are made aware of language itself, in a way which prevents us from simply reading through it to the emotion or the action' (2005: 301). Indeed, authorial control over meaning returns, as we see Joyce polishing his work 'until he had achieved the exact nuance of meaning he required' (2005: 295). More remarkably still, humanist universality reappears: 'There is a fundamental solidarity to human existence across space and time, however estranged from one another modern men and women may feel' (2005: 282). Of course, Eagleton does not directly articulate this; he 'interprets' Joyce.

Cultural studies (as called) arrived in British Peninsular Hispanism in the 1990s, with Graham and Labanyi's *Spanish Cultural Studies: An Introduction: The Struggle for Modernity* (1995).[12] The authors, adopting a Gramscian perspective, of culture as a process of struggle, identify Matthew Arnold – often a *bête noire* in cultural studies circles – as the founder of British cultural studies.[13] And they attribute the erstwhile lack of a Spanish cultural studies not to a conservative British Hispanism, but to the conservative structure of Spanish academe. This widely shared view contrasts with Jordan's enthusiastic description of a year abroad (1971–72) in Valencia, when (although not in the context of the formal curriculum) he met the ideas of 'Genette, Barthes and Todorov' (1990: 2).[14] Certainly, in the early 1980s the traditional fields of Golden Age and mediaeval literature were still very strongly represented in the British Hispanic curriculum. However, by 1990, when Jordan was writing, the expansion and diversification of the curriculum was very

---

[12] An interdisciplinary volume, which addresses the reality of a Spain of distinct nations; as with Jordan and Morgan-Tamosunas (2000), the essays and many of the referenced sources are in English. Are these cultural – or area – studies?

[13] Sociologists agree: 'A brief characterisation of what constitutes "cultural studies" would amount to an abstract of English intellectual history since Matthew Arnold: they are a blend of sociology and literary criticism' (Lepenies 1988: 195; quoted in Halsey 2004: 17).

[14] Anny Brooksbank-Jones (who was in Valencia the following year), commenting on a draft of this essay, makes much the same observation: she 'was similarly struck by the influence of French thought among arty friends'.

evidently in progress: the supremacy of Golden Age literature was over, and Mediaeval studies were in steep decline.

Turning the focus to the Americas, we reflect that early in the nineteenth century, as is well known, much of the western Hispanic world turned its back on Spain, looking elsewhere for inspiration. An example is the thought of the Argentine statesman Domingo F. Sarmiento, who particularly admired France and the USA, and who portrayed Spain as a backward country.[15] He identified the rural Spanish heritage as *barbarie*, and the new urban, mercantile future as *civilización*. While the ideas of Sarmiento and his allies have been criticized, nevertheless, they contributed to a tradition in which literature, and literary criticism, have always been central to the political struggle which is culture. Nowhere has this struggle been more evident than in Argentina, where the distinction between high and popular literature has been questioned, from within literature, since at least the 1920s.[16] Criticism, too, has focused on the social and political: as early as the 1950s the *Contorno* group produced highly (politically) theorized criticism.

Latin America has strong, diverse traditions of cultural criticism: in their different ways Pablo Neruda, Mario Benedetti, Ángel Rama and Beatriz Sarlo are all cultural critics. Moreover, irrespective of Peninsular studies, there was, by the 1980s, a well-established awareness within English-speaking Hispanism of the diversity of Spanish-American cultural production and the associated political issues: Jean Franco, John King and Gerald Martin are three obvious examples. Furthermore, 1991 saw the publication of Rowe and Schelling's *Memory and Modernity*, which explores the relationship between 'popular' and 'high' cultures – with specific reference to literature.

As we observed, the years around 1990 were certainly no Golden Age, but rather, a time of change and uncertainty. It was no longer a question of taking stock of Hispanism and debating its future direction; the Academy found its place in society fundamentally changed: external forces were increasingly evident, and academics in the Humanities discovered that they were now specialized workers engaged on the production of potential employees (as well as being competitive producers of research).

Once again, Nick Round would make an important contribution to the debate. However, the first Hispanist to articulate the realization of the new condition seems to have been Michael McGaha, a Golden Age specialist based in the United States, who in 1990 saw academics as victims of market

---

15 In *Viajes en Europa, Africa y Estados Unidos* (1851).
16 In Roberto Arlt's novels, for example.

forces, and viewed the emergence of diversity within Hispanism as threatening social fragmentation and erosion of academic prestige.[17]

Malcolm K. Read, giving a sharper political edge to the issue, replied to McGaha, saying that 'the role of education as preparation for a whole way of life, for active participating in a democracy, can no longer be assumed, but needs to be explicitly argued for and vigorously defended'; he considered McGaha typical of Hispanism: a 'curiously conservative, intellectually closed community' (1991a: 195). After briefly sketching the history of British Hispanism as an instrument of state power, he turns his attention to the current age of vocationalism, identifying in a younger generation of Hispanists (such as Paul Julian Smith) an 'untroubled ability to span radically conflicting discourses, to commodify even those analytic models which seek to expose and thereby resist reification' (1991a: 204).

In a second article, Read continues the attack, through a critique of Smith's *The Body Hispanic*. Praising analyses which are 'guaranteed to convince young Hispanists of the need to engage seriously with [...] post-structuralist texts and [...] help neutralize the powerful, reactionary elements in a discipline notable for its resistance to theory' (1991b: 140), Read, nevertheless, condemns Smith's 'eclectic liberalism' and failure to engage in 'genuine historical analysis'. Read then reproaches humanists and deconstructionists alike, for rejecting 'a theory of the subject as a site of contrasting and conflicting forces [without which] all resistance [to the patriarchal order] is impossible' (1991b: 144).

Nick Round then enters the debate, challenging Read's portrayal of the history of British Hispanism, before switching the focus to the present. Conceding Read's point, that A. A. Parker's dominating influence was insufficiently challenged in his time, he suggests that the present is not so very different:

> It is [...] what happens whenever any form of literary theory, powerfully cultivated by a few original minds, becomes a kind of half-orthodoxy among a much wider range of their colleagues. With a few of the signs changed, the picture would define, not at all unfairly, the relationship to more recent theoretical currents of a sizeable section of British hispanism in the 1990s. (1992–93: 140)

Round goes on to offer an alternative history, casting (British) Hispanism as a relatively modest, workmanlike, pluralistic and nonconformist force which (unlike French) is not part of the establishment.

---

[17] In this, he follows the line expounded by Allan Bloom, in *The Closing of the American Mind* (1987).

Then, addressing the present and the future, he warns that no single theoretical position is adequate.

> Critical theory [...] is socially useful only insofar as its practice yields
> reliable knowing: we shall not advance anyone's liberation by misleading
> them as to what the world is or has been, or where within it they are.
> [...] It remains true [...] that any academic [...] who does not make the
> linkage between professional discourse and its social effect a matter of
> conscious concern, will end up serving the established order. But this
> again enjoins vigilance and argument, rather than any particular theory.
> Finally, of course, any informed will to social action which might stem
> from academic scholarship can be made more or less effectual by the char-
> acter of the institutional channels through which it is mediated. This last is
> very evidently a political matter. The political background against which
> hispanic studies in Britain have, for the past dozen years, been carried on
> is that of a sustained attempt to monopolize those channels for other uses.
> It is no help to the resistance which has to be waged to let it be understood
> that only those with the right mix of Marxist and post-Freudian credentials
> need apply. (1992–93: 144)

Finally, he defines Hispanists.

> We are [...] the skilled producers of mental objects that are locally useful,
> we hope durable – but not, in any credible academic programme, the blue-
> prints for revolution. [...] To do this kind of thing well requires a mode
> of discussion that will blend openness and exact judgment in [...] equal
> proportions. And that cannot take place in the researcher's head or become
> fully actual merely between mind and mind: it predicates a particular
> nexus of social relations. Insofar as these relations favour creative, well-
> achieved intellectual production, they will be palpably unlike the socio-
> economic relations of the market society (though [...] inserted within these
> latter). (1992–93: 144)

A postscript then came from Stephen M. Hart who, identifying Round
with 'the anti-theory lobby in British hispanism' (1992–93: 415), judged that
the Read–Round–Smith debate marked a paradigm shift 'from the ideology
of one generation to that of the next' (1992–93: 417). Perhaps seeking to
reconcile Read with Smith (but ignoring Round's point about negotiable
roles in institutional and ideological contexts), he distinguished economic
from ideological liberation, defining academics as 'transmitters and creators
of institutionalized knowledge' (1992–93: 423). As he puts it: 'because the
milkman does not read Paul Julian Smith's works, does it make them socially
ineffective?' (1992–93: 423).

Undoubtedly, there has been a major shift, and diversification, in critical methodology and in the objects studied, since the time of these debates. The final task of this investigation is to reflect on how Hispanism is currently viewed.

Ostensibly – at least, according to the chair of the Quality Assurance Agency (QAA) Language and related studies Benchmark Group – the official view is that modern language disciplines are 'in the best traditions of serious humanistic education' (2002: unnumbered). However, in reality the QAA vision is strongly utilitarian: the main selling point is the employability of modern languages graduates. Generally speaking, in the benchmark statement (in which modern language studies are broken down into four areas of expertise), the greatest emphasis is on the practical use of the language; second in importance is knowledge of the language; cultural knowledge (of which literature is a subcategory) is third; last is intercultural awareness and understanding. Moreover, while linguistic skills and knowledges are described in detail, there is very little information indeed about what are termed 'subject-related skills' (I think that 'subject' here is probably roughly synonymous with 'culture', or 'civilization'). Essentially, the issue is ducked: this entire area is described as multidisciplinary – and the reader is referred to other 'relevant' subject benchmark statements (2002: 6).

Throughout the QAA document, modern languages are presented in instrumental, not humanistic terms: there is no reference to the individual for him/herself – only of their performance; the notions of sensibility, growth and creativity are absent; there is no sense of the discipline's intrinsic worth; the value of cultural products is specified only in terms of advantageous knowledge or skills; no moral, political or ethical dimension is attributed to education.

The pre-eminence of utilitarian, not humanistic values, is illustrated by the expected 'intercultural awareness and understanding' attributes of the good student, who must demonstrate:

> a reasoned awareness and critical understanding of one or more cultures and societies, other than their own, that will normally have been significantly enhanced by a period of residence in the country, or countries, of the target language(s); [and] an ability to describe, analyse and evaluate the similarities and dissimilarities of those cultures or societies in comparison with their own. (2002: 13)

This uninspiring language shows how far we have moved since the early 1980s: in Max Weber's terms, the new political direction which emerged then, and which was initially characterized by charismatic leadership, has now settled into bureaucracy.

Earlier in the discussion, we saw that it was widely thought that literatures were a significant part of the essentially humanistic disciplines of modern languages. Most observers, too, advocated careful modernization of the curriculum. Since English is generally regarded as a cognate discipline, and one whose recent debates about the use of theory, and development of cultural studies, are considered highly relevant to modern language disciplines, we might reflect on Hispanism's relationship with English.

In the 1980s, when the link between language and literature was deemed essential, Fishburn and Ife argued that, 'literary studies pursued in a linguistic vacuum will quickly become a branch of history, philosophy or politics. Secondly, and even more crucially, language cannot properly be studied as an end in itself' (1981: unnumbered). And yet, while the QAA benchmark statement for modern languages (which makes several passing references to literature) mentions 'subject-related skills', there appears to be no subject, as such: the reader is simply referred to other 'relevant' benchmark statements. Perhaps the English statement might be one such?

The discipline of English acknowledges many connections: to Linguistics, Drama, Communication Studies and Philosophy; it incorporates comparative literature and literature in translation; and it has interdisciplinary links, for example with Renaissance studies (English Benchmark Group, 2000: 1–3). However, modern languages are not mentioned. Clearly, wherever they (we) might be, it is not at the interdisciplinary centre of the Arts curriculum, where Nick Round thinks we should be.

Some of us (who thought we were humanists) appear to be located on the periphery of the social sciences.[18] Perhaps, then, some more theorized social science discourse should be at Hispanism's heart? Phil Swanson (like Read) thinks not:

> One might reasonably wonder if the surge in literary criticism of an extreme complexity of language, often coupled with some sort of attempted socio-political commentary, is itself an anxious desire to make literary criticism appear 'advanced' and 'productive', in a way which actually risks making it part of the very late-capitalist structures it so often appears to seek to critique. (2005: 122–3)

---

[18] Specialists in literature which addresses social questions apparently belong to a discipline called 'cultural studies', which is one of the two main branches of sociology. 'In Popperian terms, the strength of modern positivist quantitative sociology lies in the rigorous checking of clearly formulated hypotheses against meticulously collected fact. This is where the novel is at its weakest. But in the same Popperian terms, fiction of the Balzacian or Dickensian type is rich as a source of hypotheses as well as providing descriptive material of normally superior subtlety and range' (Halsey 2004: 26–7).

One possibility, which at least combines an important part of the discipline with the utilitarian project, would be the expansion of applied language studies. However, given recent developments in schools (which will surely lead to a reduction in modern linguists), this avenue, too, is unpromising.

Let us return briefly to the English Benchmark Group, to consider what they think is the nature and purpose of their discipline. English departments, while carefully taking account of temporal and cultural diversity, nevertheless maintain 'subject knowledge' principles: first, literature is socially and historically contextualized; second, the act of reading is problematized; third, while there is no canon, undergraduates should study a suitably broad selection of literature.

Modern linguists might consider this question: do we believe that English should adopt a more utilitarian view, for example by promoting the study of (say) American and African literatures, as access points to foreign societies? Alternatively, do we perhaps find that what they have to say, to some extent articulates our own beliefs?

> The subject also has a special role in sustaining in the general community a constantly renewed knowledge and critical appreciation of the literature of the past and of other cultural forms. (2000: 2)

For myself – and I suspect that Nick Round's view might not be so very different – it is rather closer to the latter. We, Hispanists of the early twenty-first century, are a community whose (essentially humanistic) task is the constant renewal of knowledge about, and the development and maintenance of links with – as well as a critical appreciation of – Hispanic and related peoples, their societies and their cultures.

List of Works Cited

Borges, Jorge Luis, 1981. *Ficciones* (Madrid: Alianza)

Dorfman, Ariel, 1995. *Reader* (London: Nick Hern Books)

Eagleton, Terry, 1984. *The Function of Criticism* (London: Verso)

———, 2005. *The English Novel. An Introduction* (Malton MA, Oxford and Carlton, Victoria: Blackwell)

Easthope, Antony, 1991. *Literary Into Cultural Studies* (London and New York: Routledge)

English Benchmark Group, 2000. *English* (Gloucester: Quality Assurance Agency for Higher Education)

Fishburn, Evelyn and Barry Ife (eds), 1981. *Language through Literature* (London: n.pub.)

Gibson, Ian, 1989. *Federico García Lorca. A Life* (London: Faber & Faber)

Graham, Helen and Jo Labanyi (eds), 1995. *Spanish Cultural Studies: An Introduction: The Struggle for Modernity* (Oxford: Oxford University Press)

Gregory, Richard, 1977. 'Psychology: Towards a Science of Fiction', in *The Cool Web: The Pattern of Children's Reading*, ed. Margaret Meek, Aidan Warlow and Griselda Barton (London, Sydney and Toronto: The Bodley Head)

Halsey, A. H., 2004. *A History of Sociology in Britain* (Oxford: Oxford University Press)

Hart, Stephen M., 1992–93. ' "Mientras que en mi casa estoy, rey soy": More on the Politics of Hispanism', *Journal of Hispanic Research*, 1: 415–23.

Hoggart, Richard, 1958. *The Uses of Literacy* (Harmondsworth: Penguin) [first published 1957]

Inglis, Fred, 1995. *Cultural Studies* (Oxford: Blackwell)

Johnson, Richard, 1986. 'The Story So Far: And Further Transformations?', in *Introduction to Contemporary Cultural Studies*, ed. David Punter (London and New York: Longman)

Jordan, Barry, 1990. *British Hispanism and the Challenge of Literary Theory* (Warminster: Aris & Phillips)

——, and Rikki Morgan-Tamosunas (eds), 2000. *Contemporary Spanish Cultural Studies* (London: Arnold)

Languages and Related Studies Benchmark Group, 2002. *Languages and Related Studies* (Gloucester: Quality Assurance Agency for Higher Education)

Lepenies, W., 1988. *Between Literature and Science: The Rise of Sociology* (Cambridge: Cambridge University Press)

McGaha, Michael, 1990. 'Whatever Happened to Hispanism?', *Journal of Hispanic Philology*, 14: 225–30

Read, Malcolm K., 1991a. 'Travelling South: Ideology and Hispanism', *Journal of Hispanic Philology*, 15: 193–206

——, 1991b. 'Writing in the Institution: The Politics of British Hispanism', *Journal of Hispanic Philology*, 15: 140–7

Round, Nicholas G., 1980. 'Thinking about Thody: Language and Culture in the University Discipline', *Modern Languages*, vol. 63(4) (December): 155–64

——, 1991. 'Overstepping the Mark: *Rayuela* and *Lo prohibido*', in *On Reasoning and Realism: Three Easy Pieces* (Manchester: Department of Spanish and Portuguese), pp. 51–66

——, 1992–93. 'The Politics of Hispanism Reconstrued', *Journal of Hispanic Research*, 1: 134–147

Rowe, William and Vivian Schelling, 1991. *Memory and Modernity: Popular Culture in Latin America* (London: Verso)

Swanson, Philip, 2005. *Latin American Fiction, A Short Introduction* (Oxford: Blackwell)

Thody, P. M. W., 1980. 'Modern Languages as a University Discipline', *Modern Languages*, 61.1 (March): 1–11

Williams, Raymond, 1965. *The Long Revolution* (Harmondsworth: Penguin) [first published 1961]

INDEX

TABULA CONGRATULATORIA

Peter Beardsell
Roger Boase
Federico Bonaddio
Anny Brooksbank Jones
D. W. Cruickshank
Catherine Davies
Rhian Davies
Philip Deacon
Alan Deyermond
John England
David Frier
Teresa Fuentes Peris
Derek Gagen
David George
Nigel Glendinning
Nigel Griffin
Maria Guterres
Richard Hitchcock
David Hook
Paul Jordan
Jeremy Lawrance
Huw Aled Lewis

C. Alex Longhurst
John Macklin
Gloria Mound
Patricia Odber de Baubeta
David G. Pattison
Juliet Perkins
Geoffrey Ribbans
Eamonn Rodgers
John Rutherford
Paddy Scott
Alison Sinclair
Cris Sousa
Eric Southworth
Philip Swanson
† Arthur Terry
Isabel Torres
Anthony Trippett
Harriet Turner
Robin Warner
Geoffrey West
Edwin Williamson
David Wood

Bulletin of Spanish Studies
Department of Hispanic Studies, Trinity College, Dublin
Trinity College, Oxford
University of Bristol, Department of Hispanic, Portuguese and Latin American Studies
University of Sheffield Library